Restoring Resilience

RESTORING RESILIENCE

Discovering Your Clients' Capacity for Healing

EILEEN M. RUSSELL

Forewords by Diana Fosha
and Daniel A. Hughes

W. W. NORTON & COMPANY

New York · London

For information about permission to reproduce selections from this book,
write to Permissions, W. W. Norton & Company, Inc., 500 Fifth Avenue,
New York, NY 10110

For information about special discounts for bulk purchases, please contact
W. W. Norton Special Sales at specialsales@wwnorton.com or 800-233-4830

Manufacturing by Edwards Brothers Malloy
Production manager: Christine Critelli

Library of Congress Cataloging-in-Publication Data

Russell, Eileen (Psychologist)
Restoring resilience : discovering your clients' capacity for healing /
Eileen Russell ; forewords by Diana Fosha and Daniel A. Hughes —
First Edition.
pages cm. — (A Norton professional book)
Includes bibliographical references and index.
ISBN 978-0-393-70571-3 (hardcover : alk. paper)
1. Resilience (Personality trait) 2. Healing. I. Title.
BF698.35.R47R87 2015
155.2'4—dc23
2015009230

W. W. Norton & Company, Inc., 500 Fifth Avenue, New York, N.Y. 10110
www.wwnorton.com
W. W. Norton & Company Ltd., Castle House, 75/76 Wells Street,
London W1T 3QT

1 2 3 4 5 6 7 8 9 0

For my husband, Mario
And my three beautiful children Gabriel, Cecilia, and Julian
The most powerful sources of my own resilience

CONTENTS

EXPANDED CONTENTS

Acknowledgements

I am grateful for the opportunity to have written this book and for everyone's patience with me during its prolonged gestation period. Writing is something I enjoy doing mostly because it is a way for me to continue to explore my experiences with patients, my understanding of the theories and techniques of psychotherapy, and my own role in the process. Now that it is done and I contemplate people (other than myself and my editors) reading it, I am both surprised by, and grateful to the readers of this book, for taking the time to sit with my reflections. I hope you find in these pages something that enlivens your work, stimulates your mind, and touches your heart.

There are so many supportive people to thank in the process of bringing a book to life. My family's support and patience has been tremendous. My children, who are still young, were very little when this process started (my youngest was not yet born) and are now more aware of what has transpired between me and my computer over these years. My experience of mothering them, of seeing the individuals they are and are becoming has sustained me personally and helped me understand what I do professionally so much more than I would have without knowing and loving them. My husband, Mario Russell, has been truly amazing. I am so grateful to him for making the sacrifices of time, money, and energy with me, for his support, encouragement, for helping me find or make the time, for asking me how it is going, for being patient, and for believing in this project, especially when I was confronting my own doubts.

My parents, Susan and Jerry McElroy have been transformational others for me many times over the years. In a field that prizes secure attachment but remains quite suspicious of its actual existence, it has sometimes been challenging even to me to really own the solidity of my first experiences with loving, kind, interested, and "good enough" true others. Among the earliest influences on my interest in resilience was their deep compassion and active caring for people in need and their attunement to how and why people struggle. Later, my father's red pen accompanied the care and time he took to help me formulate and articulate my ideas as a high school student inundated by writing projects. And my mother, one of the most generous people I know, has offered many times to help in whatever way she could to lighten the load. I so deeply appreciate their ongoing belief in and support of me, and the freedom they gave me as I found my way. My sisters, Erin McElroy-Barker and Ciara McElroy have been constant and steadfast friends, allowing for my vulnerability and my strength. And I so appreciate how they do not take me too seriously and have made me laugh heartily so often over the years.

I am very grateful to any number of my friends who patiently listened to "the book" updates from time to time, who always asked how it was going, and who were very supportive of my doing it and finishing it and remaining sane at the same time. Several people come to mind in particular to whom I am very thankful: SueAnne Piliero, Patsy Mickens, Nancy Dolan, Michelle Vago Bubrick, Barbara Lee, Lesley Pella-Woo, Skye Wilson, and Elizabeth Nystrom. I also want to thank Barbara Lee, my oldest friend, whose capacity for joy, laughter, and connection inspired my first interests in the whole subject of resilience.

The hardest thing about writing this book has been balancing it with the other exigencies of life and occasionally my own rigid insistence on balance in life. I stopped being a workhorse after finishing my Ph.D. when I felt ready to retire at 29 even though I loved my work. Having a nose to the grindstone is absolutely essential at times but it seems that in our world, it is easy to believe we should be working like that all the time. This book presented itself as an opportunity when my twin children were still very young and my youngest had not even been conceived in imagination. I wanted very much to be a present mother and in the time I absolutely had to be staring at my computer waiting for words to come, I wanted to trust my children were still being loved well. I am so very grateful to Patricia Starkle, our babysitter and part of our family for 8 years. She was the other loving, solid, secure base for my kids when I could not be there and she allowed me some mental and emotional space for this project. I also so appreciated her letting me vent and sometimes just laughing with me about myself.

I have had the great fortune of being supervised, mentored, cared for, and befriended by two wonderful women who happen to be master therapists and great people: Diana Fosha, Ph.D. and Jenna Osiason, Ph.D. This book would never have been conceived if it were not for Diana Fosha, Ph.D. Not only have I learned the content and practice of AEDP from her, but she has been an extraordinary mentor to me, encouraging me always to "do my thing," which includes this book. I am so grateful to Diana for all of her wise input and suggestions along the way and for taking the time to review the book and write its foreword. Dr. Jenna Osiason so lovingly helped me understand what I was seeing and doing in sessions with patients in concrete and very deep ways. She has both nurtured and grown with me as I have grown. I am so thankful to her for making it safe for me to bring myself into the room with her and for her very careful, astute, and intelligent listening throughout.

I have learned a tremendous amount from my colleagues, especially my fellow faculty at the AEDP Institute. I know how fortunate I am to be part of an enthusiastic, extremely talented, smart, and very compassionate group of colleagues and friends. I have learned so much from them and their work, the unique way in which they do it, the particular issues they are sensitive to, and the way they bring themselves to the task of being colleagues who are growing an institute together. I am thankful to all of them for their support, discerning feedback on the book, encouragement and, most of all, for their friendship. Fellow faculty of the AEDP institute provided not only support, but constructive and helpful feedback on the first several chapters of this book. The include: SueAnne Piliero, Benjamin Lipton, Jenna Osiason, Ron Fredrick, Steve Shapiro, Kari Gleiser, Danny Yeung, Jerry Lamagna, Natasha Prenn, Gil Tunnel, Barbara Suter, David Mars, Karen Pando-Mars, Ann Cooper, Dale Trimble, and Miriam Marsolais.

Several other colleagues provided invaluable feedback and critique on different parts of the book: Ken Benau, Russell Siler Jones, and Diana Fosha, as well as Robert Giugliano, whose additional spiritual support was essential in bringing this book to birth. I am thankful to Susan Rosengarten, who assisted me toward the end in doing a lot of cross-referencing, finding pages, checking quotes, and the like. She helped save my sanity. And a number of colleagues took the time to take my informal survey about therapists' understanding of resilience and to reflect on their own increased resilience as therapists in engaging the kind of work put forth in this book. They include: Ken Benau, David Greenan, Jennifer Edlin, Judith Levy, Judy Silvan, Bret Lyon, Shigeru Iwakabe, Anna Meyer, Karen Minsberg, Meredith Duncan, David Markowitz, Carrie Ruggieri, Susan Walton, Dan Hughes, Richard Harrison, Colette Linnihan, and Matt Fried.

It is said that experience is the best teacher. But I have also found that teaching through experience has allowed me to learn so much. Being able to watch (through videotape) the experience of the work unfolding between two other people has given me the space to reflect, to think to understand, to see, to make connections in a way that is considerably harder when you are in the thick of the interpersonal clinical encounter. A number of very gifted clinicians and very great people have given me the honor of sharing their clinical work with me aside from my fellow faculty of the AEDP Institute and I have learned so much with and through them. They include: Andrea Agee, Mary Androff, Tal Astrachan, Ken Benau, Jan Bowman, Stephen Carroll, Denise Clay, Colette Dowling, Meredith Duncan, Jennifer Edlin, Hilary Jacobs Hendel, Tom Glaser, Andrea Goldberg, Anthony Lerro, Barry Levy, David Markowitz, Betsy Kelly McCormick, Jeanne Newhouse, Lynn Norman, Jose Perez, Orli Peter, Maria

Palmer, Wendy Pollack, William Ryan, Virginia Seewaldt, Mary and Parker Stacy, Martina Verba, Patricia Williams, and Mitchell Wood.

This project has taken long enough for me to have multiple editors midwifing it at Norton, and I am grateful to Vani Kannan and Sophie Hagen for their feedback and encouragement on early drafts of chapters. I am also very grateful to Kristen Holt-Browning for her early help in the inception of this book and in her later, incredibly helpful, structuring, critical and thoughtful feedback on the entire manuscript as it was nearing the finish line. Ben Yarling's red pen on the final manuscript was intimidating until I realized how involved and engaged he was with me in a dialogue with this book as it came to fruition. I am so grateful for his careful attention, clarity, and enthusiasm. I so admire the care and attention to detail given to the last round by Trish Watson, my copyeditor. And finally, but foundationally, I am so thankful for the time, experience, and wisdom Cindy Workman Hyden offered me and for her help in imposing a more integrated architecture on what had been some haphazard wanderings, and especially for helping me find and tune my voice.

It is hard to put into words how bidirectional this work can be. Not infrequently I still have the slightly awed experience that comes with another human being coming in need, seeking, searching, struggling, and bearing heart, soul, and mind to me in hopes of getting to a better place. And in that humbling process of trying to bring my own self to the process in order to offer something that might be transformative, or at least, helpful, I take away and learn so much. Through learning something about each person I understand something more about the complexity of the human condition and about the beauty, struggle, pain, and joy of its myriad members. It goes without saying that this book could never have been written without my patients. I am grateful to all of them. There are many whose voices are not included here but who were, nevertheless, in my heart and mind through the pages of this book. I am deeply grateful for those of my patients who were willing to have transcripts of our actual work be printed here. That has been an enormous gift to me.

Foreword
by Diana Fosha

We live in challenging times. Opportunities for transformation have never been greater. At the same time, challenges to the very stability of our selves, families, social structures, and planet have also never been greater. While the last sentence could apply to any moment in time, it certainly applies to the 'now moment' we're inhabiting.

As human beings, if we are to survive, we need to meet the challenges that life throws in our path in ways that allow us to cope and keep on keeping on. However, those challenges may also end up being unexpected gifts, providing us with opportunities to—as a result of engaging them—live our lives with more gusto, more connection, with greater well-being, flexibility, and, compassion, maybe even with greater ease and with an enhanced sense of meaning and purpose.

Eileen Russell takes on *resilience* as that quality of the human spirit through which she will explore this quest to not only not be undone by adversity, but to use it as a spur to growth and thriving. This rich, inspiring book is truthful, clear, and deeply humanistic in its understanding of what it means to be resilient, even in the face of challenges that threaten to defy our humanity. No misty-eyed optimist, yet with deep faith and trust in our capacities, Russell's thinking and writing is centered, aligned, and balanced, clearly acknowledging how resilience exists side-by-side with the brokenness and the damage of trauma and neglect. Acknowledging such realities makes the belief in and the quest for resilience—its detection and, once detected, its restoration—all the more meaningful.

Eileen Russell's definition of resilience as the "self's differentiation from that which is aversive to it" is profound. In one fell swoop, with the economy of poetry, she asserts the fundamental intactness of the core of the self. Thus, *de facto*, she makes wholeness and intactness intrinsic qualities of the self, and makes the quest for restoring resilience something we do to restore things to how they are meant to be. It is an article of faith that we are wired to be whole and intact, and thus the goal of a transformative therapy in the face of things that have gone awry is to restore, and not to invent, teach, or create.

Russell makes sure that we grasp that resilience is both that which allows us to cope, adapt, and survive in situations and environments that are not conducive to human growth and thriving, and also precisely that which allows us to thrive, flourish and become more deeply ourselves. Depending on the nature of the environment in which we find ourselves, resilience can manifest as white-knuckle survival strategies that, in thwarting environments in which we feel alone and unsafe, over time morph into what we call psychopathology. At the other end of the continuum, where we hope transformative therapies reside, resilience shows up as co-extensive with "transformance," flourishing, and growth; these manifestations of resilience can really come to the fore in facilitating environments in which we feel safe, supported, and accompanied.

Each chapter of this awesome book explores a different aspect of resilience, and of the process by which resilience gets detected, restored, and enhanced. Findings from developmental psychology, interpersonal neurobiology, and affective neuroscience, as well as from positive psychology research, inform the theory of resilience presented here, and are foundational for the clinical work that flows from it. Resilience-focused clinical work comes to life through evocative and moving case presentations, both illustrating Russell's points and showing a wonderfully sensitive clinician at work. While we don't have the videos of the therapy sessions, we do have the next best thing: transcripts of the back and forth between patient and therapist, which allow us to witness and see and feel for ourselves what resilience looks like when it manifests as potential, or as promise, or as reality. We also get to experience how resilience that's seemingly lost is found, and also honored, and worked with, and supported to grow. We indeed get to witness how moment-to-moment resilience is restored through a transformational therapy.

This wonderful contribution is transmitted to you through the lens of AEDP (Accelerated Experiential Dynamic Psychotherapy), the transformative therapy model* that Eileen Russell calls her psychotherapy home, the secure base from which she launches her explorations into resilience. She shows AEDP in action in her theoretical contributions, as well as in her luminous, subtle clinical work with her patients, which we are privileged to witness. She does AEDP proud by operating steadfastly from its fundamental orientation towards healing and faith in our wired-in intactness and transformational potential. And she makes a substantive contribution to AEDP's metapsychology. Channeling Bollas†, she introduces the notion of the *self-in-transition* for the patient, and the notion of the therapist as an exemplar of one kind of crucially important *transformational other.*

Because the fundamental importance of the moment-to-moment process by which transformation becomes instantiated in the psyche of the patient cannot be exaggerated, the self-in-transition is our version of time-lapse photography. It gives us the opportunity to almost literally witness, moment-to-moment, the process by which change takes place. We see the self actually in transition—going back and forth, three steps forward, two steps backwards—between the old

---

* Fosha D. (2009). Emotion and recognition at work: Energy, vitality, pleasure, truth, desire & the emergent phenomenology of transformational experience. In D. Fosha, D. J. Siegel & M. F. Solomon (Eds.), *The healing power of emotion: Affective neuroscience, development, clinical practice* (172–203). New York: Norton.
† Bollas, C. (1979). The transformational object. *International Journal of Psychoanalysis, 60,* 97–107.

miseries, painful but familiar and thus oddly reassuring, and the
scary wonderfulness of the wished-for changes, all the more terrify-
ing for being a step into the unknown.

And in parallel, for us as therapists, we now have the beautiful idea
that we function as transformational others. That is the essence of
who we are for the people we are honored to help and accompany on
transformative journeys of healing. And, of course, implicit in these
beautiful terms is that, in the transformative process, both members
of the therapeutic dyad become transformed. Winnicott said there's
no such thing as a baby, there is only a mother-baby dyad*. Eileen
Russell says there's no such thing as a resilient person. Resilience at
its best is something that emerges when the self is together with a
transformational other devoted to that self's well-being and best-be-
coming. In other words, there is the person with resilience wired in
as a potential, and then there is the human environment in which
she or he operates at any given moment. It is that combination that
determines whether resilience manifests more as strength and flexibility (health), or as rigidity or chaos (pathology). The moment-to-
moment process of transformation involves a self-in-transition being
held (to channel Winnicott), witnessed, and worked with by a transformational other. It is thus that resilience is restored.

It is important to mention that Russell's work is also a meditation
on vulnerability in its most profoundly affirmative sense, for resilience implies the courage to be vulnerable. Resilience involves the
courage to move and be moved, to affect and be affected, and to surrender to experience in the service of growth and connection. Vulnerability certainly applies to the self-in-transition and it also very
much applies to the transformational other.

As Russell herself says, this book will work equally well whether
you are an AEDP practitioner or whether other models constitute
your home base. Regardless of what model you most identify your
psychotherapy practice with, I am reasonably certain that after read-

---

* Winnicott, D. W. (1960). The theory of the parent-infant relationship. *International Journal of Psychoanalysis, 41*, 585–595.

ing this book you will never see your patients in the same way. You also might not ever see yourself as a therapist in quite the same way.

Russell's book is both substantive and practical. It deepens and extends our understanding through the thorough and complex ways in which resilience is defined. It is practical in that it shows us how to work with resilience to make the most of it at all points of the continuum on which it exists. This book has concrete advice for how to work with resilience when it is merely a potential, or a promise; how to work with resilience when it is manifesting in moments of exquisite vulnerability, when patients are moving between the "same-old, same-old" and the potentially wonderful, yet scary, *new*; and finally, how to work with resilience just as devotedly and rigorously even when things are better, so that better-ness can be extended into thriving, flourishing, and the actualizing of potential that can sometimes exceed both our own expectations and those of the person with whom we are working.

Now, foreword complete, forward to the word. Join Eileen Russell in her marvelous explanation of resilience, how to restore it when it's been compromised, and how to help it thrive and flourish when it's online. Resilience, in Russell's work, takes both patient and therapist on a journey of growth and discovery of what it means to be human. Her moving work on restoring resilience moves us, and by moving us, moves our field—the field of the transformative therapies—forward.

Foreword

by Daniel A. Hughes

There are some old myths about resilience. These include the belief that resilience is a genetic reality. Another belief is that some have it and some don't. Some of us, though, have moved beyond these beliefs and concluded that resilience emerged within attachment relationships, and that it can still be enhanced through new attachment relationships, including therapeutic relationships. We have come to understand resilience as our ability to fight against adversity and to overcome it, often with a good friend or therapist at our side.

Now we have Eileen Russell's *Restoring Resilience*, which goes further still in developing our understanding of resilience, positioning it as a key component of therapeutic change. Dr. Russell acknowledges that resilience challenges adversities and is enhanced within the therapeutic relationship. She also makes us aware of where resilience leads us when we are overcoming adversity, describing the nature of the journey and the positive influence of discovering the place of joy and deep positive experiences in our lives.

Dr. Russell's descriptions of resilience have something in common with what Carl Rogers called the "actualization tendency," but Russell illuminates in great detail, through her descriptions of the nature of resilience and her methods for developing it, this striving for the full development of the self. Rogers spoke of the human drive toward healing, integration, and attaining our full potential, and his therapy assumed that if the therapist created the right accepting and empathic relationship, a person's actualization tendency would naturally do the work of integrative development. Russell sees this transition from the restricted self to self-at-best as the work of resilience, the capacity for which exists in all of us, ready to be expanded.

Dr. Russell shows us that the work of resilience is not finished when adversity has been processed and mastered. Even as we say goodbye to our demons, we need to learn how to live with our angels. And this may well be a frightening process, leaving us content with the safety of what is known, though it is far below our capacities for deep meaning and joy. Resilience helps us to see that we have the capacity for a full life, and that our hope to attain it need not create anxiety, but rather confidence. It enables us to flourish.

Restoring Resilience provides a therapeutic map for our patient to make the transition to self-at-best. The therapist is at the center of this map. Dr. Russell's core treatment model is AEDP, which is ideally suited for her goal of restoring resilience, but therapists from other schools of treatment will also be able to utilize her insights. She reminds us of the need to perceive our patient as being much more complex than are his symptoms, with more resources available to him than he is using, and with potential for a much more meaningful and joyful life. She reminds us of the findings of research from attachment and interpersonal neurobiology in guiding our therapeutic relationship to provide dyadic affect regulation and empathic responsiveness. Inherent within such a relationship is the patient's experience of the therapist as the transformational other who is able to guide and walk with the patient into a new life of enhanced positive experiences.

There are such similarities between the complex therapeutic relationships so carefully described by Dr. Russell and the nature of the attachment relationship that a child develops with her parent! Within the attachment relationship the parent first establishes the child's core sense of safety, then assists the child in re-establishing safety following the numerous challenges, adversities, and losses of childhood. In moving through each stressful event, the child—with the active, attuned, presence of his parent—is developing a sense of self that has the strength of resilience woven into its core. And it is from this safety and this strength, grown in the arms of her parents, that the child's open engagement with the world emerges. This safety and strength enable her to discover—truly discover in her heart and mind—not only who she is but also who she may become as she develops the fullness of her self, embracing the uncertainties and possibilities of her life.

Dr. Russell's work is both sensitive and poetic. It is also thorough, built upon a solid theoretical foundation. As she explains, therapists who are aware of and facilitate the power of resilience within their patients are probably also deepening their own capacity for resilience in the process. That's how it works. As a bonus, I believe that her readers may also become more resilient—more aware of and likely to pursue their own angels—because through her written words Dr. Russell may become, for them, a virtual transformational other.

Part 1

THE ARC OF RESILIENCE

Introduction

*Our deepest fear is not that we are inadequate. Our
deepest fear is that we are powerful beyond measure. It
is our light, not our darkness that most frightens us.*

Peoble enter therapy not simply because they are stuck and struggling but because they are ready for change and have some hope of
experiencing it. That readiness is a manifestation of each person's
innate resilience, or capacity to work *on behalf of the self*. Learning
how to identify the potential of resilience, deepen it, and put it to
use in the course of therapy is what this book is about. A primary
goal for this book is to entreat psychotherapists to find and focus on
our patients' strengths and resources to lend the work more traction,
breadth, and depth and to make it more satisfying for both therapist
and patient. This is not to suggest that the treatment model proposed
here ignores symptoms, pathology, or pain. Rather, I am suggesting
that working with what has gone wrong from the foundation of what
is right—and, perhaps, what has always been right—enhances the
therapeutic experience for patient and therapist and accelerates
healing. Moreover, working with and enhancing what is positive for

3

its own sake is a different track in the healing journey, one that has tremendous transformative potential.

This book takes as a foundational premise the humanistic notion that self-righting and healing are inborn capacities. Resilience is one manifestation of these human tendencies toward wellness. But, although self-righting and healing are proclivities and potentialities, they are not givens. Pathology (e.g., depression, anxiety, attachment issues, character disorders)—our own and others'—is real, and defenses are necessary and often, well -honed. Constriction, contraction, repression, and other forms of defensive response serve the purposes of protecting our vulnerabilities and helping us to survive in adverse circumstances. However, they also inhibit nascent potential and the thrust of expansiveness. Gaining insight into these defensive systems is not necessarily enough for people to let go of lifelong habits that have been continually reinforced, especially when the consequences of their surrender are still unknown.

Alexander and French (1946) spoke about the necessity of the patient having a "corrective emotional experience," rather than pure intellectual insight. This has been taken very seriously by the experiential or affective balance therapies (Panksepp, 2009), which commonly aim to facilitate healing and change through restoring access to bodily rooted experience and the emotions associated with them. The interpersonal context of an empathic, emotionally attuned relationship facilitates this kind of emotional experience, which then releases adaptive tendencies, and restores and even enhances the individual's innate resilience.

I am most familiar with one of these affective balance therapies, accelerated experiential dynamic psychotherapy (AEDP) (Fosha, 2000b). AEDP is a theory and a set of techniques founded on a deep belief in people's capacity for healing and change, which can be awoken in the context of secure attachment relationships that are focused on affective resonance but are capable of both disruption and repair. Being together, having connection disrupted, and repairing and restoring that connection are all affectively mediated interpersonal interactions and therefore require a comfort with and privileging of emotion as bodily rooted experience as the fulcrum of treatment.

Founded by Diana Fosha (2000a, 2000b, 2001a, 2001b, 2002, 2003, 2004a, 2004b, 2005, 2006, 2008, 2009) and elaborated with the help of several colleagues (Fosha, Siegel, & Solomon, 2009; Fosha & Yeung, 2006; Fredrick, 2009; Gleiser, Ford, & Fosha, 2008; Lamagna, 2011; Lamagna & Gleiser 2007; Lipton & Fosha, 2011; Prenn, 2009; Russell & Fosha, 2008; Shapiro, 2009; Tunnell, 2006, 2011, 2012), AEDP has been on the cutting edge of clinical explorations of the phenomenology of healing, positive affects, and the experience of the transformation of the self. It is an honor for me to share AEDP concepts with the readers of this book and to incorporate these with other psychotherapeutic theories and techniques that genuinely privilege the individual's strengths and resources and earnestly seek ways to integrate them into the psychotherapeutic process, without losing sight of the difficulty, pain, or complexity people are struggling with when they commit to any kind of psychotherapeutic endeavor.

Resilience Is Not Invulnerability

The pages that follow explore what resilience seems to be and useful ways of understanding it for clinicians. What I arrived at after three years of writing and researching this book is that the essence of resilience is the *self's differentiation from that which is aversive to it*. It is the space between the essential core self and all that would threaten, abuse, humiliate, annihilate, shame, demean, or neglect it. So much more will be said about that throughout, but in this beginning, I want to dispel some common understandings of resilience that I think are not useful for clinicians.

First, many very resilient people have *felt* broken in some way, and so it is important for clinicians to comprehend that, sometimes, even resilient people do, in fact, break—the elastic snaps, the knot comes undone, people fall apart and collapse. But this is not the dividing line between those who are ultimately resilient and those who are not, even if it is a measure of people's resilient capacity in the moment. Life probably requires us to fall apart from time to time anyway, to need others, to surrender or to be overcome, to recognize that we do not have it all together and we are not in control. Our final capacity cannot be evaluated based on these moments. Being resilient in the sense of simply persevering, being relatively unaffected, appearing to have it all together "despite," is a highly prized American ideal, but I do not think it is emblematic of maturity, development, depth, wisdom, compassion for self and others, or the capacity to really connect—to depend on and to be depended upon. This, rather, is the stuff of a whole person, whose resilience does not come at the expense of the rest of one's self. People who attain that kind of resilience, the capacity to flourish between episodes of the difficulties of life, know what it is to feel broken or lost.

And so, it is not just about being able to "move on despite." Rather, it is also about the process of trying to figure out how to move on when we cannot. How do we reknot the rope or make a new one? When broken, we forget or we cannot find our grounding, our base, our core. We feel lost. But it does not mean the ground is not there, that the core not intact. We simply may not be able to do it on our own. That's what finding and restoring resilience in therapy are all about.

Resilience and AEDP

I have chosen to write this book drawing largely on AEDP theory because this is my primary clinical approach and one that I both teach and supervise. But I hope that the reader will see throughout the book that it makes immanent sense to write a book about working with resilience from an AEDP vantage point because of AEDP's underlying humanistic emphasis on the philosophy that people are oriented toward development and capable of creative adaptation to challenging circumstances. What I hope to orient the reader to, advanced AEDP clinician and non-AEDP clinician alike, is the idea that resilience underlies even problematic adaptations and how powerful and transformative psychotherapy can be when both therapist and patient are able to see and use the kernel of truth, even of self-love in its best sense, that is at the center of our adaptations to life's challenges.

My graduate school education was very eclectic, something I did not always appreciate while I was going through it and trying to find my way while other colleagues in different schools were already strongly allied with a theoretical approach. But it encouraged me to be open to what works, for whom, when, and under what circumstances, and to try to understand why. I think of AEDP as a deeply integrative model that borrows from the theoretical and technical riches of many traditional "schools" of thought and the current influences on the field of affective neuroscience, attachment theory, emotion theory, studies of transformation, and most recently, positive psychology. Do not worry if you have never heard of AEDP—I reference different approaches and a wide variety of research to put the work into context and explain what you need to know about AEDP as it is needed. And readers who are advancing or advanced in AEDP training will find here new language and concepts.

Restoring Resilience = Change

This whole book is about change. The discovery of something that is already there does not necessarily translate into the ability to use the treasure one has found. Most of us need help validating what is ours, encouragement to live from an empowered place, companionship in our feelings and sense of connection, and a sense of kinship to trust that the painful parts of life can be born gracefully and often offer us something important to learn. The therapist's job, therefore, from beginning to end, is to see the potential, to recognize when the promise manifests, and to elaborate and encourage what is emergent to become solid and, eventually, transformational.

The Intended Audience for This Book

This book is intended for psychotherapists of all therapeutic persuasions who are interested in learning more about resilience and how it might be helpful to their practice and their patients. Positive psychology and "strengths-based" approaches have become better known in recent years, and the idea of emphasizing people's strengths is no longer new. What may be less talked about is the idea of using people's strengths to actively help them work through their struggles, instead of simply bypassing them, and to understand themselves on a deeper level and with compassion. Working to restore or enhance resilience is relevant for every clinical population, and my hope is that if you, the reader, have a patient whose life or issues are not reflected in the clinical vignettes of this book, the ideas about resilience will still inform how you think about and work with that patient. Certainly, this book should be helpful to clinicians working with people with depression, anxiety, trauma (recent and chronic), personality disorders, relationship issues, loneliness/isolation, identity struggles, and so on. I do not include vignettes of children in this book because I see only older adolescents and adults in my practice, but working with children and their families from a resilience-oriented stance seems to me to be an obvious extension.

A Note on Confidentiality

The vignettes in this book, with few exceptions, are drawn from my practice. I am deeply grateful to those of my patients who consented to allow me to use our work, including verbatim transcripts taken from videotaped sessions. I learn, teach, and supervise using videotapes, so it is hard to imagine how this book could have been written without their generous and trusting consent. What they have to say has taught me so much, and I hope it similarly enlightens the readers of this book. Their names and identifying details have been changed in order to ensure their anonymity and confidentiality.

The Arc of Restoring Resilience
and the Frame of the Book

I hope it will become ever clearer in the course of reading this book that resilience is not one time-delimited characteristic that is there or not there. Similarly, it is not simply a quality that exists on a continuum of less to more. It is also, very importantly, something that deepens and changes its expression in increasingly mature and complex ways as a person becomes healthier and more resilient. Therefore, I have come to understand resilience as existing along something like an arc. On the one end there may exist no more than *potential*, seen in momentary glimmers, and even evidenced in pathology or symptoms. As the person heals, feels safer, and develops more internal resources and intimate connections to others (including the therapist), this potential morphs into *promise*. There is a sense of possibility, an openness to a state of being on behalf of the self, in a less compromised and more safely vulnerable way. But it is still somewhat tentative and cautious. With more healing (i.e., making whole), the person is much more clearly and consciously differentiated from that which is aversive to the self. Her capacity to act on behalf of the self is considerably more open and positive, and her capacity to connect to and hold both self and other are much more elaborate and complex. This is when resilience manifests as *transformance* and, sometimes, *flourishing*. To meet the world's challenges, a person on this end of the resilience arc draws deeply from herself, is in touch with her strivings for optimal growth and development (i.e., "transformance"; see Fosha, 2009), and is open to and willing to use the external and interpersonal resources available to her, accepting that no one is an island and none of us does this journey well alone.

The analogy of the arc serves as a foundation on which the sections of the book are organized. Part 1, "The Arc of Resilience," includes this introduction and Chapter 1, which lays the groundwork for a clinical understanding of resilience, defines resilience, reframes "resistance," offers some common clinical language that will be used throughout the book, and includes the *map of resilience* as a visual representation of what is discussed and explored throughout. It also includes a transcript of a session in which the therapist chose a pathology focus over a resilience focus, examining the impact of that approach on the patient.

Part 2, "Resilience as Potential," includes Chapters 2 and 3. Chapter 2 discusses some essential theoretical elements of a resilience-oriented approach that is based in attachment theory, emotion theory, and affective neuroscience. It provides more of the language of AEDP, my home theory, and explains how and why that language is helpful and natural to anyone wanting to do resilience-oriented work. Neither Chapter 2 nor any other requires a facility with AEDP. I trust readers will take what they need in order to work from a resilience-oriented framework, and I hope that advanced AEDP readers find here some new language, subtleties, and perspective that will enhance the work they are already doing. Chapter 3 combines many of these theoretical and technical elements in the context of a transcript of an entire session with a patient that demonstrates the potential role of the therapist as *transformational other* in relation to the patient's *self-in-transition.*

Part 3, "Resilience as Promise," includes Chapters 4 and 5. Chapter 4 focuses on the importance of connection and coordination in the therapeutic relationship, pulls in a little more affective neuroscience in the form of people's social-emotional use of one another to regulate the nervous system, and discusses the importance of *empathic responsiveness* over simple attunement in an active, resilience-oriented approach. It includes a lengthy transcript of a woman terrified of her inner life and history, followed by a discussion of various techniques for softening defenses, quieting anxiety, and healing shame. Chapter 5 explores change itself. How do clinicians understand the processes of change that signal and facilitate the restoration of resilience? What are our markers that the work is progressing in the way it needs to? This chapter also draws on what affective neuroscience and interpersonal neurobiology suggest about the development of the resilient self and what that, in turn, implies for developing a resilient self later in life. Within that, the chapter examines *dyadic affect regulation* and the importance of mutual gaze and mutual vulnerability in the therapeutic relationship. These phenomena are amply evident in the transcript of a session with a woman who is wanting and simultaneously afraid to make a deeper connection with the therapist.

The final section of the book, "Resilience as Transformance/ Flourishing," comprises Chapters 6 and 7. Chapter 6 explores the phenomenon of the tremulousness of change and how people often need help embracing the newfound freedom, joy, and responsibility that comes with being more resilient, feeling better, functioning better, and having a less self-protective stance while living in the world. After two different transcripts present patients arriving at a long sought-after state of mind, the chapter discusses the function of savoring and gratitude to the building up of resilience and also to the deep exploration of the many facets of life, including those positive ones that we easily overlook in psychotherapy. Chapter 6 ends with some musings on the role of desire in the process of healing and in the creation of a meaningful life. Chapter 7 ends on a positive note, literally, by exploring the necessary and adaptive role of positive emotion and how much use can be made of that in psychotherapy without creating an artificial environment. The chapter describes how different areas of healthy adaptation are mediated by the experience of positive emotion, the idea of mature resilience as involving emotional complexity, and the possibility that growth can come from struggling in the aftermath of trauma. A case is made for an integrative approach to restoring resilience that includes the fullness of a person's story, the complexity of the human mind (if that can be captured), the depth of a person's feelings, the necessity of connection and closeness, and the intentional seeking and deepening of positive experiences. A distinction is made between transformance and flourishing. The chapter ends with a review of the *transformational spiral* and how the process of moving from languishing to flourishing, from resistance to transformance, involves many recursive experiences of healing transformation and reflecting on that healing transformation.

The final chapter to this book takes a small turn away from the focus on patients' experiences with transformative therapy to that of the therapist. It includes reflections from therapists on how this resilience-oriented work has healed the therapists themselves and enlivened their practices with renewed hope, a deeper sense of connection to their patients, and a more exquisite appreciation for how the people they work with are resilient to begin with and become even more so in the course of the work—in other words, how they too have become more resilient.

CHAPTER ONE

Reframing Resilience
Toward a Clinical Understanding

Michelangelo believed that the sculpture already existed within the stone—it was the artist's job to discern where and how the rock needed to be hewn and chiseled in order for the beauty to manifest. To see his work at L'Accademia in Florence, Italy, is a profound experience. One sees the magnificent and thoroughly complete *David* only after passing through the Hall of Prisoners that holds beautiful part-sculptures, unfinished by Michelangelo, all clearly stuck in the process of emerging. A viewer wonders what they might have been or become, imagines them more complete, and perhaps even feels frustrated that they were never born as their full selves.

The restoration of resilience is a similar process. It requires a dyadic, responsive relationship between therapist and patient that trusts that beauty, power, individuality, connection, and truth are all there for the mining. Our role as clinicians is not to put something where nothing had before existed but, rather, to make space, to proffer an invitation, and to provide the necessary and sufficiently nurturing environment for authentic experiences and expressions of self to emerge, to stretch, to grow, and to manifest to the world.

A focus on restoring resilience should start from the first moments of a therapeutic relationship. This requires a shift in perspective for most clinicians. We are accustomed to our extensive checklists

of symptoms, issues, conflicts, and safety, and only then the more
peripheral sense of what is going right in this person's life. A resilience-focused orientation shifts that figure and ground and pays
close attention to what is healthy, adaptive, likable, courageous,
unencumbered, and interpersonally related about the patient and
what s/he brings in *first*. It is from that perspective that the therapist begins to look at what has gone wrong, at the sources of suffering, at the deficits in adaptation or the costs to how the patient has
been approaching his struggles up to this point. This shift in focus
does not come at the cost of depth and complexity. Instead, it can be
seen as an added layer of complexity that more authentically rounds
out both our understanding of the people with whom we are working
and our own freedom of movement, skill, and humanity in working
with them.

This chapter explores and defines what that shift is and what it
involves. It also introduces some concepts that are extremely helpful,
even fundamental, to working toward restoring or enhancing resilience. It will define and delineate resilience specifically in a clinical
context and propose the essence of all resilience processes. These
definitions are somewhat different from how resilience is used in a
research context and, frequently, quite different from how it is used
in our common parlance. We will look at a transcript of a session in
which the therapist began by using more of a pathology focus and
then shifted to a resilience focus later, and the difference in the
patient in each of those contexts. Finally, I include here the *map of
resilience* for the sake of visual learners and to set the stage for our
ongoing conversation about resilience and what supports or hinders
healthy adaptive resilience in development and in the present day of
psychotherapeutic healing.

In most basic terms, which are elaborated and explored throughout the book, resilience-focused work starts with the assumption
that working with what is right from the beginning (1) expands the
resources of the patient, the dyad, and the work and (2) adds complexity and breadth to the process of healing and the restoration of
resilience that is not achieved if positive affects, experiences, and
self states are treated as side notes, means to an end, or simply

by-products of a therapy gone well. Some form and amount of resilience is, by the nature of our humanness, there for the mining. What it looks like and how the therapist finds it change over time as people become more resilient. The progression of this book is based on the idea that resilience is in the very least a *potential* waiting to be discovered and brought out. In the process of that discovery, it becomes a *promise* for a fuller life not yet lived. The pursuit of that promise leads to flourishing and, more important, to *transformance* (Fosha, 2008), which is the opposite of resistance and allows a person to be open to the full range of human experience, both painful and joyful.

How Therapists Define Resilience

In the course of researching and writing this book, I became curious about my colleagues' understanding of resilience and how that affected their work or approach, and also how working within an affect/experiential, healing-oriented model (specifically accelerated experiential dynamic psychotherapy, or AEDP) influenced their understanding of resilience. I sent out an informal survey to the AEDP listserv asking therapists about how they understood resilience, whether or not working in this kind of model has made them more resilient as therapists, and if and how working within such a model enhanced their patients' resilience. Their generous responses to the question of what resilience is are described below, and their reflections on how they themselves have become more resilient comprise chapter 8 of this book. I include their responses here as a good starting point toward a general consensus about resilience among clinicians—a common language we all speak. I hope to expand our understanding of resilience to be something that is more clinically relevant and useful to the process of healing and transformation.

Most people who responded to the survey defined resilience as the capacity to "bounce back" or even to flourish in the face of trauma. For example, one person defined resilience as "strength or flexibility in the face of adversity or trauma . . . like a palm tree that bends but does not break." Similarly, another likened resilience to elasticity that stretches under challenge. Another described a simple outcome that suggests infinite possible processes for attainment: "coming out sane from insane places/families." This reflects an understanding of resilience as a quality, characteristic, or capacity—a quantifiable factor. As explained later in this chapter, this understanding is reflected in the term *resilient capacity*. In the very least, it does not make sense to talk about resilience in the absence of trial, hardship, or trauma.

Some also thought about resilience more in terms of process. One therapist stated that resilience is "the capacity that is present even when a client is seemingly succumbing to hardship, feeling distressed and anguished." Several people, in referencing both their own personal traumas and those of their patients, noted that one frequently does not *feel* resilient while one is living through a very difficult situation—one is usually "just doing it." It is often only later that any of us really understand the hardship of what we have been through and can look back and marvel at how we made it through. This more process-oriented, existential way of understanding resilience is reflected in what we will call a person's *resilience potential*.

Another person defined resilience in a way that reflects our capacity to heal even if we are "broken" by trauma or adversity. She said it is "the ability to regenerate, or to make generosity out of trauma." This definition reflects an understanding of resilience not as something that is meaningfully measured at a given point in time but, rather, as a process that allows good and life to come from that which threatens or harms us. This is in keeping with the work done on posttraumatic growth (e.g., Calhoun & Tedeschi, 2001, 2006; Tedeschi, Park, & Calhoun, 1998) and is the most inclusive and perhaps the most useful way for clinicians to understand resilience, namely, that one's *potential for resilience blends with one's leanings toward growth and transformation*.

One person thought of resilience as both a quality and a potential, much in the same way that is discussed throughout this book, "a tensile quality of light and hope, deep in a person's being, which may flicker or even for a time be extinguished, but has the capacity to be rekindled if external conditions are supportive."

In fact, I think a workable clinical definition of resilience must include the possibility of breakage, breakdown, rupture, and loss. Healing involves an acquisition of more life, more energy, more hope, where formerly there was less or none. Imagine a person receiving mouth-to-mouth resuscitation. When a person loses breath and consciousness, it is highly unlikely that she will regain it on her own. But she can borrow the breath of another to vivify her own vital processes again. The body, in its own way and with its own limitations, receives and cooperates with what is offered by another until it can resume life on its own. The same is true for the mind and spirit. People look, wittingly or unwittingly, consciously or not, for signs of life, sparks of hope, to enliven their sagging spirits and their burdened minds. And they want someone to help them feel safe and worthy enough to lean on and into the other's vitality as they endeavor to make it their own.

Shifting Focus From Pathology to Healing

Resistance is the name given to motivational forces operating against growth or change and in the direction of maintenance of the status quo. Surrender might be thought of as reflective of some "force" towards growth, for which, interestingly, no satisfactory English word exists.

I will never forget the pressure I felt in graduate school in my Clinical Diagnoses classes. Having to remember lists of symptoms and the criteria required for how they should pattern themselves to comprise an Axis I or Axis II diagnostic label, and then having to apply that to brief descriptions of manufactured patients represented on paper, was at once challenging, exciting, alienating, and slightly unreal. The excitement lay in feeling that I had conquered a body of knowledge and that I was becoming like my professors and supervisors, who seemed to magically put together cryptic pieces of information and come up with a diagnosis that seemed, at the time, to explain much more than it did. The challenge lay in knowing that this skill was, in fact, important and useful in helping people to understand what is happening to them, and helping me to develop a clearer idea of what their experience is like and what treatment options might be most useful. The sense of alienation lay in the fact that none of this puzzle solving involved contact with a real human being, with the nonverbal or paraverbal communication between us, with the ineffable sense of what another is like that one knows only through *knowing* (i.e., gnosis). And, finally, the unreality stemmed, in part, from the fact that few of these descriptions ever included something that was positive about "the case."

Since Freud, we have been on the hunt for pathology. It has been a very useful search that has resulted in the field's capacity to help many people. But it requires a perceptual predisposition to pay more attention to what is wrong than to what is right. Our psychological maps have become sophisticated instruments with which we can not only locate the nature of pathology but also provide consistent, while varied, ideas about its origin. We have even evolved numerous "antidotes," in the form of therapeutic techniques, to restore health to the patient. These can be like medicine that we offer, the patient receives, and then, presumably, ideally, proceeds to get better. But now, the field is ripe for understanding better what the patient offers, what the patient brings, and what the dyad or the therapeutic system is capable of. Medicine does not work if the immune system will not or cannot cooperate—healing is a partnership. This book focuses on understanding who our partners are and what they bring to the healing process in addition to the need to be healed.

If the ultimate goal of psychotherapy is for our patients to be more relaxed, less reactive, more confident, less depressed, more goal directed, and generally happier in their lives, then we have to help them develop these parts of themselves and not simply settle for removing the blockages to them and hoping they develop on their own. The approach of peeling the onion may be sufficient for some, but for the vast majority it is not. It can go wrong in two ways. The first is that, as therapists, we do not recognize how we can be instrumental in helping our patients to develop what is nascent in them. There is no real harm done here—it is simply that both therapist and patient lose an opportunity to flourish; arguably a big loss. The second way the traditional pathology-oriented approach can go wrong is that we keep focusing on the obstacles despite nascent healing or striving. This can do harm to the extent that it discourages or undoes our partner in healing: the part of the patient that is oriented toward change, evolution, self-repair, and wholeness.

This has been made very clear to me in watching videotapes of my own and my colleagues' work. I have noticed our tendency to remark on the obstacles in response to a patient making a comment like, "I really want to take better care of myself." Well-intentioned therapists may say, "But your tendency to focus on your failures keeps getting in your way." Whatever wind was behind the sails of "I really want to take better care of myself" has just been stilled, and patients are focused, energetically as well as intellectually and emotionally, on how they continue to get in their own way. What if the therapist said, "Tell me more about *that*. What do you imagine? Where do you notice *that* energy in your body?"

Nathanson (1992) posits that the role or function of shame is to be an impediment to the affects of interest-excitement and enjoyment-joy when the environment suggests that that interest is not welcome or that joy does not resonate. The energy of joy in the body and psyche is expansive. In intending to do the exact opposite, we can stifle the potential expansiveness of our patients. A major reason this happens is how we are trained to think. Our training not only causes us to look for the pathological and problematic but also gets in our way of noticing the subtle movements and moments in which hope, joy, possibility, openness, and curiosity are present and waiting for encouragement, direction, and elaboration. We pay attention to the healthy parts when we are interested in tracking change and progress, but many therapists are less skilled in using the energy of that change and progress in a moment-to-moment way that builds on itself and creates a formidable counterweight to symptoms, defense, and despair. This is what this book hopes to counteract.

CLINICAL VIGNETTE:
"When will you ever learn not to point out the stain
on the night of the party?"

A good example of this kind of missed opportunity occurred
with a patient of mine who had come in sharing some unexpected good news about something that had happened at work.
Just before Amelia had come in,* I was thinking about how
unhappy she was in her work, how she had talked for a while
about finding another career that suited her interests and personality more, and how I was frustrated with the progress we
had made thus far in that direction. She was in a career that
was academically oriented, which bestowed a sense of importance but also chronically picked at her insecurities of not
being smart enough, particularly because she was not very
interested in much of its subject matter. Moreover, it was filled
with people who were awkward in relating to one another, fairly
judgmental, and not much fun. Amelia, on the other hand, loved
to have fun and was very creative visually and interpersonally.
Since childhood she had loved to laugh and be laughed at, and
she came alive when she was performing, a side of herself that
was consistently stifled in her more "serious" work environment. Finally, she felt more moved and connected to volunteer
work she had done in human services and the helping profes-
sions than she had ever felt in her chosen career. Consistent
with some potent messages from her childhood about what is
important, she deemed these things less valuable.

In this session, she comes in beaming. Treating it almost as
a side note, she begins to tell me about a party that she organized at work. This was a major step forward for her as she

---

* "Amelia" is a pseudonym, as are all names of patients used throughout the book.
Other personal details are also altered in order to protect patients' confidentiality and
privacy. Verbatim transcripts of videotaped sessions, however, have been approved for
inclusion in this book by patients. I am very grateful for their generosity in granting
me this permission.

continually left her personal self out of her work environment. Throwing the party felt like a big emotional and professional risk. She begins to recount how she and her partner dressed as two important figures and stayed in character and how the entire office was not only charmed but also relaxed and had a good time. They talked about it and thanked her for days afterward. It was a highlight in her work history. I spent a little time joining her and celebrating with her around this, but eventually I was seduced by the negative voice as well.

The commentary next to the dialogue may or may not be necessary or helpful at this point in the book—I include it for those who are interested. Ignore it if you get more out of just reading the transcript by itself at this point. The larger point is to "watch" and "listen" for the therapist's proclivity to follow the pathology and, more important, the patient's reaction to that type of intervention. I do not mean to suggest that focusing on pathology does not have its place but, rather, that from a resilience-oriented perspective, there are more productive ways to work with it than what is presented below.

PT: I have had a pretty good couple of weeks. . . . (My) director said, . . . "Don't you think we should throw a costume party?" . . . I was more excited by this party (**laugh, moving arms out**) than anything I have done there. [**A lot of positive affect; PT is relaxed and easily relating to TP.**]

TP: I am not surprised.

PT: And, um, I just felt really confident about it, and I was really looking forward to it, and it went off really well (*big smile*). [**Emergence of an authentic self state of confidence and strength.**]

TP: Great! [**TP joining and mirroring pride and positive affect.**]

PT: I came as. . . . We were kind of in character the whole time . . . I feel like people got a real kick out of it. [**PT beginning to elaborate on positive self-experience and recognition of positive impact on others.**]

TP: Wow, how bold! Mm-hmm.

PT: People were laughing a lot . . . our founder . . . was beyond tickled. (**PT provides more details.**)

TP: (**Laughing**)

PT: It felt really good.

TP: (**Warmly and with enthusiasm**) Good.

PT: (**Laughing, in kind of sarcastic tone that softens.**) I am embarrassed [**inhibitory affect**] that this moment, of every-thing I should have accomplished over the last couple of years, is where I felt most comfortable [**beginning of undoing of positive affect and pride with shame and defensive self criticism**], but I feel like, even though I was in character . . . I felt like I was myself more than I had been before. I was doing something that felt more natural to me. [**PT recovers, returning to good feeling around sense of true self.**]

TP: Mm-hmm. [**TP missing opportunity to go with thrust of her recovery and ask her more about feeling "more myself," "natural."**]

PT: So that was a really nice experience. [**PT likely senses TP's lack of coordination, and her energy shifts down and becomes more slow, suggesting it is time to leave this topic.**]

TP: That is great. (**Shifting to a playful tone**) So let's deal with the embarrassment about that. Why does that have to come in and mess it up? [**Again, TP moving away from "nice expe-rience" and positive affect and focusing on the inhibi-tion and negative affect.**]

PT: (**Leaning back, closing eyes**.) I know, I mean . . . [**PT's posture and facial expression are deflated in response to TP's focus on what inhibits the strong and whole parts of herself.**]

TP: (**Interrupting**) You got all this great feedback. People really appreciated it . . . you lightened a really heavy environment . . .

PT: (**Nodding and with good eye contact**)

TP: You enjoyed yourself, you felt real, you were Amelia, which is bringing your personal life into the office, which you have resisted doing.

PT: Right.

TP: **(Pause) [Silence suggests that while TP has listed all the positive things, the question is still slanted toward the negative: "What gets in the way?"]**

PT: Because it doesn't require any brains. [**PT follows the direction of the TP and answers the question. It is very easy for her to switch to talking about what is wrong. The therapeutic conversation now mirrors the conversations she has with herself.**] I feel like the accomplishments in that office are so different and more worthy of respect than what I did (**looking down, suggesting affect of shame**). I just feel embarrassed because I took so much pride . . . There are plenty of other things I should have the same all-around good feelings about, but I don't (**pause**). My boss that I have a harder time with was like, "This was great . . . I am not crazy about the stain on the carpet, but this was great." [**PT then has an association to another relationship, other than her own with her self, that consistently focuses on what is wrong with her and what she is not doing.**] And I was just like, "When will you ever learn not to point out the stain the night of the party?" (**shaking arms, throwing head back**) . . . But it was this great night, and I ended up feeling horrible about her comment about the stain in the carpet, feeling like that overshadowed everything. I guess sometimes I am looking for things to dwell on (**heavy sigh**).

A close colleague and friend of mine, Benjamin Lipton, watched the session with me and, in the gentlest of ways, pointed out the irony of my missing an opportunity to focus on how alive she was in talking about this party and this accomplishment, given my own belief in harnessing the energy of the positive. Fortunately, there were several moments later in the session that provided me with the opportunity to go back and do just that. After observing the chronic shame she feels, the strength of it, and its dynamic origins, she spoke about how she does not want to shut down. Together, we were able to draw that out, expand on it, envision it, and to allow it to calm, center, motivate, and animate her. My colleague and I both noted how much more alive she was in talking about being herself, having fun, taking a risk, and how much more energy there was within each of us and in the room. These somatic experiences of vitality and energy are markers that one is in the realm of healthy resilience and on the right path. Importantly, they also comprise a more solid self state from which the dyad can curiously explore the more painful, conflicted, shamed, or collapsed states that need integrating and healing.

TP: And that is bringing up some feelings right now. What are you feeling? [**Affective experiential focus.**]

PT: Um. I don't know. A lot of things. Just sad that I didn't get that attention or that I felt like I needed it, when it seemed like such an easy thing . . . for someone to have given. I think I felt full and like important or something. [**Some increase in self-compassion; understanding of what she needed chronically as a child but rarely got from important attachment figures.**]

TP: Mm-hmm.

PT: Uh

TP: Do you feel that now?

PT: I honestly keep thinking about my performance because that is the last time I felt these things. [**Opening of the unconscious to recent embodied experiences of feeling full or important.**]

TP: So what is that like? [**Experiential focus on emergent positive affect.**]

PT: That does make the boundaries go away . . . like I don't have to worry about anything. [**Defenses and anxiety disappear.**]

TP: So what is that like in your body right now? [**Experiential focus on relief of tension and worry and "boundaries."**]

PT: (**Gesturing toward and away from chest**) Like I can

expand and, um, like I am free (**sigh**). Like I can breath easier. [**Postbreakthrough affects**.]

TP: Mm-hmm, I can hear that. When you say you can expand do you feel that in particular parts of your body? [**Somatic exploration.**]

PT: No, I just feel like my chest isn't tight. I am not clenching any muscles. I just feel open and moving (**moving arms, smiling**). Like I don't feel trapped. I feel like I am free. I think that is probably similar to how I felt leaving the neighbors' house. (**PT then has a spontaneous memory of intensely positive, affirming experience of a visit to a neighbor's house by whom she was praised and delighted in. This experience was immediately followed by her father shaming her for allowing her pride to be evident in front of her neighbors and admonishing her for being "too big for her britches."**) [**Breakthrough of the unconscious.**]

TP: You can feel that in your body now?

PT: Yeah. It's like I don't have to care about anybody judging me. It doesn't even come into my head. And it feels strong and like I am in control and I am getting enough attention.

TP: Where does it feel strong? Where do you feel strong? [**Somatic/experiential exploration of sense of strength.**]

PT . . . I guess kind of in my core.

TP: Mm-hmm.

PT: I just feel physically strong and emotionally, that kind of like "I don't care what anybody thinks" strong. And confident, like I know I am doing something that I can do, and that I love doing.

What this latter transcript with Amelia illustrates is how an experiential, somatically-oriented focus on positive experiences deepens and solidifies those experiences of self and thereby provides context to and buffering of negative experiences, which as human beings we find far more compelling to our consciousness (Baumeister, Bratslavsky, Finkenauer, & Vohs, 2001). In the earlier transcript excerpt, the implicit therapeutic question is, What is wrong with you, and why? Amelia has plenty of answers to that, but she spins around them and loses herself. The question is devoid of compassion and true curiosity. Now, in this latter exchange, she has a much more solid and confident connection to herself, an embodied sense of the relief of tension and self-consciousness, and a freedom that she too seldom experiences. The compassion she has for herself is inextricably linked to her insights about how and to what she had to adapt at an early age. This is a much stronger, more whole, and more realistic place to start in exploring and healing the residual "pathology" of discounting and critiquing herself.

Even "Resistance" Can Be a Manifestation of Resilience

A very important point that I will return to throughout the book is this: *the seeds of resilience are often to be found in the pathology itself.* Freud (1894, 1926) commented that symptoms represent a partial failure of defenses and recognized defenses as an adaptation even as they were seen as pathological. Shifting figure and ground, a resilience-oriented approach sees symptoms as a partial success of "transformance," our wired-in strivings for growth and development (Fosha, 2008) peeking through the muck. What the person needs to become aware of or to integrate in the process restoring resilience is attempting to come through. What may become resistance over time surely started out as an expression of resilience, as the person's best effort to adapt to a circumstance that may have exceeded his or her limits.

George Vaillant's book on resilience based on the Harvard Grant Study of 268 men, begun more than 70 years ago (and still ongoing when his book was published), has an entire chapter on resilience and on what he calls "unconscious coping" (2012, p. 261). Interestingly, he uses the terms *adaptation, resilience, coping,* and *defense* interchangeably. He likens mental and emotional symptoms to physical ones, stating that "as cough, pus, and pain remind us with disconcerting regularity, the processes of illness and the processes of healing look startlingly alike" (p. 262). He goes on to say, "What makes the study of defenses so fascinating is the ambiguity of the boundary between pathology and adaptation" (p. 262). As clinicians, we are always working with and within that ambiguity. Part of what I hope to communicate in this book is how our work is enhanced by focusing on the adaptive and creative aspects of both defenses and psychopathology without denying their cost or their consequences.

In Amelia's case, her present inability to filter criticism and her feeling so in need of affirmation lest she be thrown into states of shame have a long history, beginning with being the daughter of a highly misogynistic and quite narcissistic father and a mother who said little despite being kind and generally loving. What is important is that her inability to filter the unnecessary criticism of others and her hyperawareness of the judgments (or potential judgments) of others are an expression of some part of her working very hard to make sure she is safe and connected to the relevant people around her. It epitomizes a truth that is foundational to the work of restoring resilience. Namely, what appears to be maladaptive, in its essence, is adaptive to another time, place, and interpersonal context, one in which the learning through interpersonal experience was deep, far-reaching, emotionally formative, and often repeated countless times. One can argue that this is not, therefore, resilience because she has not adapted to the current circumstances.

One can also argue that if a person adapts easily or readily to challenging situations, then perhaps the situations were not, in fact, so challenging, and their adaptation has little to do with resilience. But, as we are neither philosophers nor lawyers here, what is important is how we define resilience as clinicians, understanding that people's strengths are varied, their breaking points different, and the quality and chronicity of the adversity they experience are wide ranging and hard to capture quantitatively. Having said that, it is also important for us to distinguish between truly adaptive current behavior, thoughts, and feelings and those that are misplaced and therefore stuck. I elaborate on this later in the chapter by discussing *resilience potential* and *resilient capacity*. Briefly, the former refers to the innate possibility and force that works on behalf of the self at all times, and the latter is quantifiable factor: the maximum capacity a person has at any given point to flexibly adapt to adverse circumstances. At this point in our discussion, the key is that even in that

HOW SYMPTOMS CAN SOMETIMES BE OUR FRIENDS

A young woman patient who was married to a chronically underfunctioning man who smoked marijuana daily had always suffered with symptoms of irritable bowel syndrome and other gastrointestinal distress. Because she was a basically positive person, had lots of energy, and could push herself to accomplish a lot in the world, she managed to ignore her own needs in relation to her husband. She did what she could to manage and medicate the gastrointestinal issues. Over time, as she became more aware of her real feelings toward her husband and about being the only responsible person in the partnership, she started to understand and appreciate her flare-ups of intestinal distress as indicative (to her) that she was having difficult feelings about whatever was going on in the moment that she was avoiding. The one thing that would reliably get her to pay attention was the pain and discomfort she would feel in her stomach. What was initially relegated to an undesirable symptom came to be an ally in her attempts to live a healthier life and have more self-respecting boundaries and expectations of others. In other words, her symptoms were a manifestation of her resilience potential. And as she healed, she found more integrated ways of becoming aware of her own needs, boundaries, and feelings that did not require her to feel sick.

stuckness the kernel of resilience, of the self's working on behalf of the self, is present, there to be discovered, elaborated upon, mined, and redirected toward a different kind of resilience that involves greater safety, as well as vulnerability, and includes the possibility of flourishing rather than simply playing it safe.

A paradoxical aspect of focusing on the healing and self-righting tendencies within a person is that it often brings depth of understanding and experience while it facilitates newness and lightness. This is something that takes psychodynamically oriented clinicians a while to catch on to and trust in. Privileging the positive does not have to involve denying or avoiding the negative or the painful. Rather, when one really allows growth, transformation, and healing from within, one becomes more acutely aware of what one is healing from. *The new experience of the transformed self is felt to be new or transformed in relation to the former experiences or the former self.* There is an opportunity for a greater acceptance of what was and was not a part of one's past, and for all the complicated feelings that accompany that, such as anger, grief, loss, aloneness, compassion for the self, and even compassion for the other. As Amelia said, "It feels like I can loosen up a bit. It feels genuine. It feels like I am making room for myself."

I would like to plant the seed early in this book for clinicians to consider what it means to take seriously the idea that in many or even most cases, the expression of pathology is a manifestation, even if only a remnant, of resilient processes. This is not a novel idea— what is potentially novel is what changes if we take it seriously. If we are really curious about, turned on by, impressed by our patients' attempts to cope, if we do not simply give this idea a respectful intellectual nod but, rather, are determined to find, reframe, explore, and redirect the person's *efforts on behalf of the self,* how does it change our perception of the people we are working with, the way we work with them, the patients' sense of self, and their her experience of the therapeutic relationship and the therapeutic endeavor in general?

The Essence of Resilience

After three years of researching and writing this book and thinking a lot about resilience as I sit with my patients and those of my colleagues and supervisees, something came together as a way of understanding the essence of resilience whatever its context. Whatever else we will say about it, resilience is the *self's differentiation from that which is aversive to it.* By self I do not mean part-selves, and by aversive I do not mean that which is unpleasant or something we do not want to deal with even if it is what is best for us (e.g., going to the gym or eating kale). I am referring to the core self, very akin to what Richard Schwartz (1995) refers to as the Self. It is the true self, that "inner part," as one of my patient calls it, that sees clearly what is going on, that is evident, upon reflection, as the center of one's experiences in different contexts, over time, and in different organized incarnations of self (Damasio, 1999). By aversive, I mean that which is degrading, abusive, neglectful, enmeshed, sabotaging, hateful, annihilating, or oppressive. Resilience seems to be a spirit in us that can be tapped into and involves remaining at least somewhat separate from those things, people, events, or experiences that would wittingly or unwittingly demoralize us or disconnect us from ourselves and our hope.

Attempts to differentiate and act on behalf of the self can be more or less adaptive and more or less successful. This is a key point, because the purpose of resilience-focused therapeutic work is to never lose sight of the part of the person that wants to live and, eventually, to live well. Human beings bumble frequently and opt for the safe and the known. But that does not mean that, given the right support, opportunity, healing, and growth, they would not choose life over death, liveliness over anemia, flourishing over languishing. Many, however, have to learn to trust life and health and solidity and joy. That is the process of transformative therapy.

What is also essential about resilience is that it is both a *potential* and *capacity*. More is said about this below, but suffice it to say that all people have a potential to act on behalf of the self, adapt well to adversity, and heal from disruptive, dysregulating, or traumatic experiences. They also have a capacity, by which I mean a manifest capacity: How adaptively resilient are they in space and time? How does their resilience manifest itself? This distinction is reflected in different meanings given to the word *resilience* in the research literature, which are only very briefly mentioned below.

Finally, resilience should not be thought of as a black-and-white issue. Not only is it usually inaccurate to say a person is either resilient or not, but it is also frequently only part of the story. Often, the ways in which a person is resilient may mask the ways in which trauma, attachment problems, loss, pain, and the like have *also* made their mark. People can suffer lasting damage even if they have also been resilient. People who appear quite resilient may also have pockets of self-experience in which they hold the damage, in which they do identify with the blows against the self they have suffered (e.g., they harbor self-hatred, or have a foreshortened sense of the future). And people who have appeared to be not very resilient will often find

BROKEN AND WHOLE: HOW RESILIENCE IS
A PARADOXICAL PHENOMENON

Jacob was repeatedly sexually abused from 9 to 13 years of age by a neighbor friend of the family and passed around by the abuser to other men.* His family life was neglectful in the least and often openly hostile. He never thought he could tell anyone what was happening. After 2 years with his first psychotherapist, when he was in his mid-fifties, he reflected on how differently he felt about himself. This was triggered, in part, by talking to a woman he worked with and had known since grade school. She had spoken to a long-lost friend of theirs from high school who, when she found out she worked with Jacob, reflected on how Jacob's kindness and care toward her when she was in a very bad place were essential to her well-being at the time. Both women talked about what a good and kind man he was and always had been. The friend/coworker shared this conversation with him. He was touched by how the second woman had remembered him and was curious about how he was still able to be that way despite the hell he was going through and the total darkness with which he was accustomed to seeing his life at that time. He said to his therapist, "So, instead of being in what I would think would be a hopeless state, I was still in the midst of the burnt-out inner city planting a garden somewhere." He expressed gratitude in knowing those "oases" were there even though he does not easily remember them. The shame and self-loathing that accompanied the abuse caused him to be convinced that whatever was genuinely good about him was, in fact, false and that if people "really knew" what was going on they would hate him as he hated himself. So the true and good expressions of himself were distorted to be something other than what they really were. Only on reflection and in the wake of healing did he really see and understand that. Thinking of his younger self at that time, he said, "You did a good job. That's incredible. The tide (was) against you and you didn't drown."

* The case of Jacob is generously provided by Stephen Carroll, a colleague of mine whose work with Jacob helped restore him to his own beautiful humanity and compassionate connection to himself and others.

Here was a man no longer overtaken by or fully identified with the damage that was done to him and to his sense of self. And yet the damage was great; the fallout, substantial. From the perspective of some restored resilience, from being in a true self state, he could see that damage coexisted with goodness, kindness, compassion, and strength (i.e., resilience). As he felt and expressed pride in himself as a boy he became aware that he'd had this feeling: "I think it's always been there but I've been afraid to respond to it . . . I would come up with any excuse that I could to deny that it's real." That is the gold we are mining for in restoring resilience—that part that has always maintained a positive connection to the self despite whatever else is happening to the self.

or remember ways in which they were, but for whatever reason, this did not deeply inform their sense of self. People can be broken *and* whole, "damaged" *and* resilient. Part of the work of restoring resilience and facilitating healing is integrating those two parts.

Reflections in the Research Literature

The vast literature on resilience focuses mostly on children, defined generally as those who overcome odds and do better than might be expected given the adverse circumstances to which they are subjected (Garmezy, Masten, & Tellegen, 1984; Glantz & Johnston, 1999; Gralinski-Bakker & Hauser, 2004; Gralinski-Bakker, Hauser, Stott, Billings, & Allen, 2004; Masten, 2001; Rutter & English & Romanian Adoptees Study Team, 1998; Rutter, O'Connor, & English and Romanian Adoptees Study Team, 2004). The circumstances generally studied include physical, sexual, or emotional abuse, neglect, loss, poverty, being raised by single parents, illness, having a parent with a mental illness or substance abuse problem, and the like. Researchers in the 1970s dubbed a subgroup of these chronically stressed children "vulnerable but invincible" (Werner & Smith, 1982).

A simple, straightforward, and important finding across studies on resilient children is that as disadvantage and the number of stressful life events increase, so too do the number of protective (or compensatory) factors in the children and their environments need to increase in order to counterbalance the cumulative negative influence of stress and deprivation (Fergusson & Horwood, 2003; Werner & Smith, 1982). Garmezy (1987) termed this "cumulative risk" to emphasize the fact that many children continue to do rather well when faced with one or two major risks, but their functioning diminishes as the number of these factors in their lives increases. This is often what therapists find in their patients as well.

Thirty plus years of study has earned the field some sophistication and has opened up many more questions that have yet to be answered. What was originally a field dominated by black-and-white thinking has become one that embraces and grapples with enormous complexity—so complex, in fact, that the current, frequently cited definition of resilience is "the process of, capacity for, or outcome of successful adaptation despite challenging or threatening circumstances" (Masten, Best, & Garmezy, 1990, p. 426). Researchers of resilience have moved away from a linear, time-delimited view of resilience and have begun to define it as a multideterminined process that develops over time. In fact, Luthar and Zelazo, who write extensively about resilience, state: "Researchers must explicitly state in their reports that they are studying a process or phenomenon, and not a personal attribute of the child" (2003, p. 525). And so, the resilient child and, in the case of this book, the resilient adult are seen as existing within a web of relationships and experiences, as well as personal attributes, that are either protective or detrimental, reflecting an understanding of resilience as highly contextual, whether defined as a process or as an outcome (Wyman, 2003).

Even the research world, therefore, has found a way of talking about the process of resilience as underlying the preservation of the self, which may manifest in a range of responses and adaptations from self-protective defensiveness to flourishing. And so, here too, we will be talking about both process and outcome, potential and capacity. Resilience is both something that is manifest, observable, and even measurable, and a process that underlies attempts at adaptation in the face of stress, adversity, or trauma.

Developing a Common Language About Resilience: The Terminology of Resilience

As has already been noted, this book is not primarily about resilience in and of itself but, rather, about how resilience manifests in the therapeutic encounter and how it can be invited as a partner in healing while it also becomes more subtle, supple, and oriented toward flourishing. AEDP offers a number of terms and concepts that are highly relevant to the cultivation of resilience; these terms are defined and delineated here.

Resilience Potential, Resilient Capacity, Resistance, and Transformance

Resistance involves all the forces that work against moving forward, being open, experiencing new things, being in genuine contact with oneself or another. Some think of resistance as a manifestation of the death instinct: our innate destructive impulses toward ourselves and others. Others think of it as misguided self-protection based on fear. Whatever its origins, its consequences include the constriction of energy, of personality, and of potential. It relates to and involves our fight, flight, and freeze mechanisms. It is "defensive," and therapists usually work assiduously to get beyond it with their patients.

The quote from Emmanual Ghent's beautiful, courageous, and inspiring article in the early part of this chapter explores what is happening when patients let go and get beyond resistance themselves. Again, he states: "resistance is the name given to motivational forces operating against growth or change and in the direction of maintenance of the status quo. Surrender might be thought of as reflective of some "force" towards growth, for which, interestingly, no satisfactory English word exists" (Ghent, 1990, p. 110). A psychoanalyst, Ghent is wrestling with whatever force exists within the individual that allows one to let go of the false self. It is easy to forget that this surrender is not a once-and-for-all phenomenon. We have layers of falseness that, with experience, courage, safety, and wisdom, need to be shed in order to live more authentic, less performatory lives. But, until recently, we have been so unaccustomed to paying attention to, much less talking about, this force that we have not had a word for it. *Transformance* refers to the "overarching motivational force, operating in both development and therapy, that strives toward maximal vitality, authenticity, and genuine contact" (Fosha, 2008, p. 292). It is the inverse of resistance. It is that force that is reflected in experiences of surrender (Ghent, 1990), peak experiences (Maslow, 1971), flow (Csikszentmihalyi, 1996), self-actualization (Maslow, 1954), striving (Adler, 1964), and flourishing (Keyes & Haidt, 2003; Fredrickson, 1998; Fredrickson & Branigan, 2005; Fredrickson & Losada, 2005), as well as the processes that culminate in those ends. Unlike resistance, which typically depletes many of the self's resources and energy, transformance strivings, when realized, are marked by and provide energy and vitality to the self and expand the self's resources. It is the process that eventuates in healing in the right circumstances. I think of transformance as our most highly developed, most complex, and most currently adaptive manifestation of resilience.

If the forces of transformance remain unnamed, they remain unclear even in our experience of them. Everyone has had the experience of learning a new word after hearing it for what one believed was the first time and subsequently hearing it all over the place. Having a word for the processes within us that are geared toward transformation, healing, surrender, and growth allows us to be more aware of and attentive to them when they arise. The nominalization of the phenomenon of transformance is a crucial piece of our developing a language of healing.

As mentioned earlier, resilience is used here to denote both the process underneath adaptation and the manifest outcome of that process. It is therefore useful to have two different terms to denote these different aspects of resilience. What I have come to call the *resilience potential* refers to an innate possibility and force existing in all people that works constantly on behalf of the self to recover, bounce back, heal, or, at the very least, protect oneself from adversity, hardship, and even trauma. It underlies both transformance and resistance as these are both, in the appropriate circumstances and with the requisite resources, adaptive responses to the conditions at hand. This is similar to what the research world terms *resilience processes*.

I use the term *resilient capacity* to refer to an individual's maximum ability to bounce back, recover, heal, or protect the self at any given moment in time. It is how the resilience potential is actualized at any given time. This is a quantifiable factor that can be looked at between and within individuals and the factor therapists are looking to augment in the patients they work with. There are a number of research measures of resilience, but the most popular is Block and Kremen's (1996) Ego Resilience Scale. *Resilience potential*, on the other hand, is the inborn tendency whose existence we postulate and whose partnership we rely on in helping people to work on behalf of themselves, to heal, and to grow. It is that "something that is striving to find its way out of the dark into the light [that] has not [yet] found the key that will allow it to come into being" (Symington, 2006, p. 10).

It is important to understand that the nature and expression of the resilience potential change as the self expands. What may become resistance over time surely started out as an expression of resilience, as the person's best effort to adapt to a circumstance that may have exceeded his or her limits or resources. So this resilience potential is stuck in an unproductive gear despite its good intentions. The goal of this work is to channel the underlying self-preservational energy, which sometimes gets stuck in resistance, to more adaptive and life enhancing expressions in the present. The person has to get out of reverse or neutral and put some of the energy on behalf of the self into forward movement. In doing so, the expression of the underlying resilience potential changes from constraining and enervating conservation or resistance to flourishing and energizing transformance. *Transformance realized becomes enhanced resilient capacity.*

Is It Safe to Be Open? The Self-at-Worst and Self-at-Best

Most people can identify relationships in which they are their best and truest self and others in which their predominant feeling about themselves is something negative, and their behavior—toward themselves and the other—is regularly in accord with that. Fosha's concepts of self-at-best and self-at-worst wonderfully illustrate this interpersonal reality. Specifically, these concepts denote different ways of functioning with ourselves and others around emotional and other core affective experience (e.g., authentic self states, embodied ego states). In some contexts, the elicitation of feeling or authentic self experience triggers anxiety, and in turn, defenses come in to quiet that anxiety and continue to push out of consciousness the feelings or self states that were provoking anxiety in the first place. The self is experienced as compromised. The other is experienced as distorted (or distorting), and one's real affective experiences get cut off. This describes self-at-worst. On the other hand, we can have experiences in which we feel open to what comes up from inside us affectively, and there is relatively little anxiety and little need to defend. The other is seen realistically, and the self is experienced as effective, having access to and being informed by her own feelings. This describes self-at-best. The terms are not meant to be diagnostic judgments of a person but, rather, to capture more of the subjectivity of the person in either state. They are simple terms that can be understood by everyone ranging from the least to the most psychologically minded and self-reflective. As a patient of mine expressed (see Chapter 3), "It is a bad reflection of who I am when that happens."

These concepts describe the self's relationship with one's internal reality in the context of relationships that welcome and facilitate it or those that inhibit it in some way. "Attachment is relationship dependent" (Fosha, 2000), and self-functioning is attachment dependent. Even when we are on our own, our internalized attachments of early primary caregiving relationships (e.g., with parents) affect how we feel about ourselves in the world and how we conduct ourselves in relation to this sense of ourselves. Ideally, therapy and, more specifically, the relationship with the therapist, should be safe enough that the patient is able to be his best self, as well as willing to reveal and work with his worst self.

Frequently therapists are confronted by their patients with the question, "What's the point? Why should I go 'back there'? What good does it do me now?" This is not simply a defensive question. It is honest, self-protective, and eminently practical. It reveals a common wisdom that the simple revisitation of trauma is not in itself healing but, rather, can be, more likely, retraumatizing. Without access to greater resources—internal, external, or both—reimmersion in the traumatic experience and the paralyzing feelings that accompany it is not helpful. People simply reexperience their own powerlessness, terror, shame, and paralysis, still having no idea how to get out of them, to move on, or to feel better. This is a classic example of a negative feedback loop, in which no new (helpful) learning is introduced to provide an exit from the homeostasis of trauma.

A different approach, and one that is the basis of this book, is the engagement of another, positive feedback loop—one that takes in and integrates new information. This approach, from the very beginning, seeks to catalyze the healing process by engaging and entraining the wired-in self-righting tendencies and motivation to flourish, what AEDP (Fosha, 2008) calls *transformance strivings*. Working with the self-at-worst with a solid connection to the self-at-best allows us to work on two prongs of healing at the same time. The strong, solid, true part is being further strengthened, solidified, and elaborated, while the wounded part is offered hope, consolation, and understanding. It is not a linear model in which, once we remove the "worst" part, the "best" part has room to emerge. Rather, we are working on both parts of the system simultaneously, and they influence each other. In fact, the strengthening, nurturance, and subsequent growth of the "best" part contributes directly to the healing of the "worst" part. A self that can feel honestly and see clearly, with self-compassion, is well on the way to becoming a whole and integrated self—a self capable of and uniquely motivated to shepherd in its own lost sheep.

The self-at-worst and the self-at-best as concepts are discussed in more technical detail in Chapter 3. Here we review a simple visual psychodynamic heuristic that can serve as background for these more complicated concepts. Used by almost all therapists working from an emotion-focused psychodynamic perspective, the Triangle of Conflict (Malan, 1979; see Figure 1.1) depicts the theoretical assumption that pathology is defined by and results from the use of chronic defenses against certain impulses and feelings that elicit anxiety in the person experiencing them. Rather than having access to one's own feelings and impulses as sources of information and providers of motivation, they are blocked, presumably because cultural, societal, and familial influences have repeatedly sent the message that such experiences or expressions thereof are not acceptable. Therefore, when the intrusions and wonders of life elicit the forbidden feelings and impulses, unconsciously, the person experiences anxiety, or some kind of tension, and responds with a psychological or behavioral defense, which both modifies the anxiety and keeps the "bottom of the triangle" treasures out of consciousness, thereby temporarily restoring equilibrium. People enter therapy, according to this model, when those defenses begin to break down or one's

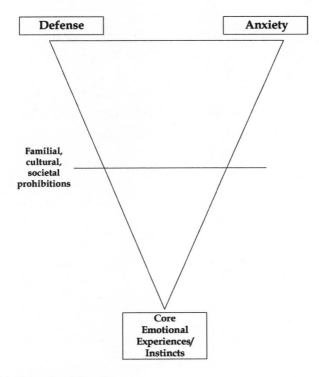

FIGURE 1.1. Triangle of Conflict.
Adapted from Malan, D. (1979). Individual psychotherapy and the science of psychodynamics. London, Butterworth.

anxiety in response to the repressed core feelings is simply too much for the old defenses to effectively moderate, or the feelings or self states themselves are simply pressing for attention.

A core principle of psychodynamic thinking asserts that these patterns of anxiety in response to feelings and impulses, as well as the defenses against them, are "learned" in childhood and are repeated in current relationships and, frequently, in the therapeutic relationship. Another way of thinking about this is to consider attachment styles as generalizable across relationships. This is depicted in Figure 1.2, the Triangle of Persons, renamed by Malan (1979) based on work by Menninger (1958). Yet another apt term for this phenomenon is *transference*, broadly understood as "unconscious repetition of earlier behaviors and projection onto new subjects" (VandenBos, 2007, p. 952). With that as our background, we will focus instead on identifying, facilitating, and working with the exception to the rule: when a person's statements, behaviors, responses, attachment styles, or feelings are "out of pattern." Transference is real, but so is the hope for and openness to a new experience with another and with oneself, which is not so predictable. In Piagetian terms, we are able to accommodate as well as assimilate.

The idea that it is unprocessed feelings or impulses that elicit this pattern of anxiety, defense, and eventually psychopathology, while very helpful and organizing, can be limiting. It is not only categorical

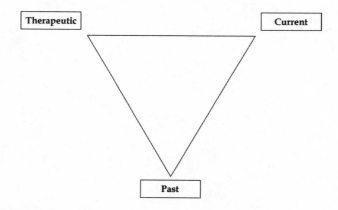

FIGURE 1.2. The Triangle of Persons.
Adapted from Malan, D. (1979) Individual psychotherapy and the science of psychodynamics. London, Butterworth.

affects or feelings (e.g., anger, sadness, joy, disgust) that can elicit anxiety and the whole pathology-engendering sequence. This same pattern can also be elicited by authentic self-states ("this is me!"), attachment experiences (e.g., closeness, longing, distance, intimacy), coordinated relational experiences (i.e., being "in sync" with another), embodied ego states, and feeling "dropped down" somatically. Collectively, AEDP refers to these as *core affective experiences*. First, they are experiential and embodied. They are core to the self in that they are real, feel real and true, and have probably been formative for the person. And they are affective in that, in the very least, they are colored by emotion even if not dominated by it. It is these core affective experiences that AEDP replaced the simpler impulse/feeling category at the bottom of the Triangle of Conflict. I will refer to core affective experiences throughout the book.

The limitation of the Triangle of Conflict and the Triangle of Persons in isolation is that they do not depict, and therefore are not capable of making sense of, the phenomenon of differential self-functioning-in-relationship. They do not address the exception to the rule. The self-at-worst and self-at-best triangles are a combination of and elaboration on the Triangle of Conflict and the Triangle of Persons (Figure 1.3). They account for the fact that intrapsychic conflict is contextualized by interpersonal experience. They can be thought

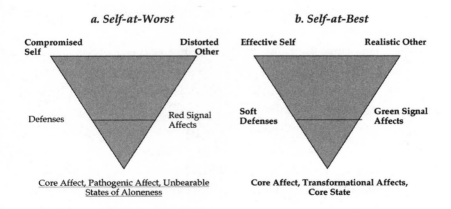

FIGURE 1.3. Self-at-Worst (a) and Self-at-Best (b).
Figure created by Diana Fosha, used with permission.

of as self states that exist within the context of relationships that either inhibit or invite fuller and truer expressions of the person.

In the self-at-worst state (Figure 1.3a), the individual has not processed emotion to completion, and anxiety, tension, or inhibition is usually high. Experiences such as shame or embarrassment, which inhibit experience and expression of deep affect, genuine relating, or connection to authentic self states, predominate the individual's experience and presentation, and the individual may make little eye contact, go on talking about something that does not feel particularly engaged or is repetitive, or just shut down. The person's reliance on defenses is stronger in order to diminish anxiety and to keep out of awareness the core experiences that are begging for attention. The individual is left in a compromised state and, as such, is limited or circumscribed in his capacity to relate to others. This is essentially the description of the classic transference neurosis. In the session dialogue presented above, this is evident in Amelia's reflexive focus on her boss's comment on the carpet and the habitual way she greets her expansiveness and vitality by saying that it is misplaced and unworthy and that therefore she is not good (i.e., smart) enough. What would it be like for both therapist and patient to focus on identifying, facilitating, and working with the exception to the rule: when a person's statements, behaviors, responses, attachment styles or feelings are "out of pattern"? Amelia's bold planning of this party and decision to "perform" by remaining in character and allowing herself to totally enjoy herself and her efforts are precisely that out-of-pattern instance we are looking for.

In contrast, the self-at-best (Figure 1.3b) has relatively easy access to one's genuine emotional experience and is comfortable expressing it. Defenses are minimal, and anxiety is essentially gone. Instead of the predominance of inhibitory affect such as shame or anxiety, characteristic of the self-at-worst, the patient usually reports experiences of curiosity, mild excitement, or a burgeoning sense of hope. (More is said in Chapter 4 about shame and its role not simply as an inhibitory affect but also as a pathogenic affect that needs to be worked with and witnessed rather than simply calmed or bypassed.) His eye contact tends to be good, and he tends to be in a thoughtful/

reflective but simultaneously communicative state, thus affectively communicating an openness to what is happening within himself and between himself and the other. The self is experienced in an effective and also accepting and realistic way, "warts and all." There is a healthy and grounded sense of pride. In addition, there is a real capacity to relate to the other as *an other* and to see him or her in a realistic way, which may or may not be positive. For example, when Amelia later had access to a very positive and affirming experience of childhood, she embodied it, and her whole physical countenance changed, as did her emotional experience and her sense of herself. In her words: "I just feel physically strong and emotionally, that kind of like 'I don't care what anybody thinks' strong. And confident, like I know I am doing something that I can do, and that I love doing."

When the other is experienced in a very positive and facilitating way, there is much opportunity for experiencing *transformational affects* and *core state*—experiences and self states that are the result of deep emotional processing as well as *the best* of the self-at-best. Transformational affects include, among other things, feeling moved or touched within oneself and feeling grateful toward another. This is not an uncommon experience for a patient following the processing of deep emotion and the therapist's facilitation and welcoming of this. Core state is a unique self state in which the person feels relaxed, accepting of oneself, compassionate toward self and other, open, grounded, in a "flow," at ease, solid but light. These states are described more completely in Chapter 2, and examples of them occur throughout the transcripts of this book.

Obviously, the self-at-best is the goal of psychotherapy. This does not mean someone feels on top of the world all the time, but rather, that someone is relatively happy, is open to her own emotional experience, has and maintains healthy and positive connections with others who allow her to be her best self, and can set limits with others who do not. It is about being able to feel real and to be real, which includes being able to identify, recover from, and repair experiences involving the self-at-worst. The more frequently one experiences the self-at-best in psychotherapy, the easier it should be to experience it and cultivate it outside of therapy. This state

PRESSURING WITH EMPATHY

Sometimes people's defenses against feeling can be more formidable. In such cases, the therapist may rely on what I call pressuring with empathy (Russell, 2004). *Pressuring* is a term borrowed from Intensive Short-Term Dynamic Psychotherapy (ISTDP) (Davanloo, 1990) that refers to a therapeutic technique of pushing on the patient's defenses in order for him to let go of them and to feel his feelings. Rather than imagining the therapist side-by-side with the patient at the top of the Triangle of Persons, pushing him to let go and drop down into affect, I have always found it more useful to imagine the therapist sitting at the bottom of the triangle, in touch with the feelings the patient may be trying to bypass or avoid. The invitation can be more insistent, as with pressuring with empathy. It is "the explicit use of the therapist's emotional reaction, more specifically the explicit self-disclosure of her own feelings of compassion, warmth, or appreciation, to help the patient feel at a deeper level" (Russell & Fosha, 2008, p.181). The pressure comes in helping the patient stay with the new feelings despite the discomfort they create, and the empathy communicates the patient's deservingness to have these feelings and the therapist's confidence that the patient can handle them. It is a lot like saying, "You don't have to run away. You can do this. You deserve it and it's good for you."

of the self is appetitive. People strive for it and know it as "good" when they inhabit it. Frequently, people settle for being and relating from a state of being that is something short of it. So identifying it, validating and actively welcoming it, and expanding it help it to feel more real, more acceptable, and more accessible to people and something to be striven for.

Transformative Therapy: The Self-in-Transition and the Transformational Other

Much of the time, in the course of a given therapy, and in the course of a given session, the patient is neither in a self-at-worst nor a self-at-best state. They are in a state that I call the self-in-transition (Figure 1.4). This is a vulnerable and fluctuating state in which there is a vacillation between the rigidity and compromise of the self-at-worst and the suppleness and connection of self-at-best. The patient is taking a risk and, in so doing, reveals his resilience potential. But he is not certain or safe enough to completely let go of his defenses. The patient is neither completely flooded by anxiety nor rigidly defended, nor is he completely open and curious about his emergent experience. Rather, his affective state is marked by a rather rapid fluctuation between inhibitory affects such as shame, embarrassment, and anxiety and expansive affects, such as signs of openness, hope, and curiosity.

These signals of hope, curiosity, and openness are revelations of the resilience potential, waiting for a place to emerge from behind the blinders of the now habitually defended and compromised self. The way to work with them effectively is to notice them and talk to them directly, to invite them and keep inviting them until they take up more and more space.

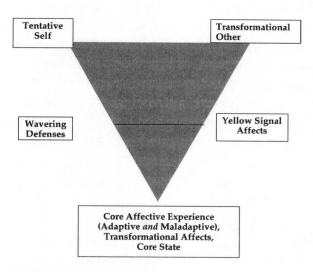

FIGURE 1.4. Self-in-Transition.

CLINICAL VIGNETTE:
"I feel like I can loosen up a bit. It feels genuine."

The following transcript is taken from the same session with Amelia, the young patient I introduced in the beginning of this chapter. At a later point in the session, after processing some of the anxiety and talking about the defense of "shutting down," she spontaneously says, "I don't want to" shut down. The therapist asks her to expand on that feeling/motivation.

PT: (**Choked up tears**) Well, because I don't want to (**smile; face in hand**). [**Emergence of healthier, resilience potential.**]

TP: You don't want to shut down.

PT: No, it's like (**wiping tears**) I know I am not happy there. I am not doing things I enjoy doing, but I am forcing myself to. I feel like the light part of me or the kid in me, I am not making any room for that (**tears**). [**PT recognizing defense against lighter, freer part of self: she makes no room. She has feelings about excluding this part of herself.**]

TP: Mm-hmm. And that's the part that has to shut down, and you are saying to me that you don't want to shut down. [**TP emphasizing motivation to let go of defense and allow emergence of transformance strivings**.] So what's *that* like right now? [**Experiential focus on resilience potential; encouraging familiarity with this part of self.**] Are you still aware of that?

PT: Yeah. Um. It's hard to get to. It's childlike . . . almost like a whiny part of me. I don't want to bring a paper home. I don't want to *not* go out to dinner with a friend because I have to read about chaos theory and the big bang (**wiping tears**).

TP: What does it feel like in your body when you say "I don't want to shut down"?

PT: It feels like I can loosen up a bit. It feels genuine. It feels like I am making room for myself, but at my peril. [**Responds to TP's invitation to notice and feel resilient part with a mixture of openness to and fear about emerging self:**

yellow-signal affects, which are a mixture of green (i.e., open/ curious) and red signals (i.e., anxious/ inclined toward closing off core experience) and will be discussed at length in chapter 3.]

The therapist continues to focus on the emerging resilient and resourced part, as long as it is not overwhelmed by anxiety and defense. For many this is a gradual process; exposure happens for longer periods each time. People, including therapists, often have to build a tolerance for their own positive affect and transformance strivings. Hope can be frightening.

At the end of this segment, the patient notices the good feelings in her body (i.e., loosening) and in her sense of connection to herself (i.e., "feels genuine") when she makes room for "I don't want to shut down." But she also becomes aware of some fear, which she later calls "dread." The therapist may have the experience of watching a Ping-Pong game. There is a rapid back-and-forth between feeling open to what is emerging from deep within the self and a fear or anxiety that encourages the erection of defenses in an effort to shut down these affects and the self experiences that accompany them. Essentially, the patient is being faced with a choice of following the familiar forces of resistance or allowing a transformational experience engendered by her own capacity to be *on behalf of herself* and the genuine, affirming, and inviting connection with the therapist and the "dyadic expansion of consciousness" (Tronick, 1998) that results from that.

In keeping with the idea that attachment is relationship dependent and self-functioning is attachment dependent, it follows that the therapeutic relationship, on a whole and in a given moment, supports or discourages the ongoing emergence of healthy and transformance-oriented aspects of self—of true self experiences. In the context of therapy, the therapist has an opportunity to be a *transformational other*. Based on Bollas's (1979) concept of a transformational object, and Fosha's (2000b, p. 8) explication of the true other, the transformational other exists within the dyadic or interpersonal moment in which she facilitates a state transformation in another that is positive (even if painful) and feels true to the self that is transforming. The transformational other is the counterpart to the self-in-transition. These are not states marked by a sense of having arrived but, rather, are dynamic and evolving even as they are defined and delineated by a given moment. They are also highly sensitive to disruption because people seem to be very attached to the known and are often made nervous by the unknown. But if the therapist is aware of this, is herself trusting in the process of transformation and compassionate about the anxiety that accompanies it, she can direct the work toward the transition and the parts of the patient that are open to it, desirous of it, motivated by it. Moreover, she can communicate a sense of trust, calm, normalcy, and rightness about it that the patient can borrow until his own trust and faith is stronger.

Bollas (1987) spoke about the transformational object as being experientially defined by the self and identified with processes that alter self-experience. The earliest experiences of this are in infancy, when the baby's physical needs are taken care of and therefore the self-experience (e.g., of hunger) is transformed (e.g., to satiety). Bollas contends that this need for transformational objects never dies but, rather, metamorphoses and chooses increasingly mature objects. These early experiences of transformation live on in our seeking of and openness to objects, experiences, ideas, beliefs, and people who are capable of transforming us. Bollas asserts that this ongoing seeking and certainty is based in infantile experience and the certainty that the object pursued will deliver the desired transformation. I contend that it is a universal, in-born need, proclivity, and hope. It is a capacity and an impulse that exist in each person, no matter what their early experience. As distorted as it may become or as problematic as the objects chosen as catalysts may be, *the tendency to seek transformational self-experiences is a reliable part of the human condition and an expression of the underlying resilience potential.*

This is a profoundly important ally to our work. It is the potential residing within our patients that is receptive to our efforts to help, understand, challenge, encourage, empathize, and elaborate the self's experience and potential, and even to have feelings on behalf of the patient. If the patient can actually receive help, understanding, challenge, encouragement, and empathy, then the resilience potential will manifest not as resistance but as transformance. Part of the challenge is helping our patients get to a place where they receive it for what it is and not for what it is imagined— or distorted—to be.

Resilience, as in the resilient capacity, is like any other human quality or capacity. It may be circumscribed by biology, but it is strengthened by and finds direction in relation to others. A child with a good ear for music may have the potential to do creative and masterful things with it if someone recognizes his capacity and interest and engages him around it, providing opportunities for exposure and exploration and joining with him in his excitement around his discoveries of himself and what he loves. In this way, the other who engages him is a transformational other. In Bollas's terms, part of the function of the transformational other is the *elaboration* of the self. Bollas would say that music itself is a transformational object for the child. And I would like to add that the parent or teacher who engages him around his transformational experience is a transformational other who does not simply identify the self but draws it out, makes room for it, engages in dialogue, and encourages its ongoing elaboration, thus allowing for greater complexity, creativity, coherence, and integration.

What that means for us as therapists is that no matter what the damage from trauma, no matter the level of pathology or defense, there is an innate resilience potential in every individual that seeks not just safety but greater health, wholeness, and well-being. It is waiting to be recognized and invited into dialogue. There is a *knowing*, no matter how unconscious, in each human being of what transformation and healing feel like, and there is a motivation to experience it. Finally, there is a recognition of it as it unfolds and in the wake of it. The awareness of and connection to one's strong, bendable but not breakable core sense of self is experienced at once as new and as always having been there. Several clinical examples of this paradoxical phenomenon of "discovering" the old, familiar, or once known appear later in the book.

The Map of Resilience

The map of resilience (Figure 1.5) is a visual depiction of what is discussed throughout this book. At the bottom, in the middle, is what I am calling our resilience potential, that capacity to be, do, and work on behalf of the self both to maintain life and psychic equilibrium and to flourish if the circumstances and our own internal resources allow for it. That potential with which we are born is met, shaped, responded to, and invited or deepened or shunned or inhibited through important experiences. These include, but are not limited to, the nature, quality, and amount of attachment relationships, the availability of other sources of interpersonal support or instrumental resources, intrapersonal resources or challenges (including temperament), the capacity to regulate emotion, and prior experience with adversity or challenge. When the balance of these is largely positive and people have had enough external and internal support to know and express their own minds, their expression of resilience (i.e., resilient capacity) looks like what we are accustomed to thinking

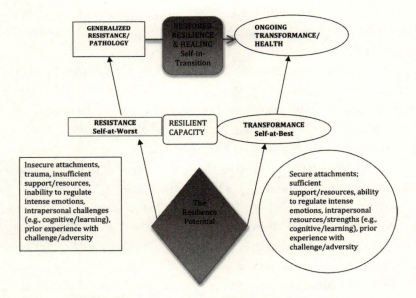

FIGURE 1.5. The Map of Resilience: From Resistance to Transformance.

about when we think of resilience. They can process what happens to them. They can lean on others when in need. They are able to keep moving along with their lives, and somehow trauma and loss seem to become integrated—not without struggle, but without defeat (i.e., self-at-best/transformance). If nothing traumatic happens that truly overwhelms such people's capacity to cope, it is reasonable that they often go through life in a transformance-oriented state: open, basically healthy, and with the potential to really flourish.

In contrast, when people do not have enough internal or external support to know and express their own minds and then encounter adversity, they rely on ways of coping that we do not typically associate with resilience. They hold things in or act things out to their detriment. They are more "defensive" and probably at some deep level do not feel like they have much choice. Rather than their mantra being "follow one's dreams," it becomes more like "just getting through to the next day." It is survival rather than thriving (self-at-worst/resistance). Over time, people begin to function in self-at-worst states much of the time, and this pattern tends to be recursive and reinforcing of itself, resulting in generalized resistance/pathology. With any luck, they come into our offices or encounter some transformational other in a different context that provides them with the hope, security, and safety to try things in a different way. This is the space in the middle—the self-in-transition—where we, as therapists, have the honor and opportunity to meet the natural healing capacities of the person before us and to journey with them toward restored resilience, healing, transformance, and encountering their own selves-at-best.

Defining Resilience in a Clinical Context

By this point it should be clear that the "trait" approach to defining resilience—the idea that one is either resilient or not—is too limited for our purposes here. In fact, the assumption underlying this book is that all people are resilient in some measure, and even symptoms and pathology can be understood as expressions of resilience to the extent that they are adaptations to maladaptive or poorly matched environments. Whether or not these adaptations enhance an individual's resilient capacity is another question. Frequently they do not, but the underlying motivation to survive, to protect the self, to get through, or to be victorious is the resilient spirit that lies within each one of us. Like all things, it needs nurturing and guidance to express itself appropriately and to create a cycle of resilience.

Resilience Is Intra- and Interpersonal, Contextual, Developmental, and Universal

In order for the reader to clearly hold in mind what is meant by resilience potential and resilient capacity, it may be helpful to review some common definitions of resilience that are not sufficiently useful in the clinical realm and to add some qualifiers that make sense of resilience in the clinical context.

The most common way of thinking about resilience is as an individual trait. One either is or is not resilient, or is more or less resilient compared with another person. In other words, resilience is *intrapersonal*. This is a very legitimate way of thinking about resilience and necessary for subjecting it to quantitative research. But beyond that, it is also an expression of a desire to encapsulate what we admire about very resilient people. We marvel at how they survived atrocities, traumas, or losses, particularly if they have not become embittered, depressed, angry, and so on. Perhaps we put ourselves in their position and cannot imagine living life as well as they do. In our linear way of thinking, we like the simplicity of A + B = C: early loss + adult trauma = pathology. We are befuddled by A + B = D: early loss + adult trauma = healthy person. And it rightly makes us curious about what else is part of this equation—what explains the exception to the rule?

This curiosity has led to a lot of good research on other factors that may mitigate the impact of trauma and loss. Combined with some wisdom from developmental psychology, attachment theory, and object relations theory on optimal human development, it can confidently be said that resilience is not just intrapersonal but deeply *interpersonal* (Bowlby, 1989; Berscheid, 2003). The sense of being loved, treasured, worthy, and the solidity of self that such repeated interpersonal experiences provide is a major source of protection against the blows of life, especially against experiences that would portend otherwise. As Bollas (1987) suggested, the experience of being transformed provides the basis of hope for future transformations.

Another important aspect of the resilient capacity is that it is *contextual*, in at least four ways. The first is that people do not tend to be resilient in every aspect of their lives, but are more resilient in some areas than in others. Everyone has an Achilles heel and a "coat of arms." Think of the person who better manages stress or failures in his family life but falls apart when they happen on the job.

The second way in which the resilient capacity is contextual has to do with time and place in life. In fact, sometimes resilient adaptations to aversive life situations have unhealthy consequences when they are used in life situations that call for different adaptations. This is what psychotherapists see all the time. The classic example of a child raised in an alcoholic, rage-aholic family who gets through by learning not to feel demonstrates how resilience in one area that allows survival through detachment and accomplishment may seriously hinder the same individual's capacity to form vulnerable, loving, and lasting relationships later in life. It would be wrong to say that such adaptations were not signs of resilience in their original time, place, and circumstance. But it would also be awkward, and a stretch, to say that such adaptations in other circumstances are still resilient per se.

The third way in which the resilient capacity is contextual is that it is frequently, though perhaps not always, defined in proportion to adversity. One person's resilience cannot really be compared with another's without knowing all of the factors that promoted or diminished the resilient capacity in each person. And finally, the resilience potential may not be obvious because its chosen expression may be maladaptive if it takes the form of resistance, or it becomes maladaptive, in fact, because the resistance is carried over to other relationships and circumstances, becoming disconnected from its original intention or motivation.

By way of example, a thirty-five-year-old woman came to treatment because she recently became involved in what felt like an important and promising relationship with a man. She was aware of how "detached" she had been from herself and others all her life and feared that this would eventually lead to the demise of the relationship. She felt strongly enough toward him that she wanted to prevent this, but she also knew she would have to overcome a lot to be more connected to her feelings and more expressive, vulnerable, dependent, and caretaking toward another. She was raised in an affluent and influential family, politically and socially. The father was dominant, explosive, emotionally abusive, highly critical, and abused alcohol. The mother was anorexic, passive, obsessive, and very detached. Anything that involved taking care of the patient or her brother seemed burdensome and too much to both parents. The patient's most basic emotional needs were chronically neglected or denied. She finally escaped by electing to go to boarding school, where she later made a suicide attempt.

A lot of work went into helping her know herself and identify and be with her own feelings, as well as regulating her anxiety around being close and vulnerable with her new boyfriend and with the therapist. Slowly, she unfolded stories that helped to explain why this very bright and capable woman feared relationships and had nurtured a tough facade, competent but impenetrable.

About a year into her treatment, she told me that something "inappropriate" had happened between her and a teacher when she was around 10 years old. She remembers his special attention and his having caressed her on a number of occasions, but she does not remember much else. A friend saw the two of them together and reported it to the principal. The teacher was fired. Her parents may never have known, but they communicated in many ways that they did not want to know. They went on about what a shame it was that this teacher was fired and how he had likely not done anything wrong. On her twelfth birthday, her parents took her and several girlfriends to dinner and the father, who had run into a business colleague, introduced his daughter to the man as "this is Lila, the sex pot." She was confused and humiliated. Several years later her father lectured her on "false memory syndrome."

Years later her parents relate to her in much the same way, ignoring what she has to say, expecting that she takes care of and makes all arrangements for them when they visit, insisting on her doing things in the ways that would be pleasing to them. She has raged and railed against them. She has even told them how much their self-absorption and unawareness of her and her needs is hurtful. But little is different. In childhood and now, her emotional detachment vis-à-vis them is adaptive and expressive of her own resilience potential to protect herself from the pain of annihilation and to resist her internalization of the toxicity of their neglect and what this suggests about her own self-worth.

I would also like to propose that resilience is *developmental*. Allan Schore notes that "a consensus has been established that development fundamentally represents the emergence of more complex forms of self-regulation over the stages of the lifespan" (2003, pp. xiv–xv). Resilience is a self- and self–other-regulatory capacity. As the self becomes more complex, so too do its ways of manifesting resilience. While some adaptive capacities may be recognized as resilient across generational lines (e.g., seeking help when one's own resources are tapped), other manifestations of resilience may be, in part, a function of age and life experience. The ability to escape into play is a wonderful expression of resilience for a child who is overwhelmed and powerless to do anything to change his or her situation. The same ability is also a positive sign for adults, but not if it is the only thing they are able to do (i.e., resilience is contextual). Similarly, an older person may be able to lean into wisdom acquired through a long life and many varied experiences to bounce back from loss or trauma such is a manifestation of the self's resilience that we could not necessarily expect from a much younger person.

The last qualification that I will offer is the *universality* of the resilience potential. Effective work in psychotherapy requires a belief in this wired-in capacity of all people. If there is nothing within the patient that is capable and desirous of healing and transformation, there is little hope that our efforts are meaningful, unless we think of ourselves as surgeons and our patients as passive recipients of our interventions. While most therapists' work is informed by an implicit, though perhaps shadowed, belief in the resilience potential, part of working with resilience clinically is making this belief explicit to oneself as a therapist and, frequently, to one's patients. Rather than a background assumption that can be easily drowned out by the symptoms, trauma, addictions, and disordered ways of relating that we see in our offices every day, it becomes a leading assumption that guides how we experience, think about, and relate to the people we work with.

Making Room for the Extraordinary and the Natural

While I have argued for the relativity of the resilient capacity (i.e., that it is interpersonal, contextual, etc.), I also want to acknowledge the likelihood that some of it is either genetic or a gift of "nature." Attachment theory explains so much, but it cannot fully explain the vast diversity of reactions to trauma. If one has been in clinical practice long enough, one has probably had the experience of marveling at patients whose abuse was profound and whose inputs of love so sparse or nonexistent and yet they are functioning far better than others whose experience might not even qualify as "traumatic."

For several years I led a training group that met five weekends a year. On one of those weekends, I and several of my colleagues were really struck by the contrast between three patients (their patients) with very similar and very severe trauma histories involving extreme sadism on the parts of members of their families. The details varied a bit, but they all involved repeated and prolonged sexual abuse, physical abuse, emotional annihilation, and profound neglect. They all had engaged in some period of self-destructive behavior. But one woman's ability to articulate her experience, to be clear about where the fault lay (as much as she also suffered with shame and self-doubt due to the abuse), and to connect with and benefit from her connections to others touched all of us weekend after weekend of watching her sessions on videotape. We could not explain this in terms of attachment theory because not one early-life relationship this woman had was remotely secure. She seems to be the exception to the rule. And what is important about this is not the comparison between her and others but, rather, what we can learn by listening closely to her and her process and to that of people like her. What does she think, how does she feel, what does she do that has allowed her to survive *and to thrive*, and how can we help others find those capacities within themselves and within their current relationships? These are the questions guiding this book.

Summary

This chapter has introduced, defined, and elaborated much of the terminology relevant to the restoration of resilience from the perspective of the approach offered here. We looked at how the shift from a pathology orientation to a healing orientation is conducive and necessary to working with resilience from the outset of therapy, so much so that even "resistance" can be seen as a manifestation of the resilience potential. That potential on behalf of the self is the essence of all resilience processes, and it is different from one's resilient capacity, which has to do with how and to what degree adaptive resilience manifests. The idea that adaptations carried over from an earlier time to the present may no longer be helpful and, in fact, may be destructive does not diminish the fact that they were the person's best efforts at the time to adapt and act on behalf of the self. The essence of resilience was defined as the self's differentiation from that which is aversive to it. The goal of a resilience-oriented transformative therapy is to transfer the pathways of how that resilience gets expressed to more currently adaptive and transformance-oriented ways of approaching life and its challenges. This was presented visually in the map of resilience, which also includes a representation of what kinds of life experiences support more resistance/conservation-oriented expressions of resilience and what kinds of life experiences support more transformance/expansion-oriented expressions of resilience.

This chapter also discussed the many angles from which to understand resilience, including that it is universal, contextual, intrapersonal, interpersonal, and developmental. In the course of therapy, glimmers of the patient's capacity to act on behalf of the self need to be recognized, attended to, supported, and elaborated. This is one of many of the tasks of the therapist in the role of the transformational other in partnership with the patient's self-in-transition, a dyadic interplay we will see over and over in the transcripts of this book. These terms are a variation and expansion on AEDP's language of the self-at-best and self-at-worst, which depict a person's relationship to her own authentic internal experience in the context an other in relationship. These and the very basic Triangle of Conflict were presented visually for ease of understanding and quick reference.

Part 2

RESILIENCE AS POTENTIAL

CHAPTER 2

Working With Resilience
Essential Elements and Theoretical Foundations

Chapter 1 attempted to define a number of concepts related to resilience and to an approach to working in a resilience-focused way. The goal was to set out a common language for us to use as the book progresses and as case histories and transcripts unfold. Assuming we now share the same language, the goal of this chapter is to explore what we do with these concepts in clinical settings and how they fit together and to begin to look at the process of working with resilience from its nascent, perhaps even disguised, form right up through to when it manifests as flourishing.

Resilience is a process, and it is a process that requires support. Research on resilience has consistently shown that those who are resilient have support. Whether it is the friendships, family support, and physical care for the elderly or the parental love and involvement and "caring others" for young children at risk, resilience appears to be much more of an *inter*dependent phenomenon than an independent/individualistic one. People who are resilient also have emotional capacities like that of self-regulation that help keep them flexible in the moment. They often have cognitive capacities that allow them to separate things out and see things clearly and a willingness and ability to learn. Thus, therapists interested in this approach need to keep in mind three essential elements to working from a resilience-oriented perspective that is psychodynamically informed and experiential: (1) a focus on attachment, secure attachment, specifically; (2) an awareness of internal and external resources available (or unavailable) to the individual; and (3) an understanding of emotion and emotional processes. These factors directly relate to some of the most basic theoretical underpinnings of accelerated experiential dynamic psychotherapy (AEDP), the model I have chosen to elucidate here as a powerful and precise way to cultivate and restore deep and lasting resilience. These three elements and how they combine are crucial to understanding how a life has been conducive to the building up of resistance and self-protection or the flowering of transformance strivings (see Figure 1.5). The more we can enter our patient's experience and understand how they have adapted and coped, the easier it is to recognize the resilience potential involved in those attempts.

And so, this chapter will explore those theoretical underpinnings, namely, attachment theory and emotion theory, and why they are so foundational to an approach that looks for and finds resilience from the beginning and works to unravel and elaborate it throughout treatment. The chapter culminates in a summary of AEDP metapsychology and interventions and why and how this model is a very natural approach for clinicians interested in resilience per se and in helping to restore and enhance it in their patients in particular. Prior knowledge of AEDP is not necessary. Readers who do not already know about AEDP have been and will be provided with an introduction to its essential principles (for those whose interest in AEDP is peaked by this book, the full introduction to AEDP can be found in Fosha 2000b), and readers who are knowledgeable about AEDP will find an elaboration of its metapsychology and approach to resilience processes (in addition, recent articles on AEDP can be found on the AEDP website, aedpinstitute.com).

Secure Attachments and the Foundations of Resilience

Research on resilience from its inception (e.g., Werner & Smith 1982) has emphasized the importance of positive connections with caring adults for kids considered to be "at risk." This research, at least until recently, did not use the term attachment very frequently, perhaps in part because one of the things that puts children at such risk is disrupted, problematic, or insecure attachment relationships with primary caregivers. But what is likely happening for those resilient children who form extraparental relationships with "caring adults" is that they are experiencing positive, secure attachment relationships with older, wiser, kind, and caring others (Alvord & Grados, 2005). These relationships can be protective or ameliorative, in the same way the psychotherapeutic relationship can be for many early or later in their lives.

Attachment theory grew out of Bowlby's observations and theory that infants and their caregivers are participants in an intricate evolutionarily determined exchange that ensures the child's survival and therefore the transmission of the parents' genes. "Bowlby's central idea was that evolution solved the problem of people's (and other primates') needs for protection and support by equipping each of us with an attachment behavioral system, an organized network of appraisals, emotions, and behaviors that increases the likelihood of establishing a close relationship—an attachment relationship, in Bowlby's terms" (Shaver & Clark, 1994, p. 109). Based on his observations, Bowlby (1980, 1982) claimed that infants are wired to look for attachment figures, become anxious when they are absent, protest when their needs are not being met, and modulate their protests based on the responsiveness of the primary caregiver in order to maintain adequate care. This is the attachment-behavioral system. What they get in return, whether attuned or not, is the caregiver-behavioral system. These patterns of behavior are mutually interdependent—one influences the other and vice versa. Parents are wired to respond to the needs of their young, and their children are wired to seek them out, particularly when in need or distress.

Ainsworth, a student of Bowlby's, wanted to operationalize the behaviors of these systems and find a way to classify different types of attachment behavior (Ainsworth, Blehar, Waters, & Wall, 1978). In her observations of infants and their caregivers, in what was called the Strange Situation, she observed that the typical response of an infant to separation from its mother was distress. Excitement and the seeking of physical proximity and comfort were the typical response to reunion, followed by a reengagement (or exploration) with the child's environment. Some groups of children showed variations on this or evidenced entirely different patterns.

There is much good clinical literature on attachment types and their adult equivalent (for two excellent summaries of infant and adult attachment relating to clinical presentations, see Wallin 2007; Cozolino 2006. See also research by Kilpatrick & Shaver, 1990, 1992). What follows is a simplified summary of the types of attachment patterns frequently referred to in the clinical material presented throughout the book. The most typical pattern, described above, was eventually dubbed "secure attachment." Again, it is marked by distress upon separation, excitement and contact seeking upon reunion, and an eventual return to interest in and engagement with the rest of the child's surroundings. Main and colleagues (Main, 1983; Main & Cassidy, 1988; Main, Kaplan, & Cassidy, 1985) explored further the adaptiveness of this kind of connection between child and parent, contending that the parent of the secure infant/child acts as a "secure base" from which to explore the novelty of his world and of his own impact on his environment and its impact on him. The child's behavior is sensitive and attuned in the way that affective neuroscientists contend is necessary for optimal brain development (Schore, 1996, 2000, 2003). When in distress or overwhelmed, he can reliably return to the parent for comfort, help, or guidance. His relationships to other people, to himself, and to the objects of his interest are preserved and encouraged. Nothing is sacrificed.

The "insecure" categories include the two types: *anxious-ambivalent* and *avoidant*. Children with these attachment styles show significant adrenocortical stress response in situations that secure children do not (Cozolino, 2006). For example, anxious/ambivalent infants exhibit distress upon separation, like their secure counterparts. However, upon reunion, they do not demonstrate as much excitement but, rather, are distressed and remain distressed for a long period of time, not initiating separation from the mother to resume exploration. They are also more difficult to soothe. In this type of attachment, the child's exploration of her environment and herself within that environment is sacrificed for the almost exclusive focus on remaining connected to the attachment figure. This corresponds to a parental behavioral pattern of inconsistency in attunement to the child, so the child does not know what to expect. Neuropsychologically, these children show a tendency toward sympathetic nervous system arousal that corresponds to irritability, acting out, dependency, and difficulty recovering from stress (Cozolino, 2006).

The avoidant type is quite the opposite. In avoidant children and infants, there is little to no overt distress at separation and little to no overt distress or excitement at reunion. These children seem almost oblivious to the presence of the caretaker and are quite focused on objects in their environment instead. However, when these children's heart rates are measured, they are just as high as that of their anxious-ambivalent peers (Sroufe & Waters, 1977). At such a young age, they have learned to suppress their emotional behavioral response. This is adaptive to the extent that most children with this type of attachment behavior have caretakers who are dismissive of their emotional expression or of them altogether. In these cases, relationships and the need for connection to others are sacrificed for the almost exclusive focus on objects in their environment and, maybe later, figments of their imagination. Cozolino (2006) asserts that some avoidant children show a propensity toward parasympathetic nervous system arousal, which is reflected in helplessness, decreased activity, and a lower heart rate. Literally, their whole selves are withdrawing (Fraley & Shaver, 1997). This is in keeping with Cicchetti and Rogosch's (1997) finding that more behaviorally resilient children turn inward and rely less on others that they rightly suspect will not be able to support them appropriately or sufficiently or without extreme cost. Their avoidance is resilient.

Let us take this last type of attachment as an example and examine how a therapist might work with an avoidant patient with a history of dismissive parenting from a resilience-oriented stance. If the patient were to relate examples of avoidant responses in his relationships or exhibit them in the therapeutic relationship, the therapist could note, explore, affirm, and elaborate on that as a very resilient response to earlier attachment environments, an adaptation that reveals a capacity to act on behalf of the self in less than optimal circumstances. She could also explore and help elaborate, in an affectively rich, somatically based way, the patient's desire to act and feel differently in current relationships, including that with the therapist.

The last attachment type to be discovered and named was the disorganized/disoriented type. It was hard to identify in the early research because children in this group evidenced behavioral patterns that frequently looked secure or insecure, but they were not as consistent as those of other children who were clearly classifiable. This inconsistency was finally explained as a mismatch between intention and behavior (Main & Solomon, 1986). So, for example, a child who was distressed at separation from the mother might begin to approach her upon reunion but freeze in his tracks for a few moments or have a look of fear or terror on his face as he approached. At first this type of attachment behavior was thought to result from overt parental abuse. In other words, the child is caught in the truly untenable position of looking for comfort and contact from the same person who may be the source of his fear or terror or pain. Interestingly, in recent years it has been found that the same confused behavior is exhibited by well-meaning parents who have a good deal of unresolved trauma of their own and may exhibit extremes of affect or behavior, like rage or terror, thus making themselves frightening to their children (Hesse & Main, 2000; Main & Hesse, 1990). The term *disorganized* denotes that, unlike the other categories of attachment, the child has no organized strategy for how to get his attachment needs met.

The importance of attachment theory to effective psychotherapy cannot be underestimated. This is mostly because attachment patterns are quite consistent over time and generalize to other relationships unless the parameters of those relationships are substantially different. In other studies by Main and colleagues (Main, 2000; Main et al., 1985), infants found to be secure or insecure exhibited similar behavior in more complex ways with the same caretaker at 6 years of age. And there is plenty of evidence that remembered early attachment patterns are later repeated with romantic partners (Fraley & Shaver, 1997; Shaver & Clark, 1994; Shaver & Mikulincer, 2011). So, those with good, secure attachments early in life tend to continue to find and make them later in life with significant others. Those with insecure attachments tend to expect significant others to either be unreliable, dismissive, or even frightening and frequently continue to find and make those kinds of attachments. As Shaver and Clark state, attachment theorists understand the continuity of attachment as "an increasingly complex and self-maintaining pattern of social interaction and emotion-regulation strategies that emerge in the context of a primary attachment relationship and then become altered and elaborated in many subsequent relationships, always with the possibility of change" (1994, p. 119). Thus, the sacrifices of relationship, of self, or of engagement with the world continue to be made, and the possibilities for expansion, exploration, self-acceptance, and deeper intimacy with others continue to be frustrated. People tend to repeat oft-used adaptations in relationships that do not call for them, or they find ones that do and thus validate and reinforce adaptations that were necessary for a child but are unproductive or counterproductive for an adult who presumably has choice.

This leads to the second reason that it is so critical for resilience-focused therapists to understand attachment theory. People come to therapy with the only tools that they have developed thus far. They approach the relationship with the therapist, consciously or not, with much the same expectation they have had of other attachment and/or authority figures in their lives. When someone with a secure attachment history comes in, the connection can feel very good to both the therapist and the patient, and the work can be more specifically focused on the life problems, issues, or struggles at hand. But, more often than not, people's attachment histories are wanting. Understanding attachment types helps us identify patterns in current and past relationships that are problematic; put defenses into the context of adapting to environments or experiences that were not sufficiently emotionally safe to allow for secure relating to another, with the self, and with the environment at the same time; and understand more clearly what is required from us as the new potential attachment figures in order to facilitate a corrective emotional experience powerful enough to generalize beyond the walls of our offices.

From a resilience-oriented perspective, it is important to balance this understanding of problematic attachment patterns with a faith in the transformance strivings of every individual we meet. People are on the lookout for different and more positive relational experiences even if they have their guard up at the same time. However well protected or difficult to access, people get themselves to therapy on the wings of *hope*. And that hope is not simply a frivolous fantasy, because the good news is that individuals can shift from insecure to secure attachment styles through good friendships and solid love relationships with a partner who is dissimilar in important ways from earlier problematic figures (Fraley & Shaver, 1997; Shaver & Clark, 1994; Shaver & Mikulincer, 2011). Change in attachment styles (for the better) is the resilience potential in action and oriented toward transformance, the process that remains open to healthier, self-affirming relationships despite multiple other messages that the self is worthless, defective, incapable, or, worst, unlovable. It is likely an observable manifestation of the brain's plasticity. Working from a standpoint focused on resilience, changing patients' attachment styles should not simply be an eventual by-product of good therapeutic treatment—it should be an integral part of treatment via the therapeutic relationship. The combination of the patient's conscious or unconscious desire to have healthier, happier relationships and the therapist's desire for him to have precisely that, along with her expertise in facilitating the experience of something different in the here and now of the therapeutic encounter is a very powerful catalyst for healing and the enhancement of resilience.

Lipton and Fosha make precisely this point in an article beautifully supported by an extensive transcript of work with a man with insecure-avoidant attachment style: "For people with histories of relational trauma, it is the very attachment experience itself—the experiential co-creation of safety and trust—that both frames and comprises the specific, detailed, moment-to-moment coloration of the therapeutic endeavor" (2011, p. 276). In other words, the experience—perhaps for the first time in one's life—of secure attachment to the therapist is itself a transformative experience that engenders resilience and, by doing so, allows for the exploration of one's life and one's self.

The Role of Emotion and Expression in Resilience Processes

Most basically, emotion is outward movement. The key characteristic is that action wells up from within the organism.

Optimal brain development is intricately linked with securely attached relationships that are marked by infant–caregiver coordination and caregiver responsiveness to the infant's or child's needs (Schore, 1994, 1996). These are essential ingredients of resilient capacity as evidenced by the research on young children, both resilient and nonresilient (Bonanno, 2004; Fergusson & Horwood, 2003; Luthar, Cicchetti, & Becker, 2000; Luthar & Zelazo, 2003; Masten et al., 1990; Masten, 2001; Rutter, 1985; Werner & Smith, 1982; Wyman, 2003). These essential ingredients are mediated by emotion and emotional communication that is both verbal and, importantly, nonverbal (Tronick, 1989). Hence, an introduction to emotion theory is also important for understanding how to build and restore resilience.

According to differential emotions theory, an emotion is a complex system that "emerges from interactions of constituent neurohormonal, motoric, and experiential processes" (Izard, Ackerman, Schoff, & Fine, 2000, p. 15), and the overarching emotional system is the primary motivational system within the human person. Differential emotions theory is one of a number of emotion theories that take a functionalist perspective on emotion. Broadly, these theories see emotion as an evolutionarily adaptive "response that organizes cognitive, experiential, behavioral, and physiological reactions to changes in the environment" (Lench, Flores, & Bench, 2011, p. 834). Similarly, Trevarthen (2005) argues that emotions are not simply reactions but essential causes of behavior and the regulation of movement.

Many modern emotion theories take as their foundation affect theory as defined and put forth by Silvan Tomkins (1962, 1963). Tomkins argued that affect results from the brain's response to a stimulus that, in turn, sets off various responses in the body that compel us to pay attention. He named nine basic innate affects, similar to many of the categorical emotions named by Darwin (1872). Affects have at least three clinically important consequences: (1) they provide information to the "organism" (i.e., the person in our case) about his or her own state; (2) that information tends to increase the display of affect (e.g., in the distressed infant, crying itself increases crying until some new stimulus elicits a new affect or a relief from the affect being felt); and (3) affective displays importantly communicate information about the person to others in their environment (Nathanson, 1996).

The experience of affect rarely happens in a vacuum. Instead, the accumulated experience of repeated distinct affects (e.g., interest- and joy) combined with responses from important people in the child's environment leads to what we would normally call *emotion*, that is, biology plus history (Basch, 1976). Nathanson states, "It is the child's dawning awareness that *affect is the link between need, its identification, and its later relief* that allows us to grow into adulthood trusting our emotions as an important source of information" (1996, p. 15, emphasis added). Inversely, depending on our own biography, affect triggers a sense of vulnerability and a series of defenses because of unmet needs or historically unmodulated affect states. Much of what we are helping people with as therapists is excessive experiences of unmodulated, ongoing negative affect (e.g., fear/distress, shame-humiliation, sadness, or anger).

The centrality of affect and emotion to clinical processes has been only recently acknowledged by a broad range of psychotherapeutic theories and techniques, from psychoanalysis to cognitive-behavioral therapy. Before this, emotion regularly was viewed through the lens of the coping research literature that suggested that "emotion-focused" coping was associated with more pathology (e.g., Billings, Cronkite, & Moos, 1983). The field now understands that both emotion-focused and problem-focused coping have their appropriate contexts and may be helpful to different people and in different situations (e.g., Marks, 2000; Vitaliano, DeWolfe, Maiuro, Russo, & Katon, 1990). There appears to be some agreement that certain ways of processing and expressing emotion are more helpful than others. *Emotion-focused processing* (as opposed to *coping*), which involves the embodied experience and expression of one's emotions and the thoughts, impulses, memories, and fantasies that accompany them, has been shown to enhance problem solving in a way that is superior to purely "rational" problem solving (Fredrickson, 1998; Fredrickson & Branigan, 2005).

The Resilient Individual as an Affective Communication System

It is thus clear that emotion is an essential aspect to our interpreting, processing of, and responding to our environment. Tronick, who with his colleagues (Cohn & Tronick, 1987; Gianino & Tronick, 1988; Tronick, 1989; Weinberg & Tronick, 1994) has done extensive research on the earliest interactions between mothers and their babies, has found that by as early as 3 months many mother–infant dyads are involved in bidirectional, mutually influencing interactions (Cohn & Tronick, 1987). Of course, this communication is preverbal and is mediated by facial expression, body language, and tone and prosody of voice, all of the right-brain functions referred to frequently by the affective neuroscientists. Tronick asserts that "the infant is part of an affective communication system in which the infant's goal-directed strivings are aided and supplemented by the capacities of the caretaker" (1989, p. 113). Tronick summarizes research that demonstrates the following qualities about infants' affective communication: (1) capable (self- and other-directed coping and soothing), (2) differentiated (e.g., prefer joyful to sad or angry faces), (3) organized (e.g., responsive to some contextual cues), (4) active (vs. passive), and (5) seeking guidance (e.g., will check with mother about how to proceed when uncertain and respond to her facial and vocal expressions of fear or reassurance).

These are the micromoments that make up attachment patterns seen in 1- or 2-year-old infants and toddlers, as well as older children and adults. The infants whose behavior is dominated by self-regulation in the face of misattunement become the older infants, toddlers, or children who are preoccupied with the parent's state (anxious/ambivalent) and have difficulty soothing themselves or being soothed, or the avoidant children who, over time, learn how to suppress the attachment needs that would elicit distress in the face of chronic misattunement or dismissal. This is their own resilient, adaptive response to a misattuned environment, but its cost, in terms of one's sense of self and other and one's capacity to joyfully engage with the rest of his environment, is potentially enormous.

We are converging on a point: the foundation of resilient capacity is the experience of self and other that is secure, predictable, and marked by a preponderance of positive affect and a sense of efficacy in relationships and in one's environment. This foundation is nurtured in caretaking relationships that are motivated to compensate for the vulnerable and relatively incapable state of the child in order to facilitate his development and simultaneously create mutual joy in the caregiver and the cared for. Both partners are wired to achieve the same end. A critical part of that end, and of the process itself, is the unmistakable preference for positive over negative affect and the motivation to return to the former when the latter has erupted. This caregiving/care-receiving process, in fact, contributes to the optimal development of the brain, which allows for flexibility in behavioral response and increasing capacity for complexity. Such complexity and flexibility are the opposite of the conservation, constriction, and rigidity that characterize people in negative affective states or relationships that are dominated by negative affect, particularly fear.

And so, if this is how we are wired from the beginning of life— that is, in great need of supportive, positive, and affectively alive relationships—it seems reasonable to assume that we remain that way throughout our lives. We can also infer—and there is evidence all the time for this in our practices—that the absence of this kind of security, vitality, and flexibility is a major piece of the experience of human suffering or emptiness. And so, facilitating the healing of suffering and engendering the kind of resilient capacity that people are wired to own involves restoring security, building capacities to metabolize negative affect and savor positive affect, restoring a sense of agency, and helping people establish, repair, and maintain supportive and meaningful relationships in their lives.

Working with Painful Emotion: Sometimes the Only Way Out Is Through

On bad days, a clinician may leave her office drained by the negative affect she has been awash in for several hours. She may feel somewhat hopeless herself about things changing for her patients or about her own capacity to really offer meaningful or lasting help. This can be due to many things, but one of them is how negative emotions are processed, or not, by the dyad. Kennedy-Moore and Watson make a very strong case for the usefulness of emotional processing in healing, while differentiating it from certain types of emotional expression that can be less therapeutically helpful: "When expression involves rumination, or passive brooding about emotional experience, it does not foster new understanding but instead intensifies and prolongs distress. . . . Ruminative expression is vague, diffuse, and stagnant, . . . It rehearses and intensifies distress, and it interferes with the implementation of active coping strategies" (2001, p. 197)

People with such ruminative tendencies usually function less well in society, have more troubled relationships, and feel more distressed generally (Kennedy-Moore & Watson, 2001). In contrast, "emotional avoiders" may be able to cope more effectively with present tasks and personal and professional responsibilities. But, while the acquisition of "skills" is very important, and while the teaching of them is often a very helpful therapeutic intervention to foster resilience, clinicians need to be able to work with people whose motivation is insufficient, whose mood is too poor, whose anxiety is too high to be able to learn, practice, and effectively use skills. This is where the therapist's skill in helping people to process unexplored emotional experiences is a key to restoring real and lasting resilience.

Kennedy-Moore and Watson (2001), themselves emotion theorists, postulate that there are at least three ways in which emotional expression may alleviate distress: (1) it can reduce distress about distress (e.g., doing it and surviving it reduces fears about feeling in general), (2) it can facilitate insight (e.g., vague feelings become clear, thus deepening self-knowledge and opening up possibilities for how to respond), and (3) it can enhance interpersonal relationships (i.e., through improved communication). Let me add that emotional expression also signals to others one's state and associated need (e.g., distress and the need for comfort or help or anger and the need for a boundary) and releases resources, including adaptive action tendencies associated with specific emotions and self-compassion. And finally, some argue that emotion is essential to action (Freeman, 2000).

Emotion Versus Emotional: Distinguishing Primary/Core Versus Secondary/Peripheral Emotion

If a key part of true resilience is the capacity to metabolize negative feeling and savor and use positive feeling, then it is important for clinicians to know what kind of affect they are working with. People can appear "emotional" but may not be processing anything at all and instead may be increasing their own distress. Getting better at distinguishing different levels or types of emotion is a very important skill for a resilience-oriented clinician practicing from this perspective. There are two keys to adaptive emotional processing versus what one might call "emoting": to be in the window of optimal arousal and feeling, and to distinguish what type of affect a dyad is working with, whether primary or secondary, core or peripheral. Let's take up the latter first.

One of the harder things for clinicians to do, especially those who may be newer to working so explicitly with emotion, is to distinguish between peripheral (sometimes seen as defensive) and *core* affects. This is where working with videotape of your own work, with a supervisor who is trained in an emotion- or affect-focused or experiential therapy, is indispensable. The distinctions I outline below are easily understood on paper but considerably more difficult to make in the room with a live person who is "emotional."

Emotion theorists and several emotion-focused or experiential therapies concur that there are important differences between types of expressed emotion that are helpful and health promoting and those that are perhaps more symptomatic of ongoing distress or character issues. For example, Greenberg and Safran (1987) discuss three types of expressed emotion: *primary*, *secondary*, and *instrumental*. Primary emotional reactions are basic emotions that have biological signatures and provide adaptive information about and for the person experiencing them. For example, anger may be a core emotion in response to some boundary violation or insult. Secondary emotions are more "defensive" and are aimed at coping and self-protection. Greenberg and Safran note that in psychotherapy patients, this is the more frequent and therefore conscious type of emotional expression. It has a sense of familiarity for the patient but is not particularly productive or adaptive. For example, the clinical observation that women have a harder time with anger and men have a harder time reaching more vulnerable feelings such as fear or sadness illustrates secondary emotion in that women may resort to feeling hurt or sad and avoid feeling their anger (i.e., core) and men may cover vulnerable feelings with anger. This is likely the type of emotional processing that is reported in the coping literature. So, it seems that cognitively oriented coping researchers and emotion-focused psychotherapists would agree that certain types of emotional processing are not all that helpful. Finally, instrumental emotional reactions are focused on influencing others' perception of the self, with little congruence between the outward emotional expression and one's internal subjective experience. Emotion-focused therapy (Greenberg, 1991; Greenberg & Johnson, 1990; Greenberg & Paivio, 1997; Greenberg, Rice, & Elliott, 1993; Johnson, 1996) works to move away from secondary or instrumental emotions toward facilitating the experience and expression of primary emotions.

Similarly, AEDP (Fosha, 2000b, 2009) presents a model of state transformation in processing emotions to completion that distinguishes four different classes of emotional experience and expression (see figure 2.1). The first and second correspond very well to Greenberg and Safran's (1987) secondary and primary emotions.

With State 1, *stress, distress, and symptoms*, the phenomenological picture is a mixture of *red signal* affects (anxiety, shame, distress), symptoms, and defense, which may include what Greenberg and Safran (1987) identified as instrumental emotional reactions but which also may be behavioral. Included in this state are defensive affects, which are certainly emotions, but they are not "core" in the moment. Because even defensive emotions are "real" and because different emotions can layer one another like parts of an onion, I like the term *peripheral* to denote affects that are not core in the moment and are thus peripheral to the affects or emotions that are most useful to pursue in the moment and will yield the most benefit for the patient (e.g., clarity, understanding, relief, adaptive action tendencies). Defenses are designed to reduce anxiety and keep out of awareness the second type of emotional experience: core affect. The challenge for the therapist is to help the patient feel safe enough (i.e., less anxious and/or less defended) to actually feel the feelings that are emerging and that have the seeds of healing built in.

State 2, or core affective experience (like Greenberg & Safran's [1987] primary emotional expression), is experienced as authentic, even if at first it feels foreign, unrecognizable, and undesired. It includes categorical emotions, as well as authentic self states, coordinated relational states (or what Stern [1998, 2007] refers to as *moments of meeting*), intersubjective moments of pleasure, and embodied ego states. I also include in this state a sense of agency, the self's energetic capacity to act on behalf of the self, the "I think I can" felt sense. In this state, affective or emotional expression has a sense of movement; involves the opening of the unconscious to memories, feelings, bodily associations, images, and novel thoughts; and has the temporality and shape of a wave that hits a peak and then comes back down, settling into the sand. In essence, core feelings are productive. They unfold, even if painfully. They are accompanied by insight into the self and others, and they almost always are followed by some measure of relief. These stand in contrast to State 1 affective states that may be expressed repeatedly but bring no new insight, do no propel the person in any healthy direction, and are almost never followed by any significant relief or increased clarity.

The idea of an optimal level of arousal, feeling, and anxiety is very important to emotional processing. This varies from person to person. Some patients need help "downregulating," such as those mentioned above who ruminate in their feelings, are flooded by them, or, more frequently, are flooded by the anxiety that accompanies the feelings. Other patients—habitual, and perhaps successful, problem solvers—often need help "upregulating" or turning up the heat of the emotional experience in order to have access to parts of themselves they have kept remote. This is especially important in circumstances that are beyond their control. In my experience in supervision, in studying my own work with patients, and in supervising others, therapists tend to underestimate the depth of real feeling that most patients are capable of—and benefit from.

In an article by Michael Bridges (2006), which I will discuss in more depth below, one of the featured patients is a woman who has been stuck for several years around reengaging relationships after a profound betrayal by her now former husband. (I had the fortunate experience of not simply reading the transcript but also seeing the videotape of the session referenced in the article.) When she finally connects to the grief she has been both holding on to and avoiding for the previous few years, she does not look like she is in a state of "optimal arousal." She sobs deeply, needs help regulating her breathing, and is, at moments, curled over in emotional pain. She is not your prototypical picture of resilience. In addition to these behavioral communications of her inner state, her heart rate at the time of this emotional expression looks like an "intense tidal wave" (Michael Bridges, September 9, 2009). Many therapists with nothing but the best intention might have moved to bring this woman back from that cliff and away from feeling, or might have unwittingly failed to shore her up sufficiently to be able to tolerate the wounded heart she describes. But what happens to this woman is what happens with some frequency in affect-oriented, experiential approaches. Her heart rate "quickly crests and recedes," and she experiences tremendous relief as well as new insights and a stronger sense of self. So, optimal arousal is determined by the individual and his or her affective range, the timing of the experience, the safety of the interpersonal moment (which implicates the therapist's tolerance of deep affect), the level of co-occurring anxiety, and the "truth" of the feelings being processed.

Michael Bridges and his colleagues at the Council for Relationships in Philadelphia have been studying their own videotaped work, specifically looking at the level of emotion in session, the amount of relief experienced by the patient postsession, and the change in heart rate from the beginning to the end of the session. Bridges lays out four key components of emotion: (1) *emotional arousal*, which involves the autonomic nervous system and the physiological reaction of the body; (2) *emotional experience*, which is the person's subjective experience of the type and intensity of the emotion they are having; (3) *emotional expression*, defined as observable verbal and nonverbal expressive behavior (e.g., facial expressions, tone of voice, gestures); and finally, (4) *emotional processing*, which involves the integration of emotion and cognition involved in insight and a change in the person's sense of self and other, as well as a greater ability to problem solve and respond in an effective way (2006, p. 552). We might call the consequence of this last factor the movement from the self-at-worst to the self-at-best. In this study, Bridges closely examines each of these factors in three different patients in an affect-oriented therapy using appropriate validated measures, in-session cardiovascular activity, and trained observer ratings of videotapes of the clinical work.

It is a fascinating study for clinicians interested in emotion-focused or experiential work as well as the process of change and transformation. The patients were all part of an ongoing clinical research study on resolving interpersonal injuries with attachment figures in the past. Each patient showed a different pattern of emotion arousal, experience, expression, and processing, as well as different outcomes. The first patient tended to *vent* in a ruminative way about whatever was distressing her in the moment. For the most part she stayed in what AEDP would call State 1 (stress, distress, symptoms). The second patient's pattern was marked by what Bridges refers to as *emotional interruption*, in which the descent into *core affect* (State 2), or adaptive emotional processing (e.g., sadness/ grief), is interrupted by a return to a more superficial level of expression (e.g., talking about past events in a detached, factual way). In other words, she goes from State 2 (core affective experience) back to State 1 (stress, distress, and symptoms). This is not at all an uncommon pattern in psychotherapy. The last patient, however, was able to move into and stay with painful experiences of grief (State 2) and, with the therapist's help, also integrate positive memories and their associated emotions, leading to a sense of resolution and eventually moving to State 3, transformational affects, and State 4, core state (more about those states below).

These patterns of expression and processing (or lack thereof) were associated with very different patterns of arousal, as indicated by the patients' heart rates. The first patient's heart rate was high at the beginning and gradually decreased over the course of the session, with little variability even at moments when she reported that she was very angry or upset. The second patient, the one whose processing was interrupted, showed a moderate increase in cardiovascular arousal in the moments that she allowed herself to cry and start to put her feelings into words (e.g., regarding an affair her sister had with her fiancé: "It's really shaken my whole") (Bridges, 2006, p. 559). This is followed by a long delay in cardiovascular recovery. In other words, it took a very long time for her level of arousal to come down despite having moved to more superficial subjects. In contrast, the third patient, who stayed with very painful affects of grief at the loss of her husband because of an affair, showed a very rapid return to baseline heart rate as she integrated positive memories that eventually helped her resolve the trauma of this betrayal and be open to loving someone else.

This is not emphasized in Bridges's article, but when one reads the transcripts, it is clear that in addition to the patients being different and expressing different levels of emotion and having different processing capacities, the interaction between each and her therapist is different, as are the interventions of the therapist. In the first scenario, the therapist is blocked out. Despite numerous attempts to ask a clarifying question or to empathize, the patient is entirely self-sufficient, while mired in her chronic, pressured negative emotions. She is sealed off, and the therapy continues that way. All of us as therapists have had experiences like this in which we feel left out, ineffective, and frustrated. Chapter 4 looks at some ways to help patients with these kinds of defenses connect to us and to themselves.

With the second patient, there is much more openness toward the therapist and even an expression of gratitude at the end of the session. For the most part, the therapist's expressions of empathy and understanding are received and used by the patient to deepen her own exploration of her feelings. However, nearing the end of the session, and perhaps because of this, the *therapist moves away from the patient's focus on her feelings* and her expression of gratitude to a collection of facts and, complying, the patient becomes more matter-of-fact and pressured in responding to the therapist's inquiry. Again, however, as evidenced by her heart rate, she remains activated for a long time. With the third patient, the therapist is not simply responsive but actively facilitating a process of experiential and emotional self awareness in the patient in a very gentle, curious, encouraging, and affirming way. For example, he says: "Yeah, that's good; you're in touch with the process now; your mind kind of immediately pops up with 'I need more consistent sleep.' I'm sure you probably do, but then you just breathe into the center of your body and go back to that place" (Bridges, 2006, p. 563). He is gentle, curious, facilitative of, and not frightened by deep emotion, and he is, as evidenced by the transcript, *using the patient's resilience potential and her current resilient capacity to further strengthen that resilience* through the process of looking at her wounded parts—in her words, her "red" and "bruised heart." She discovers that she has something to offer, that she has a new way of seeing herself and her trauma, in part because of how he sees her and how this guides how he works with her and the faith he has in the process of restoration.

One of the other striking and important things about this work is the therapist's faith in the healing power of core emotion itself. He is nowhere near passive, but he is less a director than a guide. He knows, as we all need to come to know in doing resilience-oriented work, that when one is in the realm of core affect, the patient knows more than the therapist does. The therapist *trusts deeply* (and I say more about this in the final chapter) that resilience and transfor-

GARNERING ALL OUR RESOURCES: ACCESSING SELF-AT-BEST TO WORK WITH SELF-AT-WORST

Many experiential therapies have articulated, in different ways, the importance of garnering a patient's resources before delving into the hard work ahead. Internal Family Systems therapy (IFS) (Schwartz, 1995) helps people be in touch with the self in order to work with all the parts of the self in an effort toward integration. Eye Movement Desensitization and Reprocessing (EMDR) (Shapiro, 2001; Shapiro & Forrest, 1997) works toward "resourcing" and establishing a "safe place" with a patient, particularly before facing any traumatic material. Somatic approaches like Somatic Experiencing (SE) (Levine, 1997; Napier, 1993) and Sensorimotor Psychotherapy (Ogden, Minton, & Pain, 2006) focus on helping calm and ground people in their bodies before working through trauma. AEDP uses the language of accessing the self-at-best to work with the self-at worst (Fosha, 2000b). These are modern-day, therapeutic prescriptions of ancient knowledge. The hero's journey always involves some kind of separation from the life that he or she knows, followed by a trial or initiation that needs to be faced and through which new skills and perspective are acquired. This is followed by a return to a new life that is stronger and better because of the trial and what was learned and gained through it (Bradley, 2010). Mystics have talked about this pattern as the way of spiritual growth for thousands of years: there is comfort and consolation before one is strong enough to face the desolation that eventually brings people to the other side, wiser, stronger, more knowledgeable, and perhaps able to help others along the same journey. Athletes know they need a good night's sleep and the proper kind of meal before an important competition. Babies and children frequently seek contact with or signals of safety from their caregivers before they are prepared to explore unfamiliar territory. What is instinctive for children remains organic for all of us though our ways of feeling grounded, secure, resourced, and courageous become more internalized as we mature and have sufficient security-engendering experiences.

mance are built right into core affective experiences and authentic experiences of self. He says, humbly, "If my question takes you away from your experience, go back to your experience" (Bridges, 2006, p. 13), trusting that if she stays with the emotion that is emerging and stays with herself, she will know what to do and what she can handle. The patient is able to act on her own behalf to allow herself to feel what are her own authentic and deep feelings and to discover more of her own capacities in that experience. And because she is having an experience of safe vulnerability with the therapist, her transformance strivings for growth, development, and the exploration of what she has not yet been able to explore are fully on board despite the risks of revealing herself and of feeling pain.

Safe Vulnerability

What I call "safe vulnerability" is a paradoxical phrase. There is nothing safe about being truly vulnerable. It includes being open to attack, criticism, persuasion, or temptation; being wounded or hurt; or being susceptible to physical or emotional injury. Sometimes just sheer exposure of the self can feel threatening. And yet, vulnerability is something most therapists welcome and even prize. Why? Because in order to be touched, we have to be vulnerable in the sense of being open, not fragile. We have to be in a state where the awareness of the potential for hurt, embarrassment, injury, and the like is present, but we take the risk to reveal ourselves anyway. It is in this state of safe vulnerability—as experientially determined by the patient—that the deepest healing can take place.

From the beginning, an affect-oriented, experiential therapy should aim to facilitate a patient's experience of "safe vulnerability." It is an experience of our own resilient core. There is an awareness that this revelation of self-to-self or self-to-other may hurt or embarrass or diminish or simply be associated with past hurts, embarrassments, or experiences of being diminished. Doing it anyway, facing our fears or our susceptibility to harm, requires courage enough, but to have the additional gift of this vulnerability feeling safe actually strengthens hope and our resilient capacity. It also reveals a certain amount of resilient capacity to begin with. Even in the midst of anxiety or fear or bearable levels of shame, we feel trusting and perhaps trustworthy enough to be fully ourselves.

There are many moments in therapy in which the fruits of vulnerability are lost due to either the patient's or the therapist's discomfort with the patient's level of vulnerability and the consequent return to more defensive functioning. Clinicians are compassionate, sensitive, socially skilled people who, sensing the discomfort of another, are not infrequently moved to make things feel better—to restore a sense of safety or all-rightness. But in doing this compassionate deed sometimes we help to shore up and reinforce more defensive or occlusive ways of being or relating and even unwittingly communicate that whatever is vulnerable and intensely felt by the patient is too much for us to handle. What is required is the therapist's belief in the potential power of vulnerability for healing and strengthening, as well as the therapist's own willingness to be vulnerable in extending herself in such a way that *she* risks rejection, embarrassment, or harassment from her own inner voices that tell her that such vulnerability is inappropriate, be they professional or personal.

Except in very secure people, vulnerability is almost invariably felt as something dangerous. One feels tense, flushed, and queasy, has difficulty making eye contact, and wants to "move away" by leaving the room, shutting down, or changing the focus of conversation. Vulnerable moments, therefore, if left alone, will quickly pass. People will naturally and understandably return to less vulnerable, less open states in which the work becomes more tedious, intellectual, and slow but still, perhaps, more comfortable. The therapist's neutrality in response actually increases the likelihood that such moments continue to be experienced as dangerous (even if only due to the patients' own projections) and something to be avoided. In order to make vulnerability safe for most patients, the therapist must be quite active, responsive, welcoming, and risk-taking herself.

CLINICAL VIGNETTE:
"Acceptance and an Invitation to Be Vulnerable"

The following is a vignette of a young man who is recounting a recent coffee date with his mother in which he sensed her awkwardness in being close to him. During their time together, he felt strongly his own desire to communicate his love to her in an effort to heal her and their relationship, which had been going through a very rough period up to this point. He is someone who has difficulty accessing and staying with his feelings and has had great difficulty communicating himself to others except in his caretaking of them. Even in those circumstances, the communication is more indirect and implicit. Others trust in his care for them and feel safe with him. The therapist asks him what he would want to say or do if he were face-to-face with his mother again.

PT: (The feeling is) pretty amorphous . . . hugging her comes to
    mind . . . but something more direct than that.
TP: More direct than hugging her.
PT: (**Tears**)
TP: Mm-hmm. Just stay with it.
PT: Like a direct transfer of love (**soft sob**).
TP: Mm-hmm. How do you see it?
PT: (**Eyes averted from TP**) . . . Just looking at her.
TP: Like through your eyes to hers? Mm-hmm. Can you let yourself see that right now? [**Making story experientially real in order to elicit affect.**]
PT: (**Tears; having trouble finding words**) I think it's restrained. [**PT becoming aware of his own defenses against the vulnerability.**]
TP: What's restraining it right now?
PT: I think it's being with you. [**Vertical defense; defense against the closeness with or exposure to the therapist; the defense is interpersonal more than intrapersonal.**]
TP: What about being with me is restraining it? [**Exploring whether it is something about TP in general, in the**

moment, or in the general experience of being vulnerable with another.]

PT: There are just limits on how kind of exposed I am letting myself be . . . (**no eye contact**) . . . It doesn't feel like I am able to let that down. I can push it back somewhat but am not able to let it go entirely. [**Feeling of lack of safety still predominates.**]

TP: What happens when you look at me? [**TP inviting greater contact in hopes that PT will become more consciously aware of who TP is in this moment—someone who is interested, caring, and open to him.**]

PT: (**Starting to cry again**) [**Softening of defenses; increase in vulnerability to own feelings and to TP with those feelings.**]

TP: Mmm. There's so much feeling. (**pause**) Mm. (**pause**) Can you tell me what these tears are about right now?

PT: (**No eye contact**) I don't think so.

TP: Can you try again (to look at me)? [**Pressuring with empathy.**]

PT: I am not sure. I can look at you. The first time I wasn't expecting that to happen. But now I can do that because the guard is already up. [**In the face of vulnerability he continues to refortify himself against it and the other, spending a lot of energy and losing an opportunity to feel something good or, at least, better. If the therapist lets it go here, both partners will become more "comfortable," but the potential for the patient to experience both himself and the relationship with the therapist as courageous and resilient will be lost.**]

TP: What do you see in my face? [**TP inviting conscious connection that takes in the present moment vs. the imagined other.**]

PT: (**Looking away, deep sigh**). I realize I am not looking at you when I say this, but

TP: If you try again . . . [**Pressuring defense of looking away.**]

PT: (**Eye contact, long pause**). I think (**tears**) . . .

TP: Mm.

PT: I think it has something to do with the feeling of uh
   (**pause**) . . . (**halting language; still slightly tearful**).
   One way that is going through my mind of interpreting this
   scenario is I feel like it's accepting, like an acceptance. [**The
   vulnerability has become safe enough. It is met with—
   and experienced as eliciting in the other—acceptance
   instead of rejection or scorn.**]

TP: You see acceptance in my face. [**Restating PT's tentative
   statement in a direct, mirroring, nonintellectualized
   way.**]

PT: Yeah (**tears**).

TP: And that stirs up a lot. [**Empathically reflecting PT's emotional experience.**]

PT: I don't know if it is right . . . it's like acceptance and an invitation to be vulnerable . . . brings out for me my lack of trust in it.

TP: That's what comes up in your head. [**TP attempting to
   bypass defense of intellectualizing, but on reflection,
   this was not necessary. While it may have been partly
   true, it was also likely a part of what PT was experiencing emotionally, and the reason for some of the tears:
   the pain of not feeling able to be vulnerable and safe. He
   is becoming aware of the contrast of this moment with
   other vulnerable moments in his life, which is what the
   TP hoped he would do. There is a touch of mourning-the-
   self, which is a transformational affect that comes in the
   wake of the experience of transformation.**]

PT: I think what happens is I feel pulled to be fully exposed,
   which is not a feeling that I have very often. [**An example
   among many of how patients are forgiving of their therapists' errors, particularly when they do feel safe and
   understood. Instead of using her misattunement as a
   rationale to shut down or argue a point, he simply clari-
   fies and remains open.**]

TP: So there are a lot of feelings that come up around letting
   yourself feel that a little bit, a lot I should say. You've stuck
   with this for a long time with me today (**PT tearful again**). I

can see that this is hard and you are struggling to stay with it and struggling against it, but you have really stayed with if for a long time with me today. [**Validation of his courage and openness despite forces working against it.**]

PT: It doesn't feel like it is totally in my control what I am doing here (**shy smile**).

TP: It probably isn't (**soft smile**). Is that okay? [**Acknowledgment of the dyadic and dynamic nature of their exchange; still checking for sufficient safety and asking permission.**]

PT: Yeah. I think that part of the pull is the lack of need of control (**tears**). [**Acknowledging that he feels invited by the loss of control; these are green signal affects. PT is willing to feel and to feel <u>with</u> the therapist, to be open to himself in the presence of another.**]

This last statement is very important for this young man, who had constructed a way of being based largely on having fairly tight control over what he felt, and particularly what he revealed to others. Having an experience where the invitation to the loss of control in a relationship in the context of acceptance and relative safety was not simply new for him but something he knew he badly needed, which he discussed in the next session. A similar situation happened later in the treatment in which the therapist reached out to him in a very unexpected way. And he clarified that it was not simply her seeing and appreciating him that was healing for him, but that the *surprise*, which overwhelmed his capacity to control his emotional reaction, was healing in and of itself. Each of these experiences was desensitizing him to his own emotional vulnerability with another. And the experience of surviving it and even welcoming it provided relief, hope, and a sense of himself as capable of more and as fearful of less.

The experience of safe vulnerability is the essence of secure attachment functioning at every level of our experience—the baby who is comforted while she cries, the young lovers who give themselves to one another in body and spirit, the man who unburdens his guilt with a confessor, the person who surrenders to death. But it is not relevant just to big life moments. It is relevant to how people conduct themselves and their relationships every day. Can we reach out to a friend when we are lonely or in need? Can we allow ourselves to be transparent with others and trust we have nothing to lose? Can we trust in our own abilities and still not expect ourselves to have all the answers? It is the experience of being able to hold on to ourselves, not in pride or defense, but in compassion, while facing or revealing painful, embarrassing, unformed, shamed, out-of-control, and even joyful and tender parts of the self. It is an experience that becomes a capacity over time, and with repetition and some predictability, as our sense of ourselves as capable and resilient deepens.

Once safe vulnerability has been experienced a number of times in a given relationship, it becomes an implicit expectation, so much so that a person may not even feel his or her feelings unless in contact with the other. This is the opposite of the case vignette above, where the feelings are coming and there is some defense around being so vulnerable with another—it is the experience of being *too vulnerable by oneself* and needing the help or support of another to actually feel and use one's feelings. This case is like the child who has had a rough day at school but got through it and then comes home and cries as she recounts the story and how difficult it was to a parent who is listening lovingly.

Accelerated Experiential Dynamic Psychotherapy

Because this book draws on an AEDP-oriented perspective, this section briefly introduces the basic tenets of this psychotherapeutic approach. AEDP is a model first put forth and articulated by Diana Fosha (1992, 1995, 2000a, 2000b, 2002, 2003, 2004a, 2004b, 2005, 2006, 2008, 2009, 2012). AEDP is a healing-oriented psychodynamically informed, experiential model of healing as much as of psychopathology. Fosha and her colleagues are interested in tracking the markers of change in psychotherapy, in noting what works when it works, and in exploring why and how it works when it does (Fosha, 2005). Its metapsychology is informed by affective neuroscience, attachment theory, emotion theory, studies of infant–mother interactions, models of disruption and repair, and studies of change and transformation. A number of people have written about AEDP and its application with different populations (Gleiser, Ford, & Fosha, 2008; Lamagna, 2011; Lamagna & Gleiser, 2007; Tunnell, 2006, 2011) or the importance of certain aspects of its theory to clinical application (Fosha & Yeung, 2006; Lipton & Fosha, 2011; Prenn, 2009; Russell & Fosha, 2008; Shapiro, 2009; Tunnell, 2012). There is even a popular self-help book written by one of my colleagues that is based largely on AEDP (Frederick 2009). And so AEDP continues to evolve. This book is part of its evolution.

Here I provide some of the basics of AEDP theory and technique as an introduction for many readers and a review for others. Its purpose is to set the stage for understanding the clinical approach that inspires this book and the clinical material in it. More important, a basic grasp of AEDP reveals why it is such a natural fit for any clinician wanting to understand more about the resilience of her own patients and how to work with it in the service of deepening treatment and facilitating lasting and meaningful change. For readers who are familiar with AEDP theory and technique, a number of the concepts presented in this book should deepen your understanding of resilience, transformance, and the process of healing and change.

Fundamental Aspects

There are eight fundamental aspects of AEDP (Fosha, 2012; this summary is adapted from teaching materials presented by Fosha in her week-long introduction course to AEDP). First, it is healing and transformance oriented. It is always looking for the glimmer of possibility, growth, development, openness, or curiosity that both is an expression of health and engenders the healing process. This is the most compelling reason that AEDP is such a natural therapeutic modality from which to teach about the hunt for and restoration of resilience. This is not a book about resilience per se but, rather, about resilience in therapy. You, the reader, do not have to know anything about AEDP to learn new ways of finding and restoring resilience. But in the process of that learning through this book, you will also be learning AEDP.

The second fundamental aspect of AEDP is that it is *attachment oriented* and focuses on developing a secure therapeutic attachment between therapist and patient from the beginning of treatment. Third, *dyadic affect regulation* and dyadic coordination of affective states are used for everything from actively undoing aloneness in the moment to repairing disruptions and exploring emerging affect and the anxiety that may come with it. Note that I use the term *dyadic*, which rightly implies that the patient has a real effect on the therapist that can be noted, explored, and reacted to. In fact, therapist self-disclosure of feelings, including those of appreciation, delighting in, and feeling touched by the patient, is one of the psychoanalytic taboos broken by AEDP (Fosha, 1995).

Fourth, the *subjective experience of the patient* is given center stage, and the patient is encouraged and helped to describe or articulate that experience. Fifth, AEDP focuses on *emotion and other affective change processes*. When change or transformation is evident, the AEDP therapist does not get distracted by what is not changing (as in the first case I presented of Amelia in Chapter 1). Sixth, AEDP privileges *positive affects and interactions* in order to provide vitality and energy to the process, to the dyad, and to the patient. Seventh, *metaprocessing*, which is the reflection on and processing of the experience of change and transformation itself, is unique and key and is thought to contribute to the patient's subjectively felt connection to and elaboration of the self. Eighth, *transformation*, its process and unfolding, is a quintessential focus of the work throughout.

Four States and Three State Transformations of the Transformational Process

AEDP articulates a paradigm of what frequently happens when people are helped to process emotion to completion and/or to recognize and respond to true self experiences and experiences with true others. It is best captured by the four states and the three state

EMOTIONAL EXPERIENCE
PROCESSED TO COMPLETION
The 4 States and 3 State Transformations
of the Transformational Process

STATE 1: STRESS, DISTRESS, and SYMPTOMS

Defenses and their sequelae of defensive exclusion; the sequelae of the failure of defenses; dysregulated affects; inhibiting affects (e.g., anxiety, shame)

TRANSITIONAL AFFECTS
Intrapsychic crisis

RED SIGNAL AFFECTS

FIRST STATE TRANSFORMATION
Co-creating safety

TRANSITIONAL AFFECTS:

HERALDING AFFECTS:
Glimmers of core affective experience

GREEN SIGNAL AFFECTS
Announcing openness to experience, signaling safety, readiness to shift

STATE 2: MALADAPTIVE CORE AFFECTIVE EXPERIENCE
(Need Transforming)

The pathogenic affects (e.g., toxic shame); unbearable states of aloneness (e.g., helplessness, hopelessness, despair, worthlessness; emptiness. fragmentation)

STATE 2: ADAPTIVE CORE AFFECTIVE EXPERIENCE
(Are Transforming)

Categorical emotions; coordinated relational experiences; intersubjective experiences of pleasure; authentic self states; embodied ego states and their associated emotions.

SECOND STATE TRANSFORMATION
The emergence of resilience

ADAPTIVE ACTION TENDENCIES

POST-BREAKTHROUGH AFFECTS:
Relief, hope, feeling stronger, lighter, etc

STATE 3: TRANSFORMATIONAL EXPERIENCE

The mastery affects (e.g., pride, joy); the mourning-the-self affects (emotional pain); the healing affects associated with recognition and affirmation (gratitude, tenderness, feeling moved); the tremulous affects associated with the experience of quantum change; the healing vortex of sensations associated with quantum transformations

THIRD STATE TRANSFORMATION
The co-engendering of secure attachment and the positive valuation of the self

 CALM, FLOW, EASE

STATE 4: CORE STATE and The Truth Sense

Openness, compassion and self-compassion, wisdom, generosity, kindness; understanding deeply (in both senses of the word); clarity; the sense of things feeling "right;" capacity to construct coherent and cohesive autobiographical narrative

FIGURE 2.1.
Figure created by Diana Fosha, used with permission.

transformations of the transformational process (Fosha, 2012) and is reproduced in Figure 2.1. Briefly, State 1 (stress, distress, symptoms) eventually gives way to State 2 (core affect), which is the processing of authentic emotional experience. This leads to a shift or a breakthrough and some experience of relief or lightness that follows that. The metaprocessing of that state shift frequently leads to State 3 (transformational affects), which includes a number of affects that feel subjectively positive, whether they are joyful (e.g., healing affects or mastery affects) or painful (e.g., mourning the self). Finally, usually after several rounds of processing core affect and the transformational affects that follow in their wake, people often settle into State 4 (core state), which is marked by sense of calm, ease, flow, compassion for self and others, and the integration of the deep, emotionally and viscerally felt insights of proceeding from the previous states. The transitions between these states have certain markers to alert the therapist that a shift is happening. These are called "state transformations." Now let us look at these in greater detail.

In Chapter 1, we talked about the use of the Triangle of Conflict (Ezriel, 1952). At the top of that triangle is "defense" on the left and "anxiety" on the right (see Figure 1.1). Affect-oriented experiential work focuses on regulating anxiety and reducing defenses to help people "drop down" into feeling (or core affective experience). State 1 (stress, distress, symptoms) is essentially the top of the triangle and includes anxiety or other inhibitory affects, the defenses erected against them and whatever core affective phenomena are eliciting the anxiety in the first place. To some extent the distinction between defense and anxiety is blurred because the essential point is that the person does not feel safe enough within himself or with the other to allow his authentic emotional experience to come up and be expressed. Importantly, state 1 also includes emotionality, which can both be a very partial expression of deeper affective phenomenon and/ or a cover for it. The person may appear quite distressed and expressive of that but in this state it is more often a manifestation of their disregulation than evidence that they are processing true core emotional experience. People in State 1 may appear either very regulated or not very well regulated and more obviously symptomatic.

Either way, they are not talking about what is most affectively or relationally real for them in the moment. The conversation might be difficult or might be charming, but therapists, if they are paying attention,
have the sense that something is missing or being kept at bay.

I think of the therapist's job at this point as anticipating or
imagining what the patient might be feeling unconsciously or sub-
consciously, and empathically inviting the patient into feeling.
McCullough et al. (2003) described this as trying to imagine what
affect was missing at the bottom of the triangle given what the patient
is talking about. Rather than focusing a lot of the dyad's attention on
the defenses and their consequences to the patient, the AEDP therapist focuses on what may be going on underneath or "inside" and how
to help the patient feel safe enough to feel that—to "drop down," as
we often say. The therapist may talk about "making room" to notice
what the patient might be feeling or what might be "coming up" into
consciousness. Her tone and pacing are curious, gentle, inviting, and
accepting. The first state transformation involves "heralding affects,"
which are glimmers of core affective experience (e.g., a sudden sad
face, a fist clenched in anger) and/or "green signal affects," which
include some indication from the patient that he is in some way open
to or curious about his emotional truth and perhaps ready to explore
it. (For a helpful and accessible introduction to affective-experiential
modalities, I highly McCullough et al, [2003].)

The work of emotion theorists and affective neuroscientists suggests that there are universal and intrinsic patterns that begin in
the subcortical regions of the brain and manifest in facial and bodily
changes with the full experience and expression of the categorical
emotions (Damasio, 1999; Panksepp, 1998; Tomkins, 1962, 1963).
Categorical emotions are one of the core affective experiences that
comprise State 2. They are called *core* because they are essential and
true, and when they are processed, experienced, or witnessed, one
is relieved and the work feels productive. Figure 2.1 distinguishes
between two types of core affective experiences: maladaptive and
adaptive. *Adaptive* core affective experience includes (1) categorical
emotions (à la Darwin), (2) coordinated relational experiences (e.g.,
feeling connected or not), (3) intersubjective experiences of plea-

sure (including play states), (4) authentic self states, (5) embodied ego states and their associated emotions (including affects felt only by certain "parts" of the self), (6) core needs, and (7) attachment experiences and attachment strivings. These are dubbed "adaptive" because they contain adaptive action tendencies. For example, when one is angry, the adaptive action tendency is to protect or assert the self. I would like to add that the sense of or (8) experience of agency is another core affective experience. It is people's impulse, drive, and capacity to act on behalf of themselves. Merriam-Webster's On-line Dictionary defines it as: "the capacity, condition, or state of acting or of exerting power." I do not think that agency is simply an adaptive action tendency that comes from processing core affect though it can also be that. But sometimes, people "drop down" into a felt sense of their own will, energy, desire, sense of being empowered and the capacity to act that feels like *them*. It does not have to accompany anger and the like, but is a more primary underlying capacity.

In AEDP, these core affective experiences are the focus of emotional processing, which, because they are inherently adaptive, constitute an affective change process, a *transformation*. This transformation involves having access to viscerally embodied emotional resources and information, as well as the memories, sensations, associations, insights, and other feelings that have remained unconscious as the person defended against this particular emotional experience. This coming together of feeling, bodily sensation, memory, and thinking almost invariably brings relief. That relief, whether expressed explicitly or noted in the body, then becomes the focus of attention and intervention of the work as it continues to unfold. A change has happened, and now the therapist's focus is on the patient's *experience* of that change. This is called metatherapeutic processing, or *metaprocessing* for short. Metaprocessing may be metacognitive, meta-affective, or metasomatic, depending on the focus: thoughts, feelings, or body sensations.

The special case of maladaptive core affective experiences. AEDP has made important theoretical and phenomenological distinctions between different types of core affective experience. Prior to this, and based on thinking in terms of the Triangle of Conflict, experiences of anxiety, embarrassment/shame, or even fear were thought of as top-of-the-triangle phenomena by most short-term dynamic therapists and therefore were not considered "core." But many therapists noticed that they were not easily bypassed and sometimes not even easily regulated. Moreover, patients would have the experience of not being seen or understood if they were treated simply as defenses or symptoms. It became clear that certain inhibitory emotional experiences that reflect the flight or freeze arms of the sympathetic nervous system's response to stress or threat were, in fact, core emotional experiences for the patient, around which internalized self–other dynamics and the sense of self had been consolidated. These are now called *maladaptive core affective experiences* in AEDP terminology and include (1) the pathogenic affects (e.g., toxic shame, self-hatred) and (2) unbearable states of aloneness (e.g., helplessness, hopelessness, despair, worthlessness, emptiness, fragmentation). These do not have anything adaptive built into them per se, so they do not get processed in the same way. Rather, they frequently need to be witnessed, accompanied, and approached in an effort to regulate, heal, restructure, and eventually convert to more adaptive core affective experiences (e.g., shame turns into anger or self-compassion).

Chronic experiences of fear, of being shamed, or of being left alone with too much to feel or process are formative and pathogenic. They are easily triggered in traumatized people or those with deeply problematic attachment histories, even in moments when it would seem more obvious for them to feel something more adaptive. For some, the experience of any kind of affect or connection to self is a trigger for pathogenic affect. This kind of "dropping down" should not be treated as defense but, rather, as a vulnerable revelation to the therapist of the patient's deep experience of self, self with other, or self in relation to feelings. But neither can it be treated as adaptive core affective experience, in which the unfolding and processing is organic and healthful and leads somewhere that is currently adaptive. These are experiences of being fundamentally stuck and isolated. Therefore, the therapist's response is oriented toward *undoing aloneness*. This can be done through relational, somatic, or cognitive interventions,

WITNESSING AND MAKING SPACE
FOR PATHOGENIC AFFECT

A young woman patient struggled with chronic suicidal ideation, para-suicidal behavior, and intense feelings of self-hatred. The therapist made attempts to focus on the patient's own attempts to help herself, her existential worth, the support she received from friends and professionals in a treatment program she was involved with, and the therapist's own appreciation of her. The therapist was holding the hope for the patient until she could more actively hold it herself and thought she was providing a counterweight to the heft and breadth of her self-destructive impulses. Eventually a major disruption occurred. The patient became angry, ironically but understandably, at the therapist's failure of empathy. Finally, the therapist understood that the patient needed the therapist to truly be with her in those painful states of self-hatred, witnessing them and helping to provide context, while also holding hope that it did not have to remain that way. The therapist promised to try to really understand that in these states of mind the patient really hated herself and was in terrible pain, that these states were not simply a defense but were her real feelings even if they were highly maladaptive. That promise and effort were sufficient for the patient to allow the therapist to have a different point of view without feeling so alone in these very painful states but also, importantly, without distorting the therapist's loving witness as agreement.

or all three, to orient the patient to the safety of the moment with the therapist or with another safe other or part self.

What is also very important when a patient is in this state is explicitly witnessing the pathogenic affect and the history connected with that. Quiet listening, even if it is embodied for the therapist, may leave the patient too alone and unresourced to feel again—alone—what was too much for him in the past. What I mean by *explicit witnessing* is being explicitly present to the patient's experience; communicating what it is like for the therapist to hear about it and her appreciation that the patient, who in this moment is not alone as he tells her about it and his feelings about himself; and making the link between these pathogenic affects and the current presenting issues or problems he is having.

Transformational affects: Markers of healing change. After processing core affective experiences, therapist and patient alike may have a sense of coming to the end of wave, that something is complete for the moment. There is a shift or a lightening or not much else to say. The emergence of adaptive action tendencies is an indication of the second state transformation. So are the expressions of relief, hope, and feeling stronger, lighter, or good on the part of the patient. This is an indicator to begin to ask metaprocessing questions: "What is it like to feel a little lighter (or whatever the patient's language is)?" "What's it like to have allowed yourself to express and experience so much anger at your boss here with me?" In this second state transformation we are beginning to process the experience of transformation itself.

While they may occur naturally on their own, *transformational affects* (State 3) usually emerge in response to metaprocessing questions by the therapist. At first the patient may be aware only of post-breakthrough affects (relief, lightness, strength, etc.). But if the therapist metaprocesses these affects, the patient frequently begins to feel one or more of the transformational affects. "What was it like for you to feel all that anger after so much time of keeping it buried?" "What is this relief like in your body right now?" "What was it like to have shared this with me?" "What do you make of that (particular insight)?" "What it is like to have done this important piece of work (together)?"

The transformational affects, a unique contribution of AEDP and its passion for understanding healing phenomenology, are very important to the cultivation of resilience. Such focus deepens the experience of healing, furthers understanding and insight, and contributes to the process of integration. Particularly pertinent to the process of restoring and expanding resilience, the transformational affects themselves and the processing of them increase positive affect and sense of self-efficacy, as well as compassion for the self, all of which are crucially important to the processing of self-at-worst experiences and of trauma. Transformational affects include (1) the *healing affects* of feeling moved within the self and feeling love, tenderness, and gratitude toward the other; (2) *mastery affects* of pride and joy (these are inherently expansive and feel so somatically); (3) *mourning the self*, which is grief on behalf of the self for what has been lost as a consequence of living in a limited or compromised way; (4) *tremulous affects*, which is the new and slightly nervous energy and somewhat fearful or awe-filled emotion related to the experience of transformation itself (not to be confused with State 1 experiences of anxiety or distress or any affect that is truly inhibitory); and (5) the *realization affects*, which include wonder, an exclamatory "wow" or "yes!" in response to recognizing an important truth or insight or new understanding.

Before talking about the final state transformation in emotional processing, I want to be clear that these are not necessarily linear processes. People can revert to distress or defense (State 1) at any moment. People can come into a session having had a very positive, transformational experience and be in touch with mourning the self, the healing affects of gratitude and being moved, or expansive joy or pride. Someone may come in core state. And it may appear that someone drops from State 2 into core state almost immediately, or from State 1 (distress/defense) to State 3 (transformational affects). One young woman, for example, came in talking about a recent struggle with her fairly controlling and judgmental boyfriend. At first her pace was racing—she was kind of plaintive. But within that she began to speak about something real, about her attachment needs and about how he contributes to a sense of threat in her, a feeling that she is not safe with him because he could leave at any time. She looked up at me and saw in my face that I understood her, and immediately she shifted into a profoundly different state. She began to cry from relief and felt so grateful. She spent the rest of the session between transformational affects (State 3) and core state (State 4). While it is true that she dropped into State 2 and had a brief but powerful coordinated relational experience with the therapist, a receptive affective experience in response to the therapist's understanding, and an embodied ego state in asserting her needs, it appeared to happen almost instantaneously, and the dyad did not spend time exploring or processing feelings, self, or relational states. This is what the Boston Change Process Study Group refers to as "now moment" (Stern, 1998). More is said about that in Chapter 5. The point here is that while the paradigm of the four states/three state transformations is somewhat linear, it is not strictly so, and it is most useful for the therapist to have a sense of what each state is like in order to respond accordingly in the spirit of furthering what is unfolding for the patient.

The view from here is lovely: Core state. Core state (State 4) can be thought of as the best of the self-at-best. The person is in touch with and able to express not only feelings and thoughts but also the sense of integration, perspective, calm, openness, and compassion toward the self and other that is simultaneously very grounding and a natural high. By definition, it feels good, even if there is some lingering sense of pain or grief. It is marked by the sense of truth (Fosha, 2005, 2009; Russell & Fosha, 2008). It is also the state in which an individual is most in touch with and guided by transformance strivings, which are essentially uninhibited. Obviously, it is the state of mind and heart we would like our patients (and ourselves) to live in most of the time.

The Stance of the Therapist

The fundamental source of doing meaningful psychotherapy is in the creativity of one's very being and, relatedly, in one's openness to a deep relationship with the patient.

The stance of the AEDP therapist is ideal for bringing out the innate resilience of the person with whom she is working. As mentioned above, it focuses on healing from the beginning, based on the belief that people are wired for healing and self-righting. It also trusts that, with some exceptions, most people most of the time are doing the best they can with the internal and external resources they have. We do not choose pathology or symptoms when we really know a better alternative. It follows from these beliefs and assumptions, therefore, that acceptance of the patient and his state is fundamental, as is the desire to help him transition to more adaptive ways of being with himself, in the world, and in relationships. The therapist focuses on undoing aloneness in the face of overwhelming experiences. The therapist, as subsequent chapters will show, does not hesitate to go "beyond mirroring" to helping (Fosha, 2000b, p. 273).

The therapist is not just free but encouraged to delight in and deepen positive experiences and positive self states with the patient. The AEDP stance also includes an explicit privileging and tracking of anything that is positive: signs of secure attachment, positive emotions, manifestations of resilience or transformance, and receptive affective experiences, which the patient can experience in care, concern, interest, delight, and companionship, from the therapist or others. Again, this *privileging of the positive*, as we call it, is not naïve or Polyannaish. It is, first, genuinely human and natural in secure relationships. Second, it is a way of accessing and deepening people's strengths in order to help them work with aspects of self, experience, and relating that are more problematic. And finally, and perhaps most important, it is tracking, facilitating, and elaborating on the healing process itself. Adaptive resilience, health, and healing create a different track, a different dance, a different system from that of defense, symptoms, and pathology. When this system is engaged and expanded upon, it engenders its own motivation to reproduce itself (Ghent, 1990). It is infectious in a wholly different and positive way.

My hope is that this brief introduction has made it clear why AEDP is a natural fit for therapists who want to help restore or enhance their patients' resilience. The orientation toward the phenomenology of change helps the therapist to notice from the very beginning of treatment what is fundamentally healthy and open about the patient and to partner with those positive aspects. The belief that in most situations people are doing their best with what they have and that symptoms are often the result of prior best efforts to adapt that have run their course is very accepting and leaves a lot of room for patient and therapist to marvel at how the patient has survived and what other options may exist in the present. There is a fundamental faith in people *working on behalf of themselves*, even if the behavioral manifestation is presently misguided. The encouragement of a secure therapeutic attachment to facilitate emotional processing and taking risks is consistent with our understanding that resilience is rarely a "one-person job." Rather, our need to borrow from the capacities of others as we are learning new ways for ourselves is lifelong, and it is a foundational piece of this work. Finally, the understanding that relationships that comprise, support, or undermine our functioning in the world are mediated primarily through emotion suggests that being able to *feel and deal while relating* (Fosha, 2002) is an essential piece of true resilience.

Summary

This chapter has provided some theoretical underpinnings to the therapeutic effort to help restore resilience. It discussed the importance of attachment theory to the understanding of how and why people learn to cope and to process and express (or not) their emotions and other core self and relational experiences. The experience of self that is secure and predictable and able to turn to others when overwhelmed is one that is nurtured, or not, from earliest infancy and is a foundation of resilient functioning. If it is not acquired early, it must be acquired at some point; otherwise, people must continue to function in the world in a constricted and compromised way.

We briefly reviewed theories of emotion, which posit that emotion is the primary motivational system in the person that helps organize our responses to our environment. Experiential therapies have led the way in explicating different types of emotion (e.g., primary vs. secondary) and the necessity of accessing primary, or core, emotion in facilitating change and healing (and the building up of resilience). Almost as a prelude to what is discussed in much greater detail in chapter 7, the chapter described the importance of positive affect to the self and to the health of relationships, as well as its importance as an ally in the deep and cathartic processing of very painful experiences. I introduced the concept of *safe vulnerability* and shared the short transcript of a young man who, for one of the first times in his life, was able to experience emotional exposure and vulnerability as safe enough.

The last section of this chapter provided a summary of the essential aspects of AEDP theory and practice that are relevant to the restoration of resilience. In particular, some of the fundamental aspects, such as a focus on healing from the beginning, the establishment of a secure therapeutic attachment relationship in which the full expression of the self finds a safe outlet, the emphasis on embodied affective expression to release adaptive (i.e., resilient) action tendencies, and the role of metaprocessing transformative experiences, are essential aspects of restoring and enhancing resilience. The four states and three state transformations of AEDP provide an affective and relational map of clinical phenomena that move in the direction of healing and enhanced resilience.

There was a special review of how to handle maladaptive or pathological affect in a way that does not simply bypass it or dismiss it as defensive but, rather, recognizes it as a central organizing experience of self that needs witnessing and transforming through the development of self-compassion. Mature, integrated resilience does not come through our leapfrogging over parts of ourselves we do not like or do not know how to handle. Transformational affects and core state are markers of healing change and integration that lead to more currently adaptive and resilient ways of being in the world. Finally, the stance of an AEDP therapist was reviewed and presented as a natural stance from which to conduct resilience-oriented therapy.

CHAPTER 3

The Self-in-Transition and the Transformational Other

*The memory of this early object relation manifests itself
in the person's search for an object (a person, place,
event, ideology) that promises to transform the self.*

Christopher Bollas, in The Shadow of the Object, contends that
one of the earliest experiences of the infant is of his mother "as a
process that is identified with cumulative internal and external
transformations" (1987, p. 14). Before she can become an object (or
an "other"), she is an intrinsic part of his experience of himself being
transformed. It is this experience that lives on even as object relationships come and go. This repeated experience becomes a bodily
held memory of the capacity for transformation and the seed of hope
for its eventuation over and over as one struggles with the complexity of life and the inevitability of suffering. A gambler going to the
tables (transformational object) convinced that he is going to win big
(i.e., be transformed) is a perfect, albeit unhealthy, example.

The world of psychotherapy depends on Bollas's above statement
being true, both as foreground and as background. What is foreground is the child-become-adult's ongoing need for and seeking

of transformative experiences. What is background is the capacity of objects, ideas, places, and, in this case, persons to be transformational for one another. Were it not for this powerful, dynamic exchange, patients would not come to therapy, and therapists would be burned out before finishing graduate school.

This dynamic of the self-seeking-transformation and the other—able and willing to facilitate it—is the focus of this chapter. Specifically, it explores the concept of the *transformational other*, and its counterpart in the patient, *the self-in-transition*. The self that is transitioning is moving from functioning as *self-at-worst*, in which access to core emotions and authentic self states is blocked or limited and the self is compromised, to *self-at-best*, in which access to emotional states is relatively open, the self is experienced as effective, and the other is seen in a realistic way. What this chapter should make clear is that the movement from one self state to the other is frequently a touch-and-go process that involves ambivalence and vacillation. The building up of resilience is often a gradual and bumpy ride. This is when the therapist's capacity to function as a steady, inviting, *transformational other* is so necessary. Her role is to *identify and elaborate* that which is emerging from core affective experience, to privilege hope, curiosity, and openness over anxiety, shame, or the defenses people employ to remain unaware of what is really happening for them on a deep level. It is usually in this exchange between the self who is transitioning and the transformational other that the patient has an experience of feeling as if he exists *in the heart and mind of the therapist* (Fosha, 2000b, adapted from Fonagy; Fosha, 2008).

I chose to use the transcript of one session with a patient, almost its entirety, to illustrate these concepts. It provides an opportunity to see the patient move from a self-at-worst state to a self-at-best state in which she is capable of intimacy with another and compassion toward herself, thereby strengthening her resilient capacity. Throughout much of it, there is a vacillation between the two states (the self-in-transition). The therapist is thinking, working, and relating in such a way as to facilitate the emergence and elaboration of the self-at-best (as transformational other) by paying closest attention to statements, gestures, facial expressions, and tones of voice that reveal the patient's resilience potential. This chapter is organized slightly differently from the others in that the transcript here is the canvas on which the theoretical topics are painted. Therefore, subtitles are embedded into the transcript rather than vice versa.

This transcript is from a session with a patient in her early twenties. At the time of this session, she and the therapist had been working together for approximately 5 months. She initially presented with issues and difficulty around separating from parents who were frequently neglectful, sometimes hostile, and almost always unaware of themselves and the emotional and attachment needs of their children. While charming, bright, capable of engaging, and receptive, this patient frequently had great difficulty expressing her current or past experiences in words. She knew something was wrong, but the examples she came up with to convey that sense appeared to be more benevolent than the empty, nonmirroring interactions they described actually were. This is evident in portions of the transcribed session below. She suffered with some social phobia and deep insecurity about how she was perceived by others despite being attractive and intelligent and having a history of having made relatively good, age-appropriate friendships. She also suffers with some apparently psychosomatic complaints and has a long history of migraine headaches, which are worsened by stress, particularly interpersonal. On the day of this session, she had stayed home sick from work and had a bad headache.

She opens this session thanking the therapist again for the prior week's session and for a brief phone conversation in between. She reports having had a good conversation with her mother in which she was able to observe her mother's anxiety and immaturity without becoming dysregulated herself. Describing how the conversation unfolded, she recounted her own ambivalence about scheduling a date to see her parents, which was likely conveyed to the mother through the patient's lack of clarity and tone of voice. Some emotion came into her voice and body as she then reported her mother's quick move to declare when she and the father were *not* available to see her; this felt like a "tit for tat," which was typical of the mother.

While seemingly small, these subtly dismissive moments in which the mother fails to be a grown-up (and therefore a safe attachment figure) have happened constantly over the course of her life, compromising this young woman's development and sense of self.

Self-at-Worst and Self-at-Best: Resilience as Potential

CLINICAL VIGNETTE:
"I Am On a Level That I don't Want to Be On"

PT: (**Reflecting on the mother's stating when she was not available**) . . . she was kind of asserting her individuality in a way that was neglectful of me. (**Moments later**) I really felt that empty feeling [**Unbearable state of aloneness**.] . . . It was kind of an awareness that this is what she does. Like in the past, she goes, "But that is what you are doing to me." And I would just be like, "But you're the parent!" in my head [**Expressing need for strong attachment figure**.] . . . What matters to you at the end of the day? (**as if speaking to her mother**). That's where the emptiness comes from . . . But when I hung up I wasn't stirred inside . . .

TP: You weren't what inside?

PT: Stirred. Like I was more just stirred in the moment. But it was more of just a good perception to have . . . that's why I called you . . . I was happy to get my part out.

TP: Sounds great. Sounds great.

PT: Yeah. But I don't know what I am going to do when they come to visit me. [**Increasing anxiety.**]

TP: Tell me a little more . . . (about) your internal processing of "yeah, but you're the parent." What's that like for you? [**TP focusing on partly articulated declaration of need toward parent.**]

PT: Like, kind of just like, I am wanting more that they, that she can't do. I am on a level that I don't want to be on. Like it's a different playing field. [**Starting to describe her self-at-worst functioning with mother/parents.**]

TP: Tell me more. How do you see it when you say you are on a level that you don't want to be on?

PT: Like the behavior that she is reacting to, that makes her react . . . is not my best behavior. I know that. And I'd rather her teach me, instead of tit-for-tat. [**Aware of dysregulation in presence of mother; expressing need for help—for dyadic affect regulation.**] It is a bad reflection of who I am when that happens (**starts to rub head behind ears**). [**PT describing self-at-worst.**]

TP: What's it like to say that? Do you have any feelings about that?

PT: . . . childish kind of feeling inside.

TP: Your own being childish, or your mother's?

PT: No. My mother's being childish, but my feeling more like a child because of the situation . . . (**pause**) And those inner feelings . . . or that inner monologue that I grew up with that I didn't know what to do with it. I don't know. (**pause**) Like when I have said that I am putting on a show with my parents, (**pointing finger**) that inner part sees me putting on a show. Like it's that surface the way I talk to my parents [**Reflective self function. PT recognizes false self; heralding of something more adaptive, more effective, more true. This is what the therapist wants to follow.**]

Here the patient clearly articulates that intrapsychic conflict is contextualized by interpersonal experience. She describes herself in a state that she does not like (Winnicott, 1960/ 1965) but begins to be able to clarify what the statements, attitudes, and behaviors of the mother are that either elicit that state in her or create a negative feedback loop from which it is very difficult to extricate herself. This is the self-at-worst, depicted in Figure 1.3a (Fosha, 2005). Notice that this is a triangle within a triangle. Specifically, it is the Triangle of Conflict within the Self–Other–Emotion Triangle. Briefly, the

Self–Other–Emotion Triangle captures the self's experience of the self, the other, and their dyadic emotional interaction (for more on the Self–Other–Emotion Triangle, see Fosha, 2000b).

How a dyadic pair relates to and deals with (or not) emotions that exist within and between them both is influenced by and contributes to the relative safety and comfort they feel with one another. In other words, the self–other–emotion interaction exists within a backdrop of relative openness and safety or of closedness and lack of safety that is based in part on the history of accumulated interactions between the two individuals. These are self-perpetuating dynamics. If, for example, there exists in one or both partners an ongoing sense of a lack of safety around emotion with the other, defenses will be used to cover emotions and vulnerability, thus limiting the relationship and reinforcing the lack of emotional safety. On the other hand, in a dyad in which there exists a sense of emotional safety, more will be brought forth about one or both person's emotional experiences and vulnerability, ideally leading to an expansion of the self, the other, and the capacity of each to coordinate with the other, to repair disruptions, and to metabolize intense emotional experiences, thereby increasing the resilient capacity of both partners. Tronick (1998) refers to this as "expanded dyadic states of consciousness." In contrast, the patient's and her mother's constrained or restricted dyadic state of consciousness literally limits the patient's state of consciousness (and likely, the mother's), and as she herself is aware, "It's a bad reflection of who I am when that happens."

The smaller triangle is a variation on the Triangle of Conflict (Ezriel, 1952) presented in Chapter 1. When conditions are not safe enough, the elicitation of affective phenomena triggers some form of anxiety, shame, or other inhibitory affects ("red signal affect") whose inherent discomfort leads to the erection and use of defenses (e.g., intellectualizing, changing the subject, downplaying, critique of self) for the purpose of warding off emerging affect and diminishing anxiety. Panning out to the larger triangle, it is clear how this closing off of one's own affective experiences, and the resources associated with them, leads to a compromised self. That self either distorts the other (as in the case of projection) or has needed to erect defenses because the other is already distorted, in fact, by acting or behaving in a defensive or hurtful way himself.

When, on the other hand, conditions are right (i.e., safe enough), what was once blocked affective phenomena (including self and relational experiences, categorical emotions, and self states) become expressable and expressed. This is depicted in Figure 1.3b in Chapter 1 and represents the *self-at-best*. The other is seen in a realistic way (even if not too positively), and the self is experienced as competent or effective. What makes it "safe enough" for each person is largely idiosyncratic, but optimally that person needs sufficient permission for expression, and sufficient acceptance to follow that expression. In the very least, the person needs to feel sufficiently secure that there will not be negative repercussions to sharing feelings and that if there are those are repercussions the person is willing to face.

It is important to note that self-at-worst functioning can be evoked by any number of factors. The most obvious is the patient's chronic reliance on defenses against his own experience. He brings this habitual way of relating to self and other into most, if not all, relationships. It also may be evoked by the emergence of affective experiences that have been blocked up until this point and/or the presence of anxiety, both of which can set the whole self-limiting, negative process in motion. It can be evoked by the presence of another who is experienced as critical, judgmental, shaming, punitive, and so forth. And finally, it can even be evoked in the moment by the memory of the self in a compromised state and the shame that frequently accompanies such observations and experiences of the self.

And so, in the therapeutic situation in which the patient frequently presents with his self-at-worst (at least in the beginning), the factor over which therapists have the most control is how we are perceived *in the moment* as the "other." The patient's experience of the therapist as a realistic *and* kind, compassionate, curious, nonjudgmental other is critical to shift the background to one that facilitates emotional expression and true experience of self. *This frequently necessitates an active, engaged, and explicitly empathic stance on the part of the therapist*, rather than a neutral or impassive stance that implicitly invites projection and distortion and, consequently, perpetuates the self-at-worst. In the latter case, the resilience potential remains the same, but the resilient capacity is diminished or chooses a more constrained or self-limiting expression.

Returning for a closer look at the vignette above, the patient is describing her recognition of her self-at-worst in the context of her relationship with her mother. There is a brief awareness of the pervasive and highly distressing feeling of emptiness that attends many of her interactions with her mother. There is also the appearance of a more adaptive need or desire she has in relating to her mother, which is for the mother to be the adult, the attachment figure. If our focus is on recognizing, coaxing, and encouraging the resilience potential, this should seize our attention and direct our next intervention.

The patient then goes on to describe, in a very insightful and coherent way, the dyadic nature of their mutual self-at-worst evocations of one another. Within the background of a lack of safety based in large part on the mother's narcissism, expressed in her need to fuse with her young daughter over superficial and materialistic concerns and her inability to draw out and relate to what is more authentic and vital in her daughter, the patient says or does something obstreperous. The mother, rather than setting limits, speaking from her own feelings of hurt, confusion, or anger or, rising above the childishness of her daughter, retaliates in an equally disrespectful and now passive-aggressive way. The patient is wounded but has no idea how to repair or to ask for repair, so her resilience potential expresses itself in this retaliatory, passive-aggressive way to keep her mother out and prevent her self from becoming too vulnerable with her own attachment needs that the mother has not met and will not meet. The mother, in fact, has very little ability to repair, which is one of the primary reasons the patient cannot expect or imagine it. The patient is stuck feeling young, small, frustrated, and afraid of the upcoming visit.

But, importantly, she has also revealed yet another gem of her resilience potential. She says that there is an "inner part" of herself that sees her putting on a show (i.e., being a false self) for her parents. From the perspective of working with and enhancing resilience, the therapist wants to hear more about that "inner part" than about the "show."

Before we move on to more dialogue, I want to be clear that in the above vignette, the patient is not in the moment in self-at-worst or in self-at-best. She is trying her best to communicate a frustrating situation and recalling a self-at-worst experience. In this next passage, she will be in a self-at-worst state in the moment with the therapist.

CLINICAL VIGNETTE:
"This Could Be Calm"

(Continuing where we left off . . .)

TP: Which inner part sees you putting on a show? How would you describe that part?

PT: Like really quiet and thoughtful, like an achy kind of feeling . . . like where my headaches come from I feel (**referencing migraines**). A lot more slowed down. [**PT is "dropping down" into her feelings and experience; defenses are softening and we know we are on the right track.**]

TP: (**Softly and slowly**) This part of you that observes what's happening.

PT: Yeah.

TP: And observes how you respond, and is becoming clearer and more aware that you get triggered into acting in a way that feels. [**TP inviting PT to be in touch with and share this "inner part" by (1) inquiring specifically, (2) speaking slowly and in an embodied and low tone of voice, and (3) reflecting back to the PT her experience as she has put it in her own words.**]

PT: (**Interrupting**) It feels like a sad place too (**tears**).

TP: Yeah. Mm-hmm. (**slow, low voice**) You're feeling it now as we're talking about it?

PT: I am just remembering everything . . . Everywhere I would be I would feel it. But it wouldn't match what was happening. It was like I was supposed to be on another channel.

TP: Uh huh.

PT: Yeah. I am feeling it now (**nervously biting fingernails**)

TP: (**Gently**) Is it okay to just stay with it for a moment, Melissa? [**Inviting PT into core affective experience.**] If maybe *we* just stay with it so it doesn't feel so alone? [**TP (1) asking permission if it feels safe enough to stay with affective experience and (2) countering aloneness through explicit reminder of the presence of TP through use of "we" language, which is a right-brain-to-right-brain communication.**] I have a sense that this sad part is such a wise part of you, also. [**Explicit affirmation of core affective experience, of the part of the self that felt what has happening and not happening in family situations; encouragement and reframing.**]

PT: (**Picking fingers, looking down**) [**PT clearly somewhat anxious but reflective and listening.**]

TP: What's happening right now?

PT: Well, it's just hard to believe that because of all the pain it causes people all the time (**pause; starts to cry**).

TP: That this part of you causes people pain?

PT: I don't know. I can never really stay with it. What I get on the other end is very reactive . . . [**Attachment relationships bringing out "self-at-worst"; no safe place for the core affective experience of sadness over disconnection.**]

TP: So it's hard to imagine staying with it here with me because there's a fear that it might cause me pain? Or that I might have to react to it and push it away? [**TP explicit about patient's fear of reaction/ rejection of this vulnerable self state and, by implication, is welcoming of it instead,**]

PT: Yeah, like it's making you feel uncomfortable how I'm acting, I guess. [**Distorting TP/other.**]

This is the self-at-worst in which core affect is being blocked because it causes anxiety, and defenses are prominent because of their historical ability both to reduce anxiety and to banish the core affective experiences that elicit it. Moreover, the patient sees herself in a diminished, shameful way ("its making you uncomfortable how I am acting") and the other is distorted (e.g., the therapist is uncomfortable rather than open, empathic and curious).

TP: (**Gently**) How do you see that? Do you see that in me? [**Active but gentle challenge to the projection; asking PT to pay attention to what is really happening in the moment.**]

PT: Kind of like I am neglecting you. No, I don't see that in you. But, it's making me feel like I am sidetracking (**tears**). [**Sadness pushing through some of the defense. Experientially, the patient automatically feels "off" when, in fact, she is right on. PT slightly tearful and reflective but still defended.**]

TP: What do you see in me when you talk about the sad part that sees what's going on, but she has to stay in the background? [**Dyadic affect regulation; asking PT to be both with her emotional experience and with the TP and how she really is with her in the moment.**]

PT: (**Long look at TP**) Umm. It's like you're interested and you are patient and kind of like, kind, it feels like [**PT able to take in reality of TP's presence and affective state toward her. Spontaneously uses words to describe experience of TP that befit a secure attachment figure.**]

TP: Mm. What's that like for you right now? [**Processing transformative relational experience in the moment.**]

PT: Really quiet, (**smile**) uncomfortably quiet (**slightly squirming**). [**PT is significantly slowed down and more in touch with core affective experience, but also aware of anxiety or red signal affects coming up.**]

TP: That's what it feels like inside?

PT: Yeah. My head feels like it wants to do a million different things. [**Anxiety/defense/distress.**] Like this feels like this could be calm, almost, but it's not right now. [**This is a "heralding affect" (Fosha, 2000b): an affective communication, whether statement, facial expression, shift in tone, or expression of feeling, that signals the emergence of**

some core affective phenomenon. In this case, it signals the feeling of calm.]

TP: Tell me a little more about that. This sense that it could be calm. This distressed part could be calm?

Here again, the therapist is interested more in the felt sense that something could be calm than in whatever is interfering with it being calm. The resilience potential is in the prescient sense that something is as it is not expected to be, that something other than the ordinary and known is possible. The emphasis in her question intentionally directs the patient's awareness to what is happening in her emotionally. There is an implicit value judgment reflected in this direction and emphasis: one emotional response is "higher than," or reflects a stronger or healthier aspect of self that is oriented toward change, than the other, which reflects old, habitual, relational patterns that are too frequently repeated to the detriment of the patient and of her relationships.

The statement "this could be calm" is an expression of a *receptive affective experience*, or "the individual's experience of the other's affective response to him" (Fosha, 2000b, p. 152). The therapist's exploration of the patient's *actual* experience of her when she is in touch with her sadness moves the patient away from her fear-based appraisal, which is in fact a projection, and toward a more realistic perception of engaged benevolence, which then leads to an emerging felt sense of calm. The patient cannot fully trust this yet, and so it is qualified. But this is a critical point, which brings us to our discussion of the self-at-best. In an environment of emotional safety, adaptive affect tendencies cannot and will not be expressed unless that safety is experienced by the patient and not simply offered by the therapist. As long as the patient continues to perceive and experience her environment as hostile or potentially threatening, projection though that may be, she will have access only to action tendencies that are appropriate to those perceptions, which are flight, fight, or freeze.

In contrast to the self-at-worst, the self-at-best has access to her internal experience, to her affective experience, and uses it to guide her responses to her real environment. Defenses are minimal, and there is little to no anxiety about what is emerging or present in the self. Frequently, instead, there is curiosity and openness. In part because of this access to one's affective resources, the person experiences herself as effective and the other is seen in a realistic way, even if what is happening between them is difficult (see Figure 1.3b). (At the bottom of triangle shown in Figure 1.3b are core affective phenomena, including categorical emotions, authentic self states, and what AEDP calls transformational affects and core state. I say more about these later in the chapter as it relates to the clinical material.) The self-at-best is energized by transformance strivings, the healthiest and fullest expression of the resilience potential.

It is important to be clear that the terms *self-at-best* and *self-at-worst* refer to a person's relationship to his or her own affective state or self state and experience of another person in relation to this affective or self state. It should not be confused with the colloquial "being at one's best," though there is a lot of overlap with this. In fact, the self-at-best does not have to be a happy state—frequently it is not. If my husband is angry with me and yet seeing me realistically and communicating openly about his anger, although this is not my favorite experience of my husband, in terms of his own capacity to be in relation to his feelings and to me at the same time he is in a self-at-best state. Similarly, someone can be in a self-at-best state and be weeping with pain or sorrow over injury or loss. If she is welcoming of her experience, if it feels manageable to her, and if she experiences the other with whom she is sharing her experience as open and caring, she is still in a self-at-best state. People emerge from experiences like this feeling relief and solidity within themselves and usually have much greater clarity about an emotionally evocative issue while they simultaneously feel more capable of doing something about it or even letting it go.

The goal of all therapies is that the person is in self-at-best state much of the time and the frequency with which she is in self-at-worst is considerably diminished. So what is the point of talking about the self-at-best? Is it arbitrary or artificial to work toward a person's being in a self-at-best state when the pathology with which he struggles and for which he has sought help keeps him in self-at-worst? Are we ignoring the pathology or the problem if we are focused on the self-at-best?

The main reason for looking for the self-at-best—right from the beginning of treatment and throughout—is to access its resources to help the self-at-worst. This is the essence of working to enhance resilience. *The self-at-best is the most resourceful and resilient version of that person.* It is an expression of the resilient capacity that is frequently cut off or burdened by the person's symptoms and/or chronic use of defenses. It holds a wisdom, a hope, and an ease with oneself and life that more defended self states do not.

When people are in self-at-worst states, examining their pathology or areas of conflict *can* be counterproductive. This is a closed information system. Nothing new is coming in, and so the same negative, frequently self-defeating feelings and thoughts about oneself and one's circumstances keep getting recycled. Asking someone in this state how he feels toward a more vulnerable or tender (usually younger) part of himself will likely yield a response that is, at best, confused and neutral and, at worst, dismissing, castigating, or disgusted. If, however, the person is in self-at-best and has access to his feelings and reactions, feels safe, and is able to manage what is happening inside, when he is asked, "What do you think that 8-year-old needed at that time?" or "What would you like to say to that 8-year-old girl right now, from this place?" the patient's responses are much less likely to be confused or fearful and much more likely to be marked by compassion, generosity, and a sufficient separation between the person now and the person of the other state. This differentiation is the opposite of the identification with the earlier self that frequently paralyzes people in the present. The self-at-best has access to resources, including insights about the self, that he is willing to lend the self-at-worst, who is usually in a chronic state of helplessness, much like the younger self was at the time of the traumatic, depriving, abandoning, or overwhelming situation. (For very good discussions of what is now called intrarelational AEDP, see Lamagna 2011; Lamagna and Gleiser, 2007; for people interested in facilitating working through part selves, as well as their integration, see Schwartz 1995.)

Let us return to our session where we left off. This next vignette demonstrates the *self-in-transition*, that is, the self who is neither best nor worst, neither fully open and expressive nor completely closed and defended, neither relaxed nor overwhelmed by anxiety. This self is in between and needs help and guidance to get to the self-at-best. In my experience, this is where much of the work of therapy gets done.

The Self-in-Transition: The Real Work of Therapy

CLINICAL VIGNETTE:
"If I Let It Be Like That It's Like Kind of Freeing . . .
but I Feel Really Guilty"

(Continuing where we left off . . .)

TP: Tell me a little more about that. This sense that it could be calm. This distressed part could be calm? [**Explicit focus on the resilience potential; the part at the PT's edge of awareness.**]

PT: Yeah.

TP: What makes you say that? What are you aware of? [**TP invites PT to focus on her experience of her more resilient, secure self.**]

PT: It feels very much like it is coming from my head. [**Awareness of defense.**] . . . It is not you and it is not where we are and it's not; there's nothing threatening at face value. So, it feels like if I. It feels like *my* channel is being interrupted or something. It feels like *my* head hurts [**PT able to see TP clearly and is aware of the invitation to be with her real experience, but there is still a powerful experience of anxiety and her usual defenses are in full force. It is as if the message that it is safe, which she perceives and cognitively understands, has not yet trickled down to all parts of her.**]

TP: Mm-hmm. (**pause . . .again, slow, low, soft voice**) But if you're just present in the moment between just you and me, it feels like you could be with this sad part that is aware of what is going on without it being distressing or hurtful to other people or to me or to you . . . [**TP privileging PT's awareness of what is happening in reality: her feelings and the sense of safety in the therapeutic relationship. TP returning the focus to the core affect of sadness that elicited defenses in the first place.**]

PT: I guess if I let it be like that it's like kind of freeing . . . but I feel really guilty, like dirty to let it happen. I'm really worried about it. I don't know why. It's almost like it's not allowed, like it would screw up everything. [**This is the self-in-transition and an example of yellow signal affects (see below for explication); simultaneous awareness of feeling free and guilty/worried.**]

TP: What's not allowed, just so we're both really clear?

PT: Staying with the sad feeling.

TP: Mm-hmm.

PT: (**Pause, looking away**)

The above segment of this session is the beginning of what happens for most of the rest of the session and what happens in many of our sessions with many of our patients, much of the time. The dyad has worked hard enough to move the patient out of defense and into her experience, out of her self-at-worst and toward her self-at-best. The patient's resilience potential, which is always working on behalf of her self, holds her transformance strivings, which are on the lookout for environments and relationships in which one can be one's truest self. These are emerging, and as they do, her resilient capacity (how her resilience potential is expressed) shifts from a more self-protective, conserving, closed energy to a more open, responsive energy that allows her to momentarily relax defenses, be in tune with herself and her deeper feelings and yearning, and begin to see the therapist more realistically as existing outside of her expectations. But her expectations are powerful and her self–other–emotion schema that relates to her sadness (and other true feelings) makes a strong case for self-protection, hence resistance and defense. And so she vacillates between openness to self and other and closing herself and the other down. "I guess if I let it be like that it's like kind of freeing . . . but I feel kind of guilty. I'm really worried about it . . . like it's not allowed . . . it would screw up everything." There is a dramatic difference between "freeing" and "it would screw up everything," and yet they are both uttered within seconds of each other and are felt by the patient at the same time. This is the self-in-transition, depicted in Figure 1.4.

The self-in-transition is transitioning from one self state, from one mode of functioning with oneself and others, to another mode, presumably more robust, complex, and coherent (Siegel, 2007). As Ghent describes it, "There is, however deeply buried or frozen, a longing for something in the environment to make possible the surrender, in the sense of yielding, of false self" (1990, p. 109). In Ghent's description, it is a state in which the "longing" for the possibility of "surrender . . . yielding, of the false self" is emerging but not yet fully in the lead. The self is experienced as *tentative*; whatever is emerging is not yet fully owned, and one is not completely functioning from the emerging state. Rather, whatever is healthier or more adaptive is usually experienced as existing on the edge of the person's awareness. It comes in momentarily and, in doing so, escorts a very different perspective that, when "tried on for size" arouses different feelings. But it is only being tried on—the dress has not been bought. And the question the person asks as she looks in the mirror is not simply, "Does this look and fit right?" but rather, "Would I really dare to wear something so stunning?" The excitement and the inhibition are at the same frequency and pitch.

This tentativeness accompanies the transient relaxation of defenses, which allows for the emergence of core affective experience, painful experiences of aloneness or shame, or the discovery of core state, that capacity for ease, flow, acceptance, and relaxation that we are all capable of at least from time to time. The relaxation of the defenses is due to the diminishment in anxiety and the red signal affects, like shame or embarrassment. Again, this is transient, and there seems to be an iterative process that involves letting go and clutching again, opening up and sealing over. In other words, there is a rapid alternation between *green signal affects* (hope, curiosity, openness) and *red signal affects* (anxiety, fear, shame, embarrass-ment); hence, I call these *yellow signal affects*. This is a marker of the self-in-transition. Another marker is a sense of effort and per-sistence on the part of the patient, accompanied by an implicit or explicit need for help or guidance. Finally, in choosing to privilege the resilience potential that is trying to emerge, the therapist too has a sense of effort and perhaps of excitement and risk. Both likely have a sense that something important is under way.

In emotionally safe environments the resilience potential mani-fests as transformance strivings that propel and compel the person toward greater openness and greater complexity, accepting risk as one goes. With less safety, transformance does not have an oppor-tunity to come forth, and therefore, the resilience potential usually expresses itself as creating interpersonal and intrapersonal walls. With repetition, these original manifestations of one's resilience potential can become calcifications over time, now no longer sim-ply protecting a vulnerable self from the intrusion of harmful expe-riences but also robbing him of the receipt of good, healing, safe, fertile experiences. What is unknown but contains potential for something new is *reflexively* closed off in favor of what is known and predictable, and frequently unhappy. As therapists, we want to pay attention to and make room for the expression of the resilience potential in any given moment.

The Transformational Other: The Therapist's Potential

The role of the transformational other in this self–other–emotion configuration is to identify and help elaborate that which is emerg-ing; to privilege hope, curiosity, and openness and the yet to be fully expressed core affective experience over fear, anxiety, shame, and one's characteristic defenses. The transformational other is the "something in the environment" that the self is looking for to facil-itate the surrender of its falsehood and the revelation of its truth.

The therapist must quickly identify her own confusion resulting from the rapidly contradicting statements and signals coming from the patient and recognize the opportunity therein. This is not a simple process of empathizing with and validating expressions of the patient's health and resilience that are delivered fully formed. What is being delivered is ambivalence and uncertainty, hope and also fear, vulnerability and also counterdependence. We want to accept the latter with genuine empathy and understanding. But we want to explicitly and repeatedly welcome the former and express our deep interest in getting to know these parts of the patient's self. In this way, we are working within a person's emotional and interpersonal "zone of proximal development" (Vygotsky, 1978), that place where the challenge of the next level of learning is just beyond someone's reach but perhaps with help, structure, or scaffolding is still within their grasp and something they are ready to get and grow from.

CLINICAL VIGNETTE:
"It's Right There Right Now . . . This Very Wise Sadness"

(Continuing where we left off . . .)

TP: What's not allowed just so we're both really clear?
PT: Staying with the sad feeling.
TP: Mm-hmm.
PT: (**Pause, looking away**)
TP: This sad feeling holds so much, so much truth. And it is so used to being cut off and dismissed (**PT becoming tearful**). [**TP acknowledging rightness of sad feeling and explicitly empathizing with it without challenging PT on how she cuts off her own feelings just like others did to her.**]
PT: Yeah.
TP: What is happening for you right now? [**Experiential focus on emerging affect.**]
PT: I feel like what does that say about me? If that's how I really feel, what does that say about me? [**Defense of intellectualization; self-doubt.**] That's where I go with it.
TP: You go into your head about it and you analyze it. [**TP naming defense.**]

PT: Yeah.

TP: Mm-hmm. (**pause**) What are you worried that it says about you? [**Going with the defense for the moment to understand PT's internal monologue.**]

PT: That I am a sad girl.

TP: Mm. Mm-hmm. Is there some fear that if let yourself sit with the sadness that you're not going to come out of it; that that is who you are, that you will stay there? [**TP empathically elaborating PT's fear of her own feelings. This is an intuition based on experience that people who have repressed certain feelings often fear becoming engulfed by them if they allow them at all.**]

PT: (**Soft smile**) Yeah. [**Some receptive affective experience. Smile indicates TP has understood; that is a green signal that we are on the right path.**]

TP: That it will be overpowering and overwhelming (**PT nodding, tearful**). [**Tears are further confirmation that TP is articulating PT's internal experience correctly and PT is therefore opening up and becoming more vulnerable to herself as well as to the TP.**] (**Pause, PT crying**) Mm-hmm. Rather than it could kind of move through you and come to an end like all emotions do. [**TP gently communicating an alternate possibility, namely, how emotion processes work in conditions of safety.**]

PT: (**Tears flowing**)

TP: Mmm.

PT: (**Wiping tears, crying harder**) Like if I think about it, it feels like it would define me. [**PT still moving into her head slightly, but now more "noticing" her thought process rather than being directed by it. Her tears are flowing and she is in touch with the sadness despite the fear of being defined by it.**]

TP: It's going to define you. Mm-hmm.

PT: Yeah (**wiping tears, breathing hard**).

TP: Mmm. It's right there right now. Is this the sadness, this very wise sadness? (**PT nodding while crying**) It's been seeing how disconnected everybody is for so many years (**PT crying hard**). (**pause**) Mmm. It has felt so isolated because nobody else wants to acknowledge that. Mmm. Mmm. [**Right brain-to-right brain communication; facilitating deep affect; validating feelings.**]

PT: (**Removing hands from eyes, looking up.**) [**A very clear ending of the "wave" of emotion that does not appear defensive, but rather, resolved for the moment.**]

TP: Hmm (**rising tone, as if to say "hello"**).

PT: (**Giggle**)

TP: (**Soft, warm**) What's that laugh about? Where are you right now?

PT: It's okay. [**Confirming sense of resolution; of completion of this wave of affect.**]

TP: It's okay. You feel okay?

PT: Yeah. Like I survived that. [**PT now has access to a felt sense of her own resilient capacity, derived in large part from having faced, done, and survived something initially difficult and feared to be overwhelming.**]

TP: (**Pause**) What's that like that you survived that [**TP following PT and shifting to focus on the feelings and sensations of "survival" in order to experientially deepen her own sense of her resilient self. This is metatherapeutic processing; focusing on the experience of transformation itself.**] You just went into this very deep sadness and you survived it as you said.

PT: I don't know. It's like . . . the world didn't come to an end.

Metatherapeutic Processing: Reflecting on Micro and Macro Moments of Change

Studying the process of moment-to-moment tracking of affect, the relationship, and experience through videotape of actual sessions allowed AEDP clinicians to discover that there is frequently a predictable flow to the processing of difficult, as-yet-unaddressed emotional material. There is frequently some relief or sense of lightness or renewed strength that follows processing emotion to completion (Fosha, 2000b), not unlike what happens in focusing (Gendlin, 1969) or emotion-focused therapy (Greenberg, 1991; Greenberg & Johnson, 1990; Greenberg et al., 1993; Johnson, 1996). If enough has been processed, there is frequently a state transformation in the patient that is marked by transformational affects, which, in turn, cue the therapist to focus on the patient's experience of transformation via metatherapeutic processing or metaprocessing (Fosha, 2000a, 2000b, 2009; Russell & Fosha, 2008).

Metaprocessing can be meta-affective, metacognitive, or metasomatic. It is part of the broader therapeutic process that involves alternating between waves of experiencing (e.g., sadness), which is more of a right-brain function, and reflecting, which involves more left-brain, language-mediated work. The therapist is now interested in helping the patient process the change that just happened and the changed state that is in its wake. This kind of processing helps to deepen therapeutic change and broaden the patient's scope of awareness, as well as her access to her own resources and resourcefulness. The main types of transformational affects that result from metaprocessing the experience of transformation are as follows:

- *Mastery affects*—the "I did it!" of therapy. It includes feelings of pride and joy.
- *Mourning the self*—grief over losses due to chronic reliance on defenses or inadequate caretaking by others; it involves emotional pain and empathy for the self.
- *Healing affects*—feeling moved within the self and grateful and tender toward the other.
- *Tremulous affects*—these involve sometimes paradoxical feelings such as fear/excitement and startle/surprise, along with interest or curiosity. There is frequently a sense of safe vulnerability.
- *Realization affects*—affects associated with expanded awareness and understanding when there has been a "click of rec-

ognition" (Fosha, 2009). The experience of "yes!" and "wow!" (adapted from Fosha 2009)

Typically, after a breakthrough of affect, the therapist might process *postbreakthrough affects* of feeling relieved, lighter, and stronger. These may lead to the transformational affects outlined above. Sometimes, however, as in the case of this patient and this session, while there is some relief and a glimmer of pride, there is much more to be processed. So, instead of the wave washing us up to shore, allowing us a view of the ocean and gratitude for the perspective and for being on solid ground, we only come up for air and a peak at the sun. And we prepare for the next wave.

CLINICAL VIGNETTE:
"It Fills Me Out a Little Bit"

(Continuing where we left off . . .)

TP: And before it felt so scary. You were holding yourself back because it felt so scary to go into that. [**TP believing that we might be at the end of a wave of processing and could do some metaprocessing, is slightly ahead of the PT.**]

PT: It's still a little scary.

TP: Mm-hmm. Because there's more?

PT: I guess (**PT sounds unsure**).

TP: What's making it scary right now? [**Correcting.**]

PT: Like it's embarrassing almost. [**Red signal affect.**]

TP: What's embarrassing about it?

PT: You were just looking at me, and I wasn't aware of anything else but how I was feeling, and that's a really vulnerable, embarrassing place.

TP: (**Sitting forward in chair**) Really vulnerable. [**Affirming.**] You're right. It's very vulnerable to just let go for a couple of moments and not be worrying about what somebody else is thinking and to let yourself be totally vulnerable to very deep feeling [**Undoing pathognomonic associations around**

VERTICAL AND HORIZONTAL DEFENSES

Optimal emotional functioning involves "feeling and dealing while relating." (Fosha, 2000b, p. 42) Cutting off one of these functions leads to some kind of impairment whether it be in the capacity to feel one's own emotions, in the capacity to handle life's challenge, or in the ability to relate to others. Given this, I find it helpful to think of defenses as existing on different continua and defending against different phenomena. Imagine vertical and horizontal lines or planks of wood. Imagine the vertical plank standing up in front of a person, cutting off his connection with others. Now imagine a horizontal plank, running across a person's neck, cutting off connection with the self's experience, including emotion. I refer to the former as vertical defenses and the latter as horizontal defenses. For the sake of illustration: the first are more evident in people with narcissistic and schizoid disorders and the latter are more evident in people with obsessive-compulsive tendencies and people who intellectualize. And, of course, people can use both simultaneously.

---

vulnerability; admiring and affirming PT's courage; validating sense of vulnerability]. It takes a lot of courage [**Explicitly praising and reframing capacity to be vulnerable as courageous.**]*

PT: (**Long pause**) Also, it's interesting to hear you say things like courage and wise and stuff. It's like I never paired myself with that. And like it feels really good to think that someone would think that about me. [**Receptive affective experience.**] I don't know. But I don't know if I believe it or not. [**Defense in

---

* There is a great, funny, informative, very accessible talk by Brené Brown, Ph.D., done by the TED series (www.ted.com/talks/brene_brown_on_vulnerability). Brown is a researcher who started out researching shame and then became interested in happiness and characteristics of happy people. She found that, among other things, happy people are vulnerable (i.e., open, permeable). It is a great video for clinicians learning to do more emotion-focused work, and I have recommended it to a number of my patients when they have gotten to a point in the work where they recognize that it is difficult for them to be vulnerable.

face of receptive affective experience of taking in something good from the TP and subsequently seeing herself in a positive light; again, yellow signal affects.]

TP: (**PT making good eye contact**) So if just for a moment, you could put aside your suspicion [**bypassing defenses through invitation to put them aside**] because that's there to protect you, and very understandably so [**validating origin and function of defense**] . . . and you've known me long enough and we've just been through this powerful process together, what's it like if you take it in; that your sadness is wise and I think that you're very courageous?

PT: Mm. It makes me feel like, it fills me out a little bit (**pointing to stomach/gut area**). [**Receptive affective experience and expansion of the self, physically felt in body.**]

TP: You just pointed to your stomach area. Is that where you feel that?

PT: Yeah.

TP: So if you give yourself a moment to notice that, what's that like? [**Metaprocessing the experience of transformation; of being "filled out"**].

PT: It stops my head from worrying as much, and it's more just like a "let it be" kind of feeling, like "Oh" (**laugh, rubbing head**). [**Receptive affective experience without defense; state transformation is settling in.**]

TP: So your mind relaxes a little bit and a part of you says "oh." That sounds kind of accepting. [**Reflecting experiential shift to receptive affective experience of taking in positive affirmation from TP; state shift has occurred.**]

PT: Mm-hmm.

TP: Like you can kind of take that in.

PT: (**Rubbing her head**) Yeah. But it goes away really fast (**rubbing head**). [**Here again is the self-in-transition. The yellow signal affects are the green signals "let it be" and "oh" followed by the red signal affects "it goes away really fast" and an increase in pain in her head, a likely result of tension. There is both openness/receptivity and fear/ caution.**]

TP: What's going on in your head?

PT: I feel the defenses really badly [**increased capacity for self reflective function; recognizing internal and bodily state as moving toward defense**], and so it's like painful.

TP: What are you noticing?

PT: I have a really bad headache right now. And like, I feel a wall, like it's very much there. And I see myself doing it with every word I say, almost. It's not going away. And I know I am contributing, and I just can't stop talking (**giggle**). It's just so bad. [**More definitive red signal; despite capacity to reflect, PT is beginning to feel a bit overwhelmed.**]

TP: So what would help you feel safer? [**Moving to "top of the triangle" work to help regulate anxiety; state 1 work of establishing greater safety, regulating anxiety and affect and minimizing the impact of defenses and red signal affects.**]

PT: (**Pause, rubs forehead, sad face**) I don't know. When I have felt this before, I either want to cry, throw up, hit something, or go to sleep. I don't know what to do. [**PT names coping patterns and clues TP into level of dysregulation she feels with some frequency and now in the present. These are very clear red signals and the TP's focus must shift to helping PT to regulate anxiety and feel safer again.**]

TP: Mm-hmm (**sitting back in chair, pause**). Any reactions to my sitting back? [**TP had been sitting forward in her chair and intuitively moved back in response to PT feeling overwhelmed. She then asked if PT noticed it and/ or if it has an effect.**]

PT: Like there's more time to think about; I don't feel as pressed . . . (**sigh**). [**Release of tension; dyad coregulating.**]

TP: Mm. What was in that sigh?

PT: I let go of the pain in my head (**pause**). [**Some success in regulating the overwhelming anxiety. PT can let go of some of the defenses and a new round of work can begin.**]

TP: Mm-hmm.

TP: (**A few moments later.**) I think it is not surprising to me that these defenses come up in response to doing something so profound like you just did. [**Validating the need for defenses frequently has the effect of bypassing them. Through the validation, the person feels seen and understood and therefore, the need for the defense diminishes. But the permission to defend must come authentically from the TP.**] It's so counter to your life, right? Where you are always trying to keep that sadness hidden and not offending anyone and protecting you from feeling responsible for everybody's emotional reactions (**PT nodding**). [**Nodding is a green signal affect.**] And you just let some of it leak out.

PT: Mm-hmm.

TP: A lot of it leak out. And you shared it with me. [**TP highlighting and reflecting on PT's willingness to feel and to relate to another, namely her, at the same time; initiating the metatherapeutic process—i.e., processing what was therapeutic.**]

This is a good example of recognizing and elaborating the resilience potential as well as the patient's current resilient capacity. The therapist reflects on the patient's inability to do more in the moment, her coping with feeling unrelentingly compromised in the past, and recognizes that, from a resilience standpoint, her "crying, hitting something, throwing up, or going to sleep" are her efforts at working and being on behalf of herself in environments that have not genuinely facilitated any true expression of self. This awareness allows the therapist to change direction and pace and to deepen her understanding of the patient. It also allows her to genuinely reflect this back to the patient as her tried-and-true and valid ways of being resilient in apparently normal but emotionally empty and compromised environments.

PT: (**Good eye contact; looking up at TP while head slanted and rubbing forehead**) It's hard to think I shared it with another person.

TP: Tell me?

PT: I am used to crying and writing it in my diary. And that's what always separates me from people I feel like. It's like "I know something that you don't" kind of feeling. And like the fact that we're just sitting here talking about it and that I am talking about it to a living person makes me feel good to think that I could have that with someone. [**Good, i.e., hopeful. This is an example of Tronick's (1998, 2005) expanded dyadic states of consciousness**.]

TP: Wow. So that good feeling comes back?

PT: So it makes me feel like. It would make me feel more guilty if I wasn't paying you for your time. [**This is probably a somewhat truthful statement, but in this moment it is also a defense against closeness/ intimacy.**] Just so you know, in real life I would change the subject or ask the person what they want to do and deflect it and go on feeling miserable . . . I feel like . . . if anyone were to sit with me, it would be really boring, really slow. [**Very limited, emotionally unsafe self–other–emotion configuration; the internalization of insecure attachment patterns.**]

TP: To sit with you in this place of the sadness?

PT: Mm-hmm. And they wouldn't know what to do [**Reflecting emotional communication patterns with parents, especially mother whose own anxiety overwhelms her and prevents her from being emotionally available in a helpful way.**]

TP: (**In a reflective, somewhat sad tone**) Because nobody *has* known what to do. [**Dynamic statement to PT about her real experience.**]

PT: (**Looking down, sad**) Right.

TP: (**Smile**) You've probably noticed I am not a Speedy Gonzalez. [**Playful invitation to PT to notice reality of TP with her, bringing focus back to the here-and-now and the therapeutic relationship.**]

PT: (**Giggles**) Yeah (**pause**).

TP: So there is this feeling that comes up around recognizing that you really shared it with me and I am not running away, and I am not trying to close it down, I don't think it is terrible or disgusting or anything like that. In fact, I am telling you that it's wise and you're courageous. And these little defenses come up around "well, I wouldn't entitle myself to that if I weren't paying for it," which may be true. But underneath all of that is a good feeling that comes up, and it has come up now a couple of times. [**Frequently, the good things offered by the TP have to be repeated, repeatedly. Habit, expectations derived from problematic attachment patterns, and fear of the new are formidable counterweights to good, nurturing stuff. The therapist can let it go, allowing it to be more comfortable for both herself and the patient, but a critical opportunity for growth is lost, especially if there are yellow and not red signal affects coming from the PT. The therapist as transformational other keeps working in the service of helping and accompanying the self-in-transition to truly transition.**]

PT: Mm-hmm.

TP: After sharing with me the sadness. Can you tell me what that's like? [**Invitation to notice authentic relational experience and receptive affective experience. Explicit mindful processing of current safe attachment experience and good feelings that go with that. TP is also pressuring with empathy, as discussed in Chapter 1.**]

PT: (**Rubbing head; good eye contact**) I feel the most in the present I've felt ever. [**Breakthrough of coordinated relational experience; authentic self-state. PT solidly in adaptive core affective experience, but importantly aware of glimmers of core state or glimmers of herself at her very best.**]

TP: Ever? [**TP a little shocked by PT's response, an example of quantum transformation that we should always be prepared for, even if we are not expecting it.**]

PT: Yeah.

TP: Wow. Hmm.

PT: I guess you know like when you're going through something and someone else is there too with you it kind of reaffirms that it's the present. Because this other person is seeing it too. I am not used to feeling that. I always felt like everyone is in their own separate world (**gesturing with hands**), like, but coexists. I always thought it was so amazing to learn in class (**in college**) like how people need people. And I never thought that I was one of those people. But I knew in some ways I am, but I thought it was an unhealthy dependency or something. **[Having taken in a safe attachment experience, PT is reflective about the difference between this self–other configuration and what she has been used to. She describes a chronic sense of isolation and an implied shame about her dependency needs. In contrast, now she feels "present," not alone, and she feels validated. PT is very clearly in self-at-best state.]**

The Self-at-Best: Inviting Her to Stay

This is a major breakthrough, not simply of positive feelings but of the self and of the self-in-connection. It was more than the therapist even hoped for as she pursued deepening the patient's "good" feeling around having allowed herself to feel, having allowed herself to feel with someone else, and taking in the therapist's very positive appraisal of her (i.e., wise and courageous). A more grounded, present, and embodied self emerges who, by default, has more and healthier resilient capacity than the self that walked in at the start of the session. She has more access to herself, her feelings, and her capacity to connect to another through receiving and offering her self.

An important phenomenon that is happening in these last moments, especially for those interested in mapping the emergence of resilience and the process of transformation, is the forecasting of core state. The patient in these last moments is not yet in core state. She is more comfortably and solidly in State 2, adaptive core affect. The dyad has achieved a coordinated relational experience, which she recognizes and articulates. She is also in an authentic self state (presence) that she partly attributes to the benevolent presence of the therapist. Not only is she not alone, but also her being with another makes her experience of being herself more tangible, more real. While she is in State 2, we also see glimmers of core state. Keeping in mind that the four states/three state transformations paradigm is meant to be a general guide to processing emotion to completion; it is not meant to be strictly linear. Because heralding affects are signals to us that something core is emerging even when someone is still in a state of distress, anxiety, or defense, the percolation of core state phenomena (e.g., compassion, peace, calm, presence, ease) is a very hopeful and helpful sign that we are moving in the right direction and that real transformation is in progress. *These are moments where the depth of one's resilience potential fleetingly reveals itself.* I believe that these glimmers of core state, these glimmers of resilience potential broaden and deepen core affective experiences and give people the confidence to ride the wave of sometimes very painful affect or to tolerate the discomfort of making themselves vulnerable.

How did we get here? The emergence and experience of one's core feelings (e.g., her sadness) contributes to one's resilient capacity via access to adaptive action tendencies (e.g., tears and the release of sadness) and the diminishment of anxiety around emotions and the energy-depleting defenses that are used to keep them out. Less of the self's energy has to be spent putting out fires and is freed up for other endeavors. Remembering that, in its origin, resilience is largely an interpersonal phenomenon, making the relationship explicit here and using metaprocessing to focus on the experience of transformation in the context of relationship contribute to the building up of resilient capacity.

In AEDP, there is a frequent movement back and forth between right-brain experiencing and left-brain reflection on one's experience to promote integration of the self, as well as the development of the self's narrative. In the experience of many of my colleagues and myself, this focus on the experience of change actually deepens and solidifies the insights and affective change in the person and personality of the individual having undergone a transformation. Frequently, it leads to a *cascade of transformation* (Fosha, 2008, p. 8; Russell & Fosha, 2008) or, as I prefer to think about it, an upward-moving, ever-widening spiral as the person experiences one transformation after another.

This cascade or the spiral is what happens in the rest of this transcript as the patient, who is still in transition, continues to allow herself to be vulnerable to the process of healing.

CLINICAL VIGNETTE:
"This Is What People Want to See, They Don't Want to See Something Else"

(Continuing where we left off . . .)

TP: So what does it feel like now?

PT: (**Pause**) Mm. It's like quiet and calmer, but I am still not . . . I'm like nervous.

TP: How are you experiencing the nervousness now? [**When prominent, focus on the experience of anxiety in a calm, reflective way actually has the counterintuitive effect of lessening the anxiety (Osimo, 2003).**]

PT: My head and my hands. My leg is numb, and I'm just getting really easily distracted (**sigh**). I'm basically withdrawing from you (**laugh**). [**Identifying defense; green signal affect**.]

TP: . . . I feel like in a way that's okay. Because I feel so touched by you and what you have been able to share with me today. You have taken a huge step (**PT making great eye contact**). And I feel so moved to have been part of, as you said, feeling more present in the moment than you have ever felt and to know that I have been there with you in that moment feels huge to me (**PT with big smile**).

PT: So it's okay? What do you mean that it's okay though?

TP: Well, because I feel like I've gotten more of Melissa you than I have ever gotten. And it has been very nice. And it has felt very generous to me. So if you have to kind of regulate that by backing off a little bit that also feels okay (**pause**). Maybe it's because I trust you will come back (**smiling**).

PT: Mm-hmm.

These statements contain very subtle messages. On the one hand, the therapist is again validating the patient's defenses. She is also not clinging to, pushing, or diminishing the patient (nor parts of the patient) for withdrawing. She is genuine—and I think that is key— in saying that it is "all right": basically what we've done together is wonderful, and it is enough. At the same time, she is offering a subtle invitation to stay connected in her final statement: "Maybe it is because I trust you will come back." It is reflective of the therapist's own security in the relationship and mirrors the behavior of the caregiver (mother) in one of Tronick's (1989) conglomerate descriptions of optimal mother–infant dyads:

Imagine . . . the infant abruptly turns away from his mother as the game reaches its peek of intensity and begins to suck on his thumb and stare into space with a dull facial expression. The mother stops playing and sits back watching her infant. After a few seconds the infant turns back to her with an interested and inviting expression. The mother moves closer, smiles, and says in a high-pitched, exaggerated voice, "Oh, now you're back!" He smiles in response and vocalizes. As they finish crowing together, the infant reinserts his thumb and looks away. The mother again waits. After a few seconds the infant turns back to her, and they greet each other with big smiles. (p. 112)

Tronick contrasts this with the mother–infant pair in which the child does not look back after looking away from the mother and the mother then starts to make noises and actively elicit the baby's attention, even moving her face into the baby's face, despite the baby's grimace, fussing, and pushing her away. The baby then resorts to soothing herself. These highly contrasting examples highlight the challenges we all face in making and keeping connections, and also the importance of attentive, emotionally resonant attunement to the dyadic interchange in which we are involved. It is subtle and sometimes very difficult work to figure out what are the right distances (both emotional and physical), tones, speeds, and emotional intensities that comprise the optimal range for a given patient and for a given patient at a given moment who is relating to a given therapist.

(Continuing where we left off . . .)

PT: (**Slowly and rubbing head, thinking**) That's really interesting.

TP: What's your reaction to what I am saying?

PT: I don't know. It makes me feel like I am a separate person completely from you (**nervous smile**).

TP: Hmm.

PT: But that I could affect you. It's just never really, I never really knew that. Like that I could have an effect on someone and still be someone else (**resting head on arm**). I don't know. Sounds really stupid. [**Not at all stupid. These statements clearly convey, in a way that was not understood prior to this session, the level of enmeshment in the family and the depth of this patient's compromise to accommodate her parents' real limitations**.]

TP: Not at all. Tell me a little more. I think I get what you are saying.

PT: Just that when you were saying that, I felt that filled out feeling again (**pointing to stomach**). Kind of like it's okay I guess. And when you were sharing that you were okay.

TP: Uh-huh. That I was okay despite your withdrawing? Despite your being separate?

PT: Yeah.

TP: Okay.

PT: It still feels like a huge responsibility . . . I still have that feeling that I need to tend to you (**hand to head**).

TP: If you look at me right now and you look in my face, what
about me communicates to you . . .

PT: (**Interrupting**) Nothing. It's like an alert in me . . .

TP: Right. So see if you can sit with me and look at me and notice
that in reality, in the moment, there's nothing you have to do
for me (**PT looking intently, rubbing forehead**). You don't
have to take care of me. I'm okay. I feel close to you, I feel connected to you, even if you're moving away a little. I trust what's
happening here (**PT removes hand from head**). I trust you
(**PT raises eyebrows as if this is a new thought**). What
happens inside?

PT: It feels really safe (**nodding yes**). Feel really, um, like "what
was the big fuss about?" But if I didn't have to describe it, it
would feel, I don't know. I feel more here I guess (**looking at
TP**).

TP: (**Warmly, smiling**) Welcome back.

PT: (**Rolling face into crook of arm on arm of chair; soft
giggle**) Thank you (**looking up**). I don't think I ever was
here. [**State 3 Transformational affects, specifically, the
healing affects of gratitude toward the other and feeling moved within the self; also the realization affects
around recognizing she has never been really present.**]

TP: Wow. What's making you say that right now?

PT: (**Sitting up, crying**) Because I've never felt like this with
anyone.

TP: Mmm (**pause**). Wow. There's a lot of feelings around that.
What's coming up as you tell me that Melissa?

PT: (**Wiping tears, still crying**) Like I've been hiding and I
don't know why. I mean I do know why. There's not as much
shame as there should be. I mean it's not as bad as I think.
[**Another transformational affect arises in the wake of
the realization affects described above. Specifically, PT
is in the process of mourning the self, grieving the loss
of what might have been, of what she might have had or**]

**experienced had she not been hemmed in by the inter-
personal rules and demands for compliance of her family of origin and of her own defenses. Mourning-the-self,
even though painful, is healing and transformative. It
is not a hopeless anger directed at the self, but rather a
grief for the self.]**

TP: Mm-hmm.

PT: Like this is what people want to see, they don't want to see
something else. 'Cause that feels real. [**Emergence of a brand
new experience-based understanding of what people
actually desire of and for her.**]

TP: What is this that people want to see? What are you recognizing right now?

PT: Just, I guess, just how I feel inside. My feelings.

TP: Mm-hmm. What are these tears about right now?

PT: I don't know. I guess it's more like I feel sorry for myself.
   [**Emergence of self compassion.**]

TP: Tell me more.

PT: Like what I was doing that I thought was good was actually
not. I wish I knew better.

TP: Well now you do.

PT: Yeah, but I am afraid that it will go away.

TP: Mm-hmm.

PT: Or like I'll jinx it.

TP: (**Slow, low voice**) It is not an untypical reaction when you
have gone through something so powerful. Because it feels so
new and you kind of worry that, "oh my gosh . . ." instead of
really trusting that you just did something really powerful and
really real. And we did it together and I witnessed it, so it can't
remain a figment of your imagination if it is real.

PT: Right. Okay.

TP: How's your head? [**TP aware of the session coming to an
end and wanting to check in and wind things down.**]

PT: Really bad, probably from crying.

TP: What are you feeling right now?

PT: Dread about interacting with my parents.

TP: Are they coming this weekend?

PT: I guess so.

TP: I know this may be a little hard for you to take in. But I really want to thank you so much for sharing with me something so deep and so private and so true to yourself. Something you've had to protect for so long. It really does feel like a privilege to me.

PT: (**Slightly tearful soft smile, pause**) How did you know it would be hard for me to take it in (**laugh, looking away**). Yeah.

TP: Is any little part of you taking that in?

PT: (**Good eye contact, pointing to head**) I think it will reverberate. Like I'll remember you said it. I'm glad you said it, cause (**pause**)

TP: You'll take it with you?

PT: Yeah.

TP: Good. That was my hope.

PT: Thank you.

The patient returned the next week, and when the therapist asked her what her reaction to this session was, she stated, "It was like the whole universe shifted for me."

Summary

This chapter explored and elaborated the concepts of the self-in-transition and its partner, the transformational other, the respective roles of patient and therapist when they are knee deep in the therapeutic task of discovering and elaborating core experiences in which the resilience potential is buried. It followed a powerful session almost in its entirety and traced the micromovements toward transformation and healing (and away again) to illustrate how the movement to deeper and more open expressions of resilience often come about in a one-step-forward, one-step-back kind of way. But the trajectory toward healing and restored resilience nonetheless moves forward. Shifting from a self-at-worst to a self-at-best state requires the therapist to be aware of and responsive to small articulations of openness, curiosity, and the heralding of the possibility of something more (e.g., "this could be calm"). It requires the therapist to trust that a more resilient, flexible, stronger self is there in the patient and that it also requires the patient to allow herself sufficient vulnerability (i.e., safe vulnerability) to allow the dyad to explore it together.

Part 3

RESILIENCE AS PROMISE

CHAPTER 4

Connection and Coordination in Softening Defenses and Quieting Anxiety

The ability of the self to transition, to recognize other possibilities or paths, and to dare taking them depends on so many factors. While there was a lot of back and forth in the transcript of the session presented in Chapter 3, on the whole the work was smooth. There were few of those awkward silences in which the patient has nothing more to say and the therapist is trying to figure out what to say or do. This is in part because of how the therapist read the signals of the patient, which of them she chose to privilege (i.e., those revealing resilience potential), and how she responded to those signals. But it is also a session that happened in the context of an ongoing dyadically generated interchange and way of being with one another that, while as unique as any other dyad, had a few key ingredients that allowed for such deep and transformative work to happen.

Part 3 is named "Resilience as Promise" to convey the idea that once the conditions of safety are both provided and at least partly received, the therapeutic process is on its way, and the forces of transformance are engaged enough to bring about a more adaptive and healthier expression of resilience than has previously been attained. When the self is beginning to transition, the therapist's stance can shift slightly from the provision of safety and invitation to a stance of responsiveness, welcome, elaboration, delighting, and highlighting the changes that are under way. Of course, I do not mean this in a strictly linear way. At any given moment, someone may return to a more defensive way of functioning or to a state of distress, overwhelm, or shutdown, where they rely on old ways of protecting themselves. We need to track resilience in whatever way it presents itself and respond accordingly. The larger point is that as people heal, their manifest resilience, their resilient capacity, changes and becomes more adaptive, less constrained, more expansive, more autonomous, and more integrative of the self. And with that, the therapist's role as the transformational other changes as well.

In the spirit of alternating between experience and reflection (Fosha, 2000b), this chapter, following an experiential chapter in which we were immersed in rich clinical material, reflects on our understanding of what happened in that exchange, why it was effective, and what it illuminates about the process of restoring resilience. Specifically, this chapter focuses on what is likely happening neurologically in a safe connection. It also looks more closely at patterns of coordination, disruption, and repair, the limits of the term *attunement*, and the need for *empathic responsiveness* when people are transitioning and yet ambivalent about that. It presents a case and transcript of someone who goes back and forth between resistance and transformance (i.e., another self-in-transition). Finally, it explores techniques for softening defenses, calming the anxiety, and diminishing the shame that can threaten to stall or silence transformance strivings and the development of a greater and healthier resilient capacity.

"Using" the Other: Affective Neuroscience and The Polyvagal Theory of Emotion

Affective neuroscience has increasing influence on the thinking of modern psychotherapists. Long dead is the dichromatic version of the debate about nature versus nurture, which, in its insistence that the pathology–health continuum was determined by genes/biology or the (family) environment, prolonged a false dichotomy, and failed to appreciate the complicated ways in which these influences actually effect and are effected by one another. That interchange is the focus of today's affective neuroscience, which has begun to articulate how the structures of the brain, wired to develop as they must, are helped or hindered by the environment. As a result, we have clearer ideas about how and why things go wrong and how the optimal development of cognitive and self-regulatory capacities and positive views of self actually occurs in the minds of young children, even infants. A few neuroscientists (Porges, 1997, 2001, 2005, 2009, 2010, 2011; Schore, 1994, 1996, 2000, 2003, 2012; Siegel, 2003, 2007; Siegel & Hartzell, 2003) go so far as to say that the development of these capacities and their associated brain structures are literally dependent on other brains.

Chapter 5 looks more carefully at other aspects of affective neuroscience and interpersonal neurobiology and their relevance to the cultivation and restoration of resilience through psychotherapy. Our focus here is on some of the neuroscientific findings that inform, support, and, in the very least, have incredible parallels with clinical work focused on resilience.

Stephen Porges (1997, 2001, 2005, 2009, 2011) has studied the evolution of the autonomic nervous system and writes about the importance of its ventral-vagal complex to the regulation of emotion. The vagus nerve is a primary nerve of the parasympathetic nervous system. Porges postulates that human beings have evolved a hierarchically organized series of responses to threat or stress. In what is, in fact, the third but "highest" level of response (i.e., most evolved and newest), the organism engages the ventral-vagal system, which is responsible for signaling others in the environment regarding movement and emotion through its control over facial expressions and vocalization. Porges refers to this as the "social engagement system."

To summarize, the ventral-vagal system helps people self-regulate and seek and use the help of an other to dyadically regulate and engage in nonthreatening moments. When that strategy fails, humans revert to a phylogenetically older system, the *sympathetic nervous system*, which was adapted to mobilize fight or flight response strategies. If that is not sufficient to avert the stress, threat, danger, or attack, we rely on our earliest adapted stress response, which utilizes the *dorsal vagal* system to immobilize the body, engaging a freezing response and even feigning death. These coping systems are hierarchically organized such that we rely on older, less evolved coping systems during threat. If used chronically, these older systems of fight/flee and freeze are literally dangerous to the central nervous system.

On behalf of the self, our bodies are literally wired to engage/ connect, flee, fight, or freeze. In Porges's words, "The phylogeny of vertebrates illustrates a progressive increase in the complexity of the neural mechanisms available to regulate neurobehavioral state to deal with the challenges along a continuum, defined by survival on one end, and positive social-emotional experiences on the other" (2001, p. 124). This comports with my contention that there is a wired-in resilience potential that works on behalf of the self, underlying a panoply of responses to the environment that range from resistance (or conservation/protection) to transformance/flourishing (or expansion). Each level and type of coping is a manifestation of one's resilience potential and resilient capacity in a given moment. The problem, of course, is when the older, less evolved system of coping is utilized in a situation that could be resolved through a more evolved, more communicative coping system. As Porges points out, the environmental situation influences our neurophysiological state, but also our neurophysiological state influences our capacity to deal with the challenges at hand. If we are regularly in a fight, flight, or freeze state when the situation does not warrant it, our ability to respond effectively to our environment and the people in it is seriously compromised. And so the challenge becomes how to harness the energy of the defense used on behalf of the self to respond to the environment in a more adaptive, evolving, and open way.

It might be most useful at this point to refer back to the clinical example in Chapter 3 for an example of what Porges is talking about. At some point, Melissa says that it is hard to stay with her feelings because they must be making the therapist feel uncomfortable. The therapist asks her explicitly to use her own *social engagement system* to check for the safety that is, in fact, there rather than what her autonomic nervous system is (transferentially) prepared to find. When she does this, she is aware of the safety and acceptance being offered and even a part of her that can access a feeling of safety in herself. She says, "This could be calm." It is as if there is something starting to happen in her parasympathetic nervous system to counter the overdrive of her sympathetic nervous system. But it is not yet enough for her to actually feel calm and engaged simultaneously.

A few minutes later, after dropping into the sad feeling and allowing herself to cry in the presence of the therapist, she says, on reflection, "You were just looking at me, and I wasn't aware of anything else but how I was feeling, and that's a really vulnerable, embarrassing place." In the moment, she was able to use the therapist (i.e., to relate or be related to) to feel, to connect with herself, and not to defend vertically (against the other) or horizontally (against the self). But this capacity to use the other to help regulate the self is new and still unfamiliar and so elicits anxiety upon reflection. Importantly, however, from an experiential perspective, she has still *had the experience*. Her mind will find different ways of making sense of it, rationalizing it, questioning it, accepting it or not. But she has still had the experience of feeling and dealing while relating. She has a number of such experiences in this session, followed by some anxiety and defense. But each time, she trusts a little bit more, takes in a little bit more, lingers a little longer. Finally, she says, "It stops my head from worrying as much, and it's more just like a 'let it be' kind of feeling, like 'Oh.'"

An important feature of Porges's theory is his emphasis on the role of the parasympathetic nervous system on the regulation of emotion and stress. So much is expressed through our face and the tone of our voice. And so much is received from and understood about the other, our partner in dialogue, through the eyes' attention to the other's face and the ears' extraction of tone and inflection in the other's voice. These are the nonverbal, right-brain-mediated communicators of information and critical components of what Siegel (1999) refers to as "interpersonal neurobiology," our brain's capacity to affect and be affected by other brains. As clinicians, particularly those of us with experiential orientations, this "social engagement system," as defined by Porges, is not only an essential means by which patients communicate their states to us but also an indispensable tool in our own kit to help people feel safe and to engage us and them in an effort to facilitate healing and the building of resilience. In the example in Chapter 3, when the therapist senses that the patient is too much in a sympathetic mode of flight, the therapist sits back to literally give her more space, and she is able to relax a bit and continue to engage.

Finally, a very important inference from Porges's work is the necessity of helping people to change state in order to engage in more meaningful, fruitful, and less fraught exploration of their own experience, as well as some clues about how to do that. Unregulated anxiety is counterproductive. Melissa in Chapter 3 says, for example, "I feel the defenses really badly, and so it's like painful . . . I have a really bad headache right now. And like, I feel a wall, like it's very much there. And I see myself doing it with every word I say, almost. It's not going away. And I know I am contributing, and I just can't stop talking." People dominated by fight/flight/freeze neurophysiological states may not even be capable of engaging with us to let us help them. Once their nervous systems are in survival mode, the fact that help is at hand may not even be recognized. An interesting point made by Porges is that the ventral-vagal complex allows for brief moments of excitation of the heart and mobilization without having to revert to the sympathetically mediated fight/flight state. In other words, the vagal brake allows us to mobilize while remaining socially engaged even when under stress. This is our optimal mode of functioning and, in the words of Fosha, involves "feeling and dealing while relating" (2000b, p. 42). It is only when the vagal brake is not working sufficiently well or the stress has gone on too long or without relief that the sympathetic nervous system takes over and engagement with a potentially helpful other is much less likely.

In most cases, if the clinician actively and intentionally brings the patient's focus to his connection with her, particularly if the connection is strong (e.g., requests to make eye contact or listening to the voice of the therapist), soon after the patient begins to feel anxious a calming effect occurs, allowing for engagement while dealing with the source of stress. The patient does not go into a panicked (fight/

flight) state, suggesting that intentionally keeping the social engagement system humming in the face of stress engages the vagal brake and allows for a more resourced and resilient response to stress or threat than might be available if the patient were left alone staring at the floor, unable, on her own, to prevent the slide into a sympathetic overload in which the capacity "to deal" is diminished and from which it is difficult to return. On the other hand, if intimate interpersonal connection is a source of threat for the patient, looking away may be a more helpful behavioral response to downregulate sympathetic activity (Stephen Porges, personal communication, June 16, 2009).

Part of dyadic affect regulation is finding what works with our individual patients to keep them engaged with themselves and with us. And people defy our expectations. For example, a young woman I worked with was the object of hatred and severe physical, emotional, and psychological abuse. Early on in the work, she would regularly dissociate; I could see her go blank and look absent. I noticed that she would then look very deeply into my eyes, not through me as dissociative patients can often do. I asked her what happened when she looked into my eyes, and she told me it was calming. Mutual gaze has been a crucial part of our work together. On the other hand, I have worked with many individuals with far more experiences with secure attachment in their histories who, in order to be with themselves and their feelings and to be able to tell me what is going on, need to look slightly away.

From everything discussed thus far, it seems reasonable to assume that resilient individuals can more regularly and more reliably use the ventral-vagal response—or the vagal break—to threat or stress and, less regularly, resort to other, more closed forms of coping (Cozolino, 2006). In other words, they can use another person (e.g., the therapist, a friend, a parent, a partner) to regulate themselves. The *polyvagal theory of emotion* describes what is going on in the brain and the body during resilient responses to stress. Moreover, it can guide our thinking about what we would like to help our patients develop in their stress response repertoire. While it may not be a mandate, the theory strongly suggests that working directly and actively to help shift people's responses to threats and modes of coping is not only good psychological treatment but also healing and restorative of the body and the brain. In the very least, it implies that therapists' use of tone of voice, eye contact, pacing, facial expression of emotion, and breathing may be of essential importance in helping people to regulate and access their most adaptive way of responding.

All of this suggests a high level of coordination or being "in sync" with our patients. Being aware of how connected they are to themselves, whether or not they are connected to and effectively communicating with us, their level of anxiety, their capacity for emotion regulation, and their willingness to use us, their therapists, to help regulate them requires fairly precise moment-to-moment tracking of affect and of the relationship (Fosha, 2000b). It also requires being aware of ourselves, tracking our own affect, our own connectedness or lack thereof, and our own ability and willingness to correct missteps, to repair disruptions, and to be flexible and adaptable to the moment (i.e., to be resilient) (Wallin, 2007).

The next section looks more closely at this dance of coordination, disruption, and repair that happens in all relationships. Important in its own right to development, the psychotherapeutic process, and the restoration of resilience, it is also discussed here in the larger context of, and as a sort of prelude to, processes of change in interpersonal relationships that foster enhanced resilience. That discussion continues in Chapter 5.

Coordination, Disruption, and Repair

Several infant researchers contend that dynamic interactions between the parent and child become internalized expectations of the relationship, and perhaps of other relationships, based on repetition, salience, "thickness" [i.e., number and variety of time-activity contexts that are experienced by a dyad (Tronick, 2003)], and the level of affect attunement of the typical interactions between the partners (Beebe & Lachman, 1994; Stern, 1985; Tronick 1989, 1998, 2003, 2005). Cycles and patterns of attunement, disruption, and repair are believed to influence not just the going-on-being (the unique and idiosyncratic way of being in relation with another) of a particular relationship but also our expectations of other relationships, our sense of self, mood tendencies, and our proclivity, or not, toward psychopathology. Is an important relationship regularly in sync or not? Is it marked by too much disruption? Is it capable of the repair of disruption? We do know that healthy, securely attached relationships are marked by approximately a third of their time in a coordinated state and the rest in disruption and repair.

Tronick's work with infants suggests that from our earliest beginnings we are motivated to be in coordination with one another, and we experience it as painful, frustrating, or, in the very least, quite uncomfortable to not be; we therefore work to repair and to reestablish coordination (Beebe & Lachman, 1994; Cohn & Tronick, 1987; Tronick, 1989; Weinberg & Tronick, 1994). Given the importance and ubiquity of this pattern of change in all of our important relationships, it is important to be precise about what we mean by each of these phases of the change process. Because *attunement* is complicated and deserves its own section, I will start with disruption. For our purposes, I consider *disruption* any internal, external, or interpersonal event, feeling, impulse, or behavior that literally disrupts the coordinated, affectively synchronized state in which the dyad, up to this moment, existed. Some disconnection has entered the relationship and is frequently marked by negative affect on the part of one or both partners. *Repair* is any effort, communicated facially or bodily, through tone of voice, gesture, behavior, or statement on the part of one or both members of the dyad, that has the intention and/or the effect of returning the dyad to a state of coordination and connection.

Attunement, it turns out, has a very precise meaning that I believe is less relevant to psychotherapy than its use in the literature suggests. Daniel Stern first defined *affect attunement* in his book *The Interpersonal World of the Infant* (1985) when referring to infant–parent communication. Since then, it has informed almost every affectively and/or psychodynamically oriented approach to psychotherapy. Unfortunately, it is sometimes used interchangeably with empathy, the single most important ingredient in all forms of psychotherapy. But Stern was clear to distinguish it from empathy. While empathy involves the mediation of cognition (i.e., imagining what someone is going through, needs, etc.), affect attunement "is the performance of behaviors that express the quality of a shared affect state without imitating the exact behavioral expression of the inner state" (1985, p. 142). It is not necessarily verbally mediated, and the expression of the shared affect state can be communicated in a different modality (e.g., vocal vs. facial) than the original communication and is therefore not simply imitation. An example of affect attunement is a parent exclaiming "wheeeeeeeee" while the child swings excitedly on a swing. The exclamation, intonation, duration, and punctuation frame and mirror the child's internal experience of excitement. As Benjamin notes, "The parent is in fact taking pleasure in contacting the child's mind" (1990, p. 38) and not necessarily having the same feeling toward or about the object, action, or reaction that the child is having.

The Limits of Attunement

What Stern meant by affect attunement is a very special, dyadically focused intersubjective experience, much like Tronick's dyadic states of consciousness. Two people are focused on one another, having an experience of the other, of the relationship, and perhaps of something or someone else to whom they are both relating. There exists, however briefly, some kind of matching or mirroring of subjective affective states, and that gets communicated one to the other. This is a very specific kind of experience, marked by positive affect, within that synchronized phase, referred to more broadly by others as coordination (Tronick & Cohen, 1969; Tronick, 1989, 2005) or ongoing regulations, which consist of matching, attunement, responsiveness, and minor moments of "disjuncture" followed by a return to coordination (Beebe & Lachman, 1994)—essentially a back and forth, an exchange, a flow that "feels" basically good to both partners. This distinction is important because there is room for more than simple, pure "affect attunement" in the coordinated or synchronized phase of the interaction. And given the complexity of adult relating, with its residuals of earlier relationships and attendant defenses, as well as cognition and choice, it gives us as therapists more room to be and to do than what is really meant by "affect attunement" as we more colloquially use it. In addition, if we trust too much in the healing power of simple attunement, that all we need to do is "get" what someone is feeling, we lose many opportunities to be more effective and more helpful. From this perspective, "attuning" is only the first step. Harmonizing means we each play our own separate instruments and our own separate parts together in a way that creates something rich and beautiful. For this reason, I use the phrase coordination, disruption, and repair.

Strictly speaking, there is no scaffolding in the attuned caregiver's response. They are attuning, like different instruments with one another, trying to hit the same note. And this is wonderful and necessary. There is no complementary response—when one is in a happy state, a complementary response is perhaps not needed. But affectively *attuning* to someone in a negative state—and our patients are frequently in negative affect states—frequently elicits in us a need, desire, or instinct to "do" rather than simply be. This is true, perhaps most obviously, in the example of a baby screaming from hunger. An empathic mother is not simply going to attune to her baby's distress—she is going to feel her own distress and be moved to feed the baby, thus relieving both her distress and the baby's. Less obvious, but more apt, is a clinical example. Borrowing from the transcript in Chapter 3, at a certain point the patient is so overwhelmed that she says that when in the past she has felt this way she was only able to, "cry, throw up, hit something, or go to sleep." The therapist's empathic attunement to this kind of overwhelm leads her to inquire about what would help her feel more safe, and to sit back in the chair, thus giving the patient more space. That kind of responsiveness is not captured by the terms *attunement, matching,* or *synchrony,* or even *empathy.* It is a complementary or compensatory responsiveness that depends on the other's capacity to be attuned, as well as her role as an (potential) attachment figure, her relationship of love, care, and concern, and simply being in less need or more capable at the moment. Let us call this, what is frequently referred to incorrectly as "attunement," *empathic responsiveness.*

The Conditions of a Secure Therapeutic Attachment:
Empathic Responsiveness in Coordination and Disruption

Empathic responsiveness is not limited to unequal pairings. For example, several years ago, when my daughter was a little more than 1 year old, my sister came over and was telling me, through tears, about something that made her very sad. Sitting on the living room floor with my kids wandering around us, my daughter started to pay attention, and she gently moved toward my sister, kissing her on the cheek, and throwing her arms around her neck. My sister and I were both very touched. Even at that young age her capacity for affective attunement to my sister's distress did not lead her simply to her own expression of sadness but, rather, moved her out of herself in a gesture of compassion or empathy toward a beloved adult that was not just resonance but actual empathic responsiveness. In empathic responsiveness, our attunement elicits our empathic capacity to imagine or understand the need of the other and combines with some ability to move out of the self to help or to offer something, or simply to be a consciously comforting presence.

Even around negative affect or distress, it is still possible to have harmonious, coordinated interaction. What this looks like is a balance between self- and mutual-directed (Beebe & Lachman, 1994) or other-directed (Gianino & Tronick, 1988) regulatory behaviors. Harmony does not exist without two different parts being sung. This is very important in the context of both the infant–caregiver dyad and the patient–therapist dyad. These are not equal relationships, and in part because they are not, simple attunement may not be enough to maintain coordination or even to repair a disruption, especially when one is in a negative state. How we express the care that arises with empathy or what we do to respond to the feelings of the other is the other crucial piece that is rarely discussed in expositions of affect attunement.

At the age of 10 a patient found and read her mother's diary. In it the mother stated, "I am so sad that my husband does not like my little daughter." Reading that statement, my patient inferred several things she had long suspected: (1) that he was not her "real" father; (2) that the stepfather did not, in fact, love her, as so much of his cruel and controlling behavior suggested; and (3) that the mother was attuned enough to feel the feelings the child frequently felt and to feel for her, but she did not "get it" enough to do anything about it, not even to communicate that empathy to her child. She neither moved in to comfort nor intervened in his abusiveness, nor did she leave.

Something more than attunement is frequently needed in stratified relationships in which one is usually in greater need than the other. At times, simply having our feelings reflected back to us is sufficiently helpful. But at other times, our attunement leads to behaviors that are not matching the distress of the other but complementing it, filling the gap, scaffolding the learning, providing alternate strategies, or simply offering comfort. To my mind this is an intrinsic part of all attachment relationships; attunement is simply the first and necessary step to move us toward empathic responsiveness.

CLINICAL VIGNETTE:
The Sinkhole: Resilience as Promise

The following is an extensive transcript of two sessions with a single woman in her late thirties. Her social isolation had been lifelong to some extent but worsened in adulthood after moving to a city where she had no family and no friends from childhood. Most of her weekends were spent alone in her apartment. This isolation stood in contrast to her professional life, where, although she was still occasionally inhibited and had difficulty promoting herself or asserting her needs with superiors, she was a well-respected, talented entertainment executive, managing myriad technical and creative tasks, as well as interpersonal drama among the staff members, with some deftness and a sense of humor. In the year leading up to these sessions, she had made strides in reaching out to potential friends at her workplace and elsewhere, as well as finally dipping her toes into the world of Internet dating. In the face of these outward-moving instincts and desires, she still frequently confronted a lethargy and detachment that convinced her that being home was really the only desirable thing. Talking in "parts language" had been helpful to her in the past and so was used again so as to deepen interest in the "resistant" or frightened parts of her, as well as deepen compassion for them. In parts language, borrowed largely from Schwartz's (1995) internal dynamic systems model but also elaborated in Lamagna and Gleiser's (2007) intrarelational approach to AEDP, aspects of self-experience are worked with as if they are persons in their own right deserving of a listening ear. She comes in one early summer morning stating:

PT: So I think we should just dive back in to what we started last week . . . I mean I guess just trying to communicate with that part that is so buried, um, and trying to find out what (**pause**) it has to say, or how to stop fighting it so much, I guess . . .

PT: (**A few minutes into the session**) In thinking about it, but being scared to kind of look at it alone. You know, kind of having this feeling of "I'm gonna wait for Eileen on that," you know, but definitely having this feeling of it still being around, you know, which is why today, yesterday, I was thinking we should just keep going. [**Safety established with TP; safe attachment figure with whom PT explores frightening territory.**]

TP: Mm-hmm. So how are you noticing it today? How is it with you today? [**Experiential focus.**]

PT: I mean I guess there is this feeling of a (**fingers to solar plexus, pause**) of a lack or a (**voice getting choked up**) or a, I don't know, like a hole in my center that everything is falling into. [**Maladaptive core affective experience. Patients frequently describe these experiences of unbearable aloneness, chronic shame, terror, in very stark, dark terms like a black hole, falling far down, feeling lost, frozen, etc.**]

TP: (**Sympathetic**) Wow (**pointing to own solar plexus**), in here? [**Dyadic somatic mirroring.**]

PT: Yeah.

TP: What do you feel as you say that? As that image, that feeling comes to mind? (**Pause**) It sounds scary. Is it?

PT: (**Pause**). It's kind of like it would be if so much of myself wasn't already in there (**voice choked with feeling**).

TP: What are you feeling right now?

PT: (**Pause**) Feeling lost.

TP: Down in there?

PT: (**Nodding**)

TP: It's very hard for you to talk to me right now?

PT: Yeah. It feels like I'm kind of slipping into it.

TP: Mm-hmm.

This does not sound very resilient. It sounds frightening and potentially hopeless and helpless, not ideal grounds for nurturing one's resilient capacity. But this is where a depth-oriented, experiential, attachment-focused way of restoring resilience is quite different than a focus on shifting thoughts to something more positive. Clearly, this experience is very real for this woman, and therefore "core." It is part of the truth of her experience, perhaps especially in relationships or in their chronic lack of attunement or coordination. But as with any trauma, simply staying with it for the sake of staying with it is not necessarily helpful. What is restorative for her own resilient capacity is to be able to stay with it while staying with another at the same time. In other words, undoing the aloneness that accompanied trauma in the first place is very healing, as is having one's trauma witnessed by another who is caring, compassionate, and moved. From a resilience standpoint, part of why undoing aloneness is healing is that it facilitates the differentiation of the self from that which is aversive to it. The patient is no longer entirely that old feeling of being lost and alone, even unable to feel. She is now, at least at moments, partly connected to an other, a different relational feeling and self state in a different time and place.

It is also important to distinguish this from what some call "secondary emotions" (Greenberg & Safran, 1987). While, by itself, feeling lost is not adaptive and does not contain adaptive action tendencies within it, these feelings are not defensive in a traditional sense. They are essential aspects of the person's experience and in that way have to be dealt with as primary emotions. How we work maladaptive core affective experience (State 2 maladaptive) is by being very present to and with the patient in the moment *and* in the memory in order to transform the traumatic/unbearable experience. Actively helping to undo aloneness, diminish shame, and reduce the present experience of terror is called for in working with *maladaptive core affective experiences* referred to in Chapter 2.

(A few moments later . . .)[*]

TP: I have this image of a well. I don't know if that is similar to what you are imagining? [**TP attuning to PT's emotional experience and offering an image arising from her own unconscious; something for both to imagine, explore, and work with.**]

PT: I guess it's more of a, like a well is too contained, it's more like a sinkhole, 'cause it could get bigger. [**TP's offering allows PT to elaborate more precisely her own image that matches her felt sense and feels "right."**]

TP: Can you imagine a tree or something nearby? [**Dyadic regulation of affect and empathic responsiveness; TP using her own affect to help determine her response. She has a sense of danger, vastness, and unbearable (i.e., too much) aloneness. She is actively participating in the image in order to undo the aloneness without taking PT out of this important exploration of her interior life.**]

PT: (**Small nod**) Yeah (**pause**).

TP: I guess the image that is coming to my mind is of my having a rope that is about this thick (**gesturing with fingers to indi-**

---

[*] Few moments later" indicates that some of the actual dialogue is omitted for the sake of clarity and conciseness.

cate very thick rope) and tying it around that tree in a really tight knot [**Beyond mirroring: TP actively helping to undo aloneness and fear through empathic responsiveness.**]

PT: (**Nodding**)

TP: And putting it down the sinkhole to you.

PT: (**Silence**)

TP: What's happening?

PT: I grab the rope (**pause**) [**Transformance strivings coming on board; this is an expression of the resilience potential and her resilient capacity in the face of challenge.**]

TP: Do you need me to pull?

PT: (**Tears starting; face very sad; voice sad**) Yeah.

TP: That's okay. That's what I was prepared to do.

PT: (**Nodding**)

TP: So I am pulling and I have the tree to back me up.

PT: (**Wiping tears**)

TP: What do you see now?

PT: I guess I feel the struggle to get over that rim (**pause**) and kind of the question of whether it's worth it. [**Unbearable state of aloneness; despair, helplessness, hopelessness.**]

TP: You need help getting over the rim? [**Choice point; TP focuses on struggle, not the loss of the struggle. Also making acceptable the need for help.**]

PT: (**Pause**) Well I can see myself getting over the rim. But then I can't stay there.

TP: What do you mean?

PT: It's like kind of getting up and falling back.

TP: You feel weak?

PT: (**Nodding**) Yeah.

TP: You are trying. It takes all your strength to get up, but you just fall backwards because you just don't have the strength in your legs. [**Putting into words PT's experience of overwhelm, weakness, need, and aloneness; recognizing and elaborating.**]

PT: (**nodding**) [**Green signal.**]

TP: Does it feel not safe to stay by the side of the sinkhole? Or does it feel okay to maybe just stay there for a few of minutes? Like what if we just sat there together? [**TP actively attempting to undo aloneness in the moment and in the memory by inserting herself and using the language of togetherness; also checking on capacity and felt sense of sufficient safety.**]

PT: I mean we can sit, but it feels like it's (**pause**) kind of crumbling away towards us, kind of growing.

TP: Okay, so we need to move. [**TP taking the lead. While in adaptive core affective experience, the TP can step back a little and allow the PT's experience to unfold, in maladaptive core affect; the TP has to remain very active to make sure she is a presence in the PT's awareness so as to delimit the pull of the trauma vortex.**]

PT: (**Nodding**)

TP: Can I help you walk? Can you let yourself lean on me?

PT: (**Pause**) I don't know if I really want to go (**becoming tearful**).

TP: What's holding you there? [**Acceptance, exploration.**]

PT: I don't know. I guess it feels like there is so much down there.

TP: Mmm. Mm-hmm.

PT: Or something important there.

TP: Mm-hmm.

PT: That I can't just turn around and walk away from it. [**Now, feeling less alone/more resilient, PT wants to face aspects of herself lost in this sinkhole. This is what she was unable/unwilling to do on her own, and what a resilient decision that turns out to have been!**]

TP: Okay.

(A few moments later . . .)

PT: We could stand there by the edge.

TP: It feels safe enough?

PT: Yeah.

TP: Do you want to throw in some kind of net or fishing pole or something? Is there something in there right now that is ready to be rescued or pulled out, like you were?

PT: I think Ellen is in there, the 2-year-old (self) (**thoughtful pause**). She crawls out on her own [**emergence of a resilient and joyful young part of PT that we had done work with in the past**] . . . and I pick her up.

TP: You pick her up. What is it like for you right now to pick her up, to hold her? [**Experiential exploration of intrapersonal relatedness.**]

PT: It is comforting.

TP: What are you feeling?

PT: I guess I am really surprised that she was down there. And that she doesn't seem upset by it at all. So I guess I am relieved that she is not traumatized.

TP: Mm-hmm. You think she didn't know enough to know that it was kind of scary down there?

PT: Yeah. I guess it's just confusing because now I really feel like I don't know what is down there. It seemed so, seemed so scary I guess or so all consuming. And (**pause**) and she just crawled right out. [**Something/someone safe and resilient emerges from the maladaptive core affective experience; integration of a fragmented part.**]

This is a very beautiful and hopeful moment in the session. The patient comes in with a sense of the importance of exploring a "buried" part of her, but also of the need to not do that by herself, the need for help. She accepts it from the therapist and becomes stronger and more resolved in her exploration. Much to her surprise, and the therapist's delight, what emerges or becomes unburied is an essentially unscathed part of her. The shadow turns out to be her strength, her faith, her joy. It is like a personification of the resilience potential itself, the part of her that has always been clearly differentiated from the darkness, loneliness, void, and shameful self states Catherine had become so accustomed to. This is a "now moment" (Stern, 1998; Mayes, 2005) between herself and a part of herself. As discussed greater detail in Chapter 5, this is a moment of opportunity for the patient to do something different, but authentic, that is responsive to the developing relationship between her self and her own resilient core.

(A few moments later . . .)

PT: I guess she doesn't understand why she would be scared. Actually, she's not. I don't know if I have ever seen her scared. She is more content. She is more a source of comfort for me than me feeling like I am comforting her.

TP: So how are you feeling right now? What are you aware of?

PT: My body is feeling pretty calm. [**Some post-breakthrough affects.**] There is still a little of the anxiety (**pointing to solar plexus**) but, and there is still that pressure between my eyes (**pointing to forehead between eyes**), but um, the sadness is gone. [**Referring to the tears that she never labeled sadness earlier in session.**] (**Pause**) And I want to look over the edge and see what is down there. [**Green signal affects; PT is becoming increasingly resilient and in touch with her exploratory drive. She indicates a more open, less fearful or inhibited curiosity and a sense of readiness to push ahead.**]

TP: Does it feel safe enough to do that?

PT: (**Pause**) Yeah, but I don't see anything.

There is a moment of pause in the work. The patient indicates she is ready but is not sure how to proceed. The therapist comments about how eager both she and "Ellen" seemed to come out of the sinkhole when given the chance and sufficient safety. In an effort to keep the exploration moving, she offers:

TP: So I have two thoughts . . . one is of you issuing an invitation to anything that is in the sinkhole, saying "It's okay to come out. We're here and we are not going to reject you." But you have to be ready to do that, to mean that . . . And my second thought is that maybe it is okay for you to go in there. [**TP participating and helping but not directing, trusting that if given different options, the patient will have a sense of what is best.**]

PT: Mm-hmm.

TP: If I am here, you know, kind of like your experience last week, of "I am not gonna go there, not without Eileen."

PT: (**Nodding**)

TP: So if I am here and I have a big rope, and Ellen is hanging around on the grass, then maybe you could go in there.

PT: Mm-hmm. I don't know. I am not scared to think about going in because I feel like I won't see anything. Like, I don't know, maybe it is better protected than I thought, or more contained than I thought, and (**pause**). Yeah. I guess I never thought that it was. I always felt like it was impossible to come out if I went in. That was the, that was the fight . . . to try to stay away from it and not look at it and not even know where it was.

TP: What are you afraid is really in there?

PT: (**Long pause**) I guess some type of abuse, some sort of betrayal by someone that I loved and that I still love.

TP: Do you think of anyone in particular?

PT: (**Long pause**) I think of my family. I guess I think of three people closest to me then, which would be my parents and Kevin (her oldest brother).

TP: And then is when?

PT: Definitely before the divorce, probably before Deidre left (oldest sister by 10 years), so the first 5 years. [**PT revealing that she does have quite specific fears about what she will find/remember.**]

TP: What is it about your experience, I don't mean rationally, that makes you think that or intuit that? Like, is there something you notice in your body or images that you have?

PT: To think what? Like to pinpoint the time frame or the people or . . .?

TP: To pinpoint the timeframe, to have a sense of, just as you articulated it, that maybe there was a betrayal by someone I loved, either your parents or Kevin, before age 5?

PT: (**Pause**) I guess because there is a feeling of loss. Like there is a feeling that something. I don't know. Some part of me fell down that hole, got sucked into that hole, ran into that hole, before I really could understand what was happening. Like that it was all emotional, and not intellectual. (*PT*: Choked up?)

TP: And that's what it *still* feels like.

PT: Yeah. Well I guess, I look at Ellen and I say, I feel like "where did my sense of safety go?" Like she is almost oblivious to, like why should she worry about anything?

TP: Mm-hmm.

PT: Like that's what I need from her. That's what I love about her.

TP: Mm-hmm.

PT: Because I don't have that. [**PT in touch with and curious about an intact, resilient, solid experience of self that resides in a very young version of herself. She is overly differentiated from it and not enough in touch with the fact that it is also her self.**]

After a lot of courageous work, the session ends in a bittersweet place. This exploration has been very important and helpful, and gaining more access to a courageous and secure part of herself goes a long way toward restoring, rather than simply building up, a solid resilience. But the work is far from complete. It leaves the patient and therapist with at least as many questions as they started the session with and with the painful and stark reality that the patient does not, in fact, lead her life from a position of security and safety. At the same time, it makes clearer what needs to be integrated and how much sadness and pain have resulted from living her life out of touch with whatever part of her feels secure and curious in the world.

Chapter 1 addressed the idea that the seeds of resilience are very much interpersonal. This is true throughout life, as is evidenced in the research on the myriad benefits of social support to people going through any number of trials or challenges. In this session, Catherine comes in acknowledging that something is coming up in her that is too frightening for her to face on her own, but she at least has the courage to ask for help in exploring it, and she is able to make use of the help the therapist offers. These capacities alone are expressions of resilience. As the patient approaches her fear, she finds a part of herself that is not afraid and has never been, that has a capacity for joy and trust. It gives her courage but also makes her very curious. If that part resides in her, why has it been buried? Why did she have to jump into that sinkhole? What was she escaping or hiding from? Those questions themselves express some differentiation and portend greater resilient capacity. She is not simply, organically afraid and socially isolated. She learned to protect herself from something *outside of herself.* That means that she was adapting and not simply flawed. *That* means she has the capacity and willingness to act on behalf of herself, which suggests a certain level of care and concern for the self rather than isolation or disregard. And while she is still disturbed and saddened by the possibilities of what might have stifled her so, she now wants to know and feels ready to know, which is also, in its turn, a sign of restored resilience.

(A few weeks later . . .)

PT: I guess last night, as I was trying to sleep, I was thinking about coming here today and thinking about, well, what should we talk about. And I had that image again of the sinkhole.

TP: Mmm. Mm-hmm.

PT: And Ellen kind of crawling out of it, and just kind of picking her up and standing by the edge of it. I guess in terms of what we were saying that so much energy goes into that or repressing that or . . . So, I guess I'd kind of like to go back to that area.

TP: Good. Great. Where do you want to start? Do you want to start with the image that came to you last night and we'll kind of see where it goes?

PT: Yeah, I guess. There really isn't any other.

TP: So paint the scene for me again. I mean I have a fairly clear image, but I also realize . . . .

PT: . . .but the hole seems to be, like the edges seem more solid this time. [**PT already starting from a more resilient, solid place. The image itself is less fragile and frightening.**]

TP: Hmm.

PT: It seems like just a hole rather than something that is possibly growing.

TP: Mm-hmm.

PT: And it actually doesn't have the, I don't know. There is no fear really, as I stand there. Actually there might be a little curiosity. [**Green signal affect. PT now needs less leading, guiding, structuring, and explicit use of the TP this time. Feeling more capable herself.**]

TP: Mm-hmm.

(A few moments later . . .)

TP: So how do you notice the curiosity right now? Is that still there? [**Focus on experience of the green signal affect; the tendency that counters the fear and moves her forward. Also, this is an invitation to notice her adaptive action tendencies.**]

PT: Yeah. I mean the curiosity is kind of like in my stomach I guess (**pointing to stomach**), kind of deeper down than where the fear or anxiety usually is.

TP: Hmm. What's it like right now? What does it feel like?

PT: It's like an energy that is kind of (**gesturing with her hands**) stretching a little and kind of pushing against me.

TP: Mm-hmm.

PT: And some of that anxiety or trepidation is back. [**Yellow signal affects.**]

TP: What does the curiosity want you to do? [**TP focusing on green signal vs. red.**]

PT: It wants some action, I guess.

TP: Mm-hmm.

PT: Whether it is walking over there or . . . It's kind of like "well, do something."

TP: Is it possible right now, Catherine, . . . to just put the fear and trepidation aside . . . like what we have done in the past, not to banish it, it certainly can jump in if it feels, if there is a need to protect you, but just putting it aside to make room for this curiosity, that kind of energy?

PT: When I do, it feels like the curiosity fills in that space (**motioning to solar plexus where fear resides**). Like I can feel it in my arms now too. [**Expansion of strength, courage, and sense of competence in the body; literally an embodied experience of resilience.**]

TP: Mm-hmm. What's it like there right now in your arms?

PT: Kind of a tingling.

TP: So if this could express itself what would it do?

PT: I mean it would move me. I kind of see it almost pushing me.

TP: Mm-hmm. And can you let it move you?

PT: Well, I have to put Ellen down before I get any closer to the edge. [**Another marker of enhanced resilient capacity. She is now the protector of the young child self that she is used to being comforted by.**]

TP: How come?

PT: Because I don't want her near it.

TP: So you put her down?

PT: Yeah.

TP: And what do you notice?

PT: I worry about her wandering away or getting hurt or separated.

TP: Is that distracting you right now from moving?

PT: Yeah. I wish I knew that she would just stay put.

TP: Is there anyone or anything with whom she could stay put? That you would feel secure, she'd feel secure?

PT: My first thought was of a playpen to put her in, but then (**pause; interruption**) you showed up.

TP: Mmm.

PT: And kind of crouched down to her. And kind of I know she will be safe with you, but I also have the selfish side of "what if I need you?"

TP: Mm-hmm.

PT: (**Playfully**) So I guess I will leave her with you and you had the foresight to bring a playpen just in case (**laughing**). [**What emerges with restored resilient capacity is not only a more confident and solid sense of self but also creativity and creative problem solving. There is even room left over to laugh and feel somewhat relaxed. Chapter 7 explores in detail positive affect, problem solving, and an expanded behavioral repertoire allowing more flexibility.**]

TP: (**Laugh**) Good thinking!

PT: (**Laughing**) Well, yeah, you're a mom, you know these things.

TP: Plan B.

PT: Yeah.

TP: And that feels okay?

PT: Yeah.

TP: Good. So where is the curiosity now?

PT: I don't know. It's like I can't keep the anxiety completely separate and I can't get the curiosity to come back in. [**Yellow signal affects and the self-in-transition.**]

TP: Mm-hmm.

PT: I mean it's still there kind of near me, but I am not feeling it.

TP: You know, I just get that.

PT: (**Nodding**)

TP: You know there is this big dark sinkhole, and there is this curiosity, which got a little bit bigger before. But maybe as you put Ellen aside and you get closer to doing it, like anything, you feel more anxiety. [**Validating defense/ anxiety and allowing it.**]

PT: Yeah.

TP: So I am wondering if it feels possible to actually approach it with both the anxiety and the curiosity, knowing that I am there and Ellen is there and if you need something, you know, I can step in. [**Shoring up her resources once again in light of mounting anxiety; solidifying the self-at-best to work with the self-at-worst. Also, regulating anxiety by acknowledging and accepting it as part of the process of change.**]

PT: (**Long pause**) So I take a step closer.

TP: Mm-hmm. How far away are you now?

PT: Probably another step I would be able to see down into it and two steps I would be right on the edge of it.

TP: Okay.

PT: But it just seems kind of black hole kind of black. [**Back in territory of maladaptive core affect experiences, which obviously this patient needs to explore as, in her words, "so much of myself" is in there. Also, however, here she is observing it in a mindful way rather than being immersed in or engulfed by it or identified with it.**]

TP: Mm-hmm.

PT: And I guess I feel like there isn't any lead-up to it. That it is just gonna, like I won't be able to see it until it is right there.

TP: It's just a matter of having to face it.

PT: Yeah.

TP: Mm-hmm.

PT: (**Pause**) So I take another step.

TP: Good for you. What are you noticing now?

PT: That my head really doesn't want to go. [**Reemergence of the defense or fear; viscerally felt by the patient.**]

TP: Your head doesn't want to go. The rest of you feels more willing, but your head is holding back?

PT: Yeah.

TP: How do you notice the greater willingness in the rest of you?

PT: Because there is still some of that tingling in my arms and torso, and it definitely stops right here (**hand horizontally across neck**). And my eyes feel kind of squinty, like I want to close them. [**Some dissociative phenomena.**]

TP: Mm-hmm.

PT: Heavy.

(A few moments later . . .)

PT: The body has never really been all that important. It is hard to kind of start taking it seriously now. [**PT referencing her historical disregard for her body, which was associated**

**with multiple and self-limiting somatic complaints when
she was a younger woman.**]

TP: Hmm. (**Pause**) But there is a lot of sadness there and a lot of
energy. This body feels really stuck. [**Explicit empathy for
part of her that wants to move or to know or to feel.**]

PT: Actually, the body jumped into the hole. [**More resilient
image in response to encouragement/empathy.**]

TP: Wow. And what is happening now?

PT: It is like we fell a ways, but still landed in the dark.

TP: And what is it like there right now?

PT: I guess it is like a hole, like dirt walls, and it is very dry. There
isn't really anything unpleasant about it. And, I can see that
there is a tunnel, but I guess the light is more coming from
above, like I can't see into the tunnel very well.

TP: So the sinkhole leads to a tunnel.

PT: Yeah.

TP: Mm-hmm. What is happening in your body right now?

PT: Still that same kind of readiness, I guess. So I just crawl right
in there.

(A few moments later . . .)

PT: It makes me sad. It brings the sadness back. Like the head
just seems so sure that there is nothing there.

TP: Mmm. What is sad about that right now?

PT: Because I feel like there is, but if I can't convince the head
that there is I won't find it.

TP: What are you feeling right now?

PT: Feeling like a sad ache in my chest.

TP: Mm-hmm.

PT: I still have the tingling in my arms. And my eyes feel kind of
angry, but I feel like that is the eyes as part of the body, rather
than being part of the head. Like the head is being a jackass.

TP: What is the head so scared of?

PT: I guess it's that same idea, like there is nothing worth messing up what we have now.

TP: Mm-hmm. But that is its response, right?

PT: Yeah.

TP: It kind of wants to keep everything status quo. It feels safer that way.

PT: Mm-hmm.

TP: Because something feels not safe. So much of your body feels like, "Okay I am ready for something else."

PT: (**Nodding**)

TP: I am either ready to know something else, I am ready to do something differently, I am ready to discover, I am ready to take in what I am feeling more, whatever it is. And the head is just saying, "I am not."

PT: Yeah.

TP: Or maybe it is habitual. "I am so used to being in charge and in control that I am really reluctant to relinquish control." [**Trying out different possibilities to see what PT connects with.**]

PT: Mm-hmm.

TP: Even though I am in a relationship here, and this other part really wants and needs and is craving something else.

(**A few moments later . . .**)

PT: It's like the head always goes for the worst case scenarios and kind of, I don't know, I guess is still stuck on the idea that it must be some, one cataclysmic event that I am repressing or something. [**Content of the fear: the discovery of Big T trauma.**]

TP: You know I think that the head does a very good job of doing its job, right? I mean that is all of our head's jobs, which is to use that (**PT nods**) prefrontal cortex and plan and strategize and think through possibilities. And it protects us in that way. And it protects the body . . . [**Reframing the defense by verbalizing its intent, which is basically benevolent toward the self.**]

PT: But also as you say, I think it is just some stubbornness. The head is used to always knowing everything, and always coming first over feelings. [**PT identifying as defense rather than anxiety or fear.**]

TP: You know I have to tell you, and I don't know if this is helpful or not, but your description and your tone of voice today in describing your head feels so much like how you described your father last week. [**Offering dynamic connection as another, but hardly only, perspective.**]

PT: (**Curious**) Hmm.

TP: And that knowing better and kind of being tough, but also in denial of being tough. But kind of "but I really know best" and not really hearing or taking the feedback from other people. It is a bit of a know-it-all.

PT: (**Eyes widening**) Yeah.

TP: And it is kind of okay with that. But in that, it is not supple. It is not adjusting itself to the other person in the relationship. And as you said last week, in fact you think your father has adjusted a bit and is more supple and more responsive and more aware of you and attentive to your nonverbal cues and signals, but it is difficult for you to behave differently with him because your conglomerate experience is that he's like that.

PT: (**Nodding**) Right.

TP: Like the way he was when you were young, needing to be in charge, right all the time.

PT: Yeah. It's a lot to think about (**smiling**).

A couple of weeks after this session, the patient was talking more about how her father responded to her about any assertion of her own ideas, needs, thoughts, and so forth. He was regularly and easily moralizing and quick to fault her for doing things intentionally to hurt or upset or disappoint him. She experientially remembered the feeling of being reprimanded for being hurtful in saying things that she thought were innocuous and simply her thoughts. She felt fear, a deep self-consciousness, and a feeling of being trapped and untrustworthy. She realized that the way she learned to feel about herself, her thoughts, feelings, and instincts, was that they were likely "bad" or would be hurtful to other people. Hence, the painstaking care she needed to take to communicate herself, coupled with the suspicion that others would not be genuine about their responses to her (stemming mostly from her relationship with her mother), made social contact thoroughly exhausting. Since that time, the fear of some "cataclysmic" event that remains out of her consciousness has almost never come up, and her desire for and courage in seeking relationships and social interactions has increased, frequently eclipsing the fear or the lethargy, but sometimes having to fight to be heard.

Restructuring Defenses and Quieting Anxiety: Getting Out of State 1

Stuck points or periods of stasis are part of development—intrapersonal or interpersonal. And so, as many of my artist patients describe their own experience, stasis and maybe even times of regression are "part of the process" and nothing, per se, to worry about. But all clinicians know that experience of building frustration and perhaps anxiety or boredom in a given psychotherapy in which the patient seems to have stopped growing, moving, changing, or benefiting from the work. In my experience, these are usually signals that something has to change and that, perhaps, I need to do something differently to start that process.

In addition to the generalized stuck points that last weeks to months, there are moments in a given session in which defenses are front and center or secondary emotions are being expressed that go nowhere. And so, obstacles are either relatively engrained and entrenched or simply of the moment. I am continually reminded that underestimating what people are capable of is a mistake through repeatedly discovering that when I have allowed someone to linger a long time in a more defensive state, or fail to help them regulate their anxiety, they frequently report later that the session felt unproductive, or they worried they were boring me, wished I had done something more, or do not remember it, or that it was not nearly as helpful as other sessions.

If the focus of the therapist is on deepening primary affect, or core affective experience, in order to draw on the resources contained within, she will always be working to help regulate anxiety, move away from ruminative, secondary, or defensive emotional expression, and modulate the distress of the patient. But while these interventions are very helpful and welcome in hindsight by almost everyone, they are not always welcome in the moment, especially if the therapist is encouraging the patient to let go of long-cherished defenses.

Some questions are helpful in engaging people emotionally and moving them from State 1 (stress, distress, and symptoms resulting from defenses and their failure) to State 2 (core affective experience). They are too many and too unique to fully list here, but the following are some, organized by whether the patient is primarily in defense or in anxiety.

Helpful Questions When Someone Is Defending
Against Feeling:

- Are you aware of how you are feeling inside as you tell me about this?
- What is happening in your body right now as you tell me this?
- There is such a look of X on your face as you tell me this? Are you aware of feeling X or is there something else?
- I have such a feeling of X as you tell me this. Does that resonate with you at all?
- My body feels so X as you tell me this. Do you have any reactions to that? Does that resonate with anything that is happening for you, or is it just my reaction?
- I know you are used to X (naming defense in a colloquial non-pejorative way) when you have strong feelings, but I wonder if you would feel safe enough here with me, just for the moment, to make a little room to let yourself have this very important feeling.
- It seems that this feeling has so much to tell you and us about yourself and what is important to you (or what you

need). I wonder if we could just take a few moments to pay attention to it.

Helpful Suggestions/Statements When Someone Is Experiencing Red Signal Affects (Anxiety, Tension, Shame, Embarrassment):

- Notice what that is like for you right now?
- It takes a lot of courage for you to let yourself notice and feel X with me right now. It seems very natural that some hesitation comes up in your body as you pay attention to something that you have been unaware of (avoided, etc.) for so long. [A little encouragement goes a long way, and besides, it is true.]
- Where do you notice that anxiety (. . .) in your body right now?
- It is so important what you are letting yourself start to feel. I want to reassure you that we will do this at a pace that you can tolerate. A little anxiety is pretty natural, but too much might shut you down or cause you to want to run away. So you need to let me know what feels like too much and we will slow down or even take a break. How does that sound to you?
- I can see that this experience brings up some shame or embarrassment for you, but it is important for you to understand that I am not sitting here in judgment of you. In fact, (quite the opposite), . . . I admire your courage given how X this is for you; (or) it is most imponant for me and for our work that you are free to tell me everything and that honesty is freeing for you and helps us in our work.

In working with defense, anxiety, or distress, the therapist needs to strike a careful balance between *encouraging* the parts of the self that want to allow for what is emerging and *reassuring* the parts that experience it as threatening or frightening. The major goal is creating safety within the therapeutic relationship, as it is experienced by the patient, to explore and express aspects of the self's experience that have remained unapproachable or unwilling to be exposed up until this point. This, of course, is the substance of secure attachment relationships of any kind. There is a mutual experience of care, concern, and sufficient acceptance, curiosity, openness, and safety to explore and to seek and find comfort and reassurance when our discoveries prove overwhelming or threatening.

One of the most important things to keep in mind in helping people regulate their anxiety and relinquish their defenses is the issue of their own felt sense of safety in the relationship. A therapist can be as gentle and kind as they come, but frequently some patients persist in dealing with therapists as if they are judgmental, indifferent, withholding, scolding, or worse. This is especially true if trauma reactions get triggered unwittingly by the therapeutic exchange. Encouraging patients to focus on the reality of what is happening in the moment can be very helpful, but hypervigilance does not dissipate so easily for most, particularly those with deeply problematic attachment histories. At best, the burgeoning sense of safety exists side-by-side with the caution, inhibition, or overt fear, as illustrated in the transcript above. For this reason, and because I believe working with resilience requires a deeply collaborative approach, asking permission if it would be okay to take a step or explore a possibility is enormously useful. It reminds people that they have an essential voice in the relationship, helps them feel in control of the pace at which this often very affecting work will unfold, and communicates the respect of the therapist for the patient's own unique process while being clear about the ultimate goal and the approximate path.

Osimo (2003) discusses how sometimes just having people put their anxiety experience into words actually diminishes it. It may also be that, from a polyvagal/social engagement perspective (Porges 1997, 2001, 2009), actually remaining engaged facially and verbally (including paraverbally) with the therapist while having a stressful, sympathetic nervous system response invites the parasympathetic system into the mix and thus calms the system.

Healing Shame: Undoing Aloneness and Working With Toxic Emotions

As discussed above, the experience of shame is frequently not bypassed or assuaged easily, in part because it is a central organizing experience about the self in the world. And so, it can be very difficult to find and connect with more resilient parts of the patient for both patient and therapist. As with excessive anxiety and tough defenses, it is therefore important to be able to work with these more paralyzing negative emotions that may block transformation strivings and glimmers of resilience potential.

Important life stories of connection or, more aptly, disconnection are associated with shame, helplessness, or despair. At times, the emergence of shame in a therapeutic moment is habit—the person's reflexive reaction to being seen. In such moments, reassurance, affirmation, or pressuring with empathy may be enough to put it aside in order to process the emotions of the moment or to take in something good. At other times, the emergence of shame and its cousins needs to become the focus of the work in the moment because life continues to be filtered through that distorted lens, and experiences that might otherwise be positive or even healing are not experienced as such. Moreover, shameful or helpless self states tend to be recursive: people act in a way that is compromised and wind up feeling ashamed of being and appearing ashamed or inadequate.

Nathanson (1992) writes that shame functions as an impediment to interest-excitement and enjoyment-joy—it is the experience of interest-excitement and enjoyment-joy suddenly interrupted. Somatically, one's gaze is averted, perhaps the head drops, the body slumps, and the skin flushes. The person becomes self-conscious in a painful way and wants attention turned away from the self.

A young male patient struggled with obsessive thinking; perfectionism; discomfort with what he perceived to be the imperfections of the women he was involved with; fantasies of fame, grandeur, and sexual bliss; uncertainty about a career path; and a fear that he would hurt or disappoint the women he was involved with. The only child of parents who loved him but were not emotionally expressive or accessible, he had no one to talk with and no way to talk about his father's infidelity and the parents' very complicated relationship. In late adolescence, after years of having seemingly random physical challenges, he was finally diagnosed with a progressive, degenerative disease that would require him to need assistance with everyday tasks and also required a lot of self-care in order to maintain capacities he still had. He continued to lead a fairly normal life, earning a master's degree and working for a time. He finally had to leave a job because he could no longer manage the physical tasks most people take for granted. Because he was entitled to disability and his parents could afford to supplement his income, he took some time to pursue other interests in the arts. He would talk about the daily living with (and adapting to) the disability and how it figured into concerns about viable work and his ability to be in a love partnership and a father. But it was not until we really stayed with the shame or, in his words, humiliation of the disease itself that we began to really understand the part of him that feared hurting a woman. While other conflicts also contributed to this fear, the sense of humiliation about what he could not do, what he might not be able to do, the needs he would have to direct toward a partner, and the possibility of not achieving a typical male role of being a provider were all too painful to deal with. They remained deeply private and stoked the sense of being "toxic" to another. It was profoundly and quietly freeing for him to share all of these concerns and feelings with himself and, moreover, with me and to *simultaneously* "feel loved and accepted" (in his own words).

Lyon and Rubin (in press) point out the uniqueness of shame as an emotion in that the action tendency is to freeze or hide. Rather than increasing the life force, it diminishes it. This is why it is referred to in AEDP as a "maladaptive core affective experience." The intention in working with it is to undo this paralysis or the aloneness that accompanies it in order to free up energy for more adaptive emotions. And yet, shame is part of every life. Our experiences of being shut down or of wanting or needing to hide need to be witnessed with care, love, and acceptance to counterbalance the shutdown. But it is also healing to be joined in our humanity and its vulnerability to painful exposure when we experience shame. Lyon and Rubin also talk about the importance of paying attention to the connection with the therapist, having access to resources about the patient (from intelligence, to perseverance, musical ability, etc.), alternating between past and present, and completing self-protective responses that may have been aborted in the past.

Helpful Questions and Statements for Working with Maladaptive Core Affective Experiences

- I can see this is very painful for you. I so appreciate your sharing it with me. It feels very genuine and true that this has been your experience.
- What is your experience of me in this moment?
- Internally you are judging yourself. I just want you to know explicitly that I don't feel any judgment toward you right now. In fact, quite the opposite. I am so touched (admiring, etc.) that you are sharing this very vulnerable part of yourself with me. . . . Can you take that in? What is that like for you?
- As you are sharing these important and formative memories of being (shamed, frightened, helpless, etc.), are you also aware that you are here with me in my office right now and that you are safe right now?
- I am so glad that you are now finding a way of sharing some of this shame with me so that you don't have to continue to carry this burden completely on your own. I can imagine this has been/ felt very isolating for you.
- Is there anything you would like to say or do with that (younger, former, or name the patient gives to an earlier self-experience) part of yourself that felt so ashamed (alone, frightened, hopeless, etc.)?
- Can you feel even a little bit of compassion for that self that went through X right now?

The ultimate goal of work with State 2 maladaptive affects is to help people move into an embodied experience of *adaptive affects*, especially in the context of the experiences that were in some way self-annihilating. Compassion toward the self, anger on behalf of the self directed at others who may have been persecutors in some way, helping younger selves distinguish between their actions and their selves (the traditional distinction between guilt and shame respectively), gratitude over connections, grief over losses, and even awe or admiration about how one survived are all adaptive affective experiences that both mark and facilitate healing from shame. They also, importantly, create some space between the self and that which is aversive to it—the essence of resilience. So, rather than being engulfed by a feeling, a self state, or a toxic relationship, one can process feelings around it, and the self can remain separate from it in some way that preserves the self.

But getting to more adaptive core affective experiences (on behalf of the self) already requires some separation and self-compassion to even be possible. When someone is presently engulfed in maladaptive core affective experience, it is common that they do not have any of that separation or compassion. They may even hate the former or shamed self. This is where the therapist's explicit holding of the compassion is so important. A woman patient was so distressed about a mistake she had made that would cost her and her family money they did not have. As she described to me what had happened, it was clear she was not being negligent, lazy, or careless—she had made an "honest mistake." But she was so angry at herself, and all she could do was call herself an idiot. Of course, the things she had missed that led to the mistake were as clear as day with 20/20 hindsight. I worked hard to see if I could offer her a more compassionate and forgiving perspective, but she could not take it in emotionally. The best we could do in that session was get her to a place where she was open to asking herself what it would be like to be more self-forgiving the next time she was in the process of castigating herself. Sometimes, all we can do is plant the seed.

Themis is a word derived from ancient Greek that refers to a culture's definition of "normative expectations, ethics, moral order, social values and convention" (Bradley, 2010, p. 53). Jonathan Shay (1994) used this term to talk about the systemic betrayals of themis by Vietnam veterans. Bradley (2010), in a fantastic seminar on trauma and resilience, points out that this is often a key part of trauma itself, whatever type it is. People's expectations of what is right and wrong are profoundly violated. The leads to a lack of trust in others and, frequently, in oneself and one's judgment. Maladaptive core affective experiences are often the consequence of themis. We can see this in the example of the patient in this chapter in a particularly sad way. She learned over and over that she could not trust herself, her perceptions, or her reactions to situations and people. She had to shut down to stay safe and prevent further shame or alienation, from her father in particular. This is a combination of shame and a violation of themis. Optimally, a normative expectation is that we can trust our reactions, thoughts, and feelings to have import and meaning and to be welcome by those who love us.

Summary

This chapter has focused on the sometimes slow and plodding aspects of resilience-oriented work that require a lot of activity and focus on the part of the therapist. We reviewed the use of the other in the context of the polyvagal theory of emotion and how it may apply to the clinical realm and the role of the therapist's nonverbal and verbal presence in helping to regulate patients whose anxiety is high and whose fight/flight/freeze mechanisms have been triggered. While these defensive mechanisms are expressions of the resilience potential working on behalf of the self, in nonthreatening situations these are maladaptive, and the goal of our work is to help people move toward increasingly healthy and currently adaptive expressions of resilience. We also reviewed the concepts of attunement, disruption, and repair and how pure attunement is often not sufficient to help people develop more to more adaptive ways of functioning and feeling. Rather, empathic responsiveness is frequently what is called for, particularly when people are stuck in negative and painful places. The chapter concluded with some explicit suggestions for how to work with anxiety (or, more broadly, red signal affects), defenses, and shame and other unbearable and toxic emotions that frequently burden people.

CHAPTER 5

Recognizing, Facilitating, and Responding to Occasions of Change

Resilience can remain only a potential. As it is recognized and brought out, it contains and expresses the promise of transformation. When one is able to fully engage it, it is expressed finally as transformance, the force underlying growth, development, and receptivity to life-enhancing experiences and relationships. Often, when tranformance is fully engaged, people are in a state of flourishing. How do they get there, and how do we help them get there?

The goal of the psychotherapeutic endeavor is healing. And healing, by definition, involves *change*. We know that psychotherapy research consistently shows that the "nonspecific" factors, including and especially some experience of the therapist's empathy on the part of the patient, constitute a meaningful portion of the efficacy of the work (Greenberg, Watson, Elliott, & Bohart, 2001; Orlinsky, Grawe, & Parks, 1994). So while we can continue to come up with techniques and interventions to make psychotherapy even more effective, we should be equally interested in understanding how and why those "nonspecific factors" are, indeed, efficacious—are themselves *very precise* techniques and interventions. What is happening in the healthy, healing-promoting psychotherapeutic relationship? What happens moment to moment in the exchange between two people that is, in fact, very specifically potent? It

therefore makes sense to return to our origins and look closely at
the mutually influential, security- or non-security-engendering,
intensely affectively driven relationship between young infants and
their primary caretakers.

This chapter focuses on processes of global change. It starts by
reviewing some of how the brain develops optimally in responsive
attachment relationships and allows for the development of emotion regulation, which is an essential part of resilient functioning in
the world. It then looks more specifically at the importance of right-
brain-to-right-brain communication to the developing brain and to
the healing brain of a patient in psychotherapy. From there we will
explore models of the process of change, specifically, therapeutic
change, whether it is the step-by-step or the quantum-leap variety,
and how a resilience-oriented therapist must become a very good
detector of transformance and glimmers of resilience potential in
the sometimes small, but terribly important, moments of change.

The Development of the Resilient Self: What Interpersonal Neurobiology and Affective Neuroscience Have to Say

Alan Schore (1994, 1996, 2000, 2003) has written extensively about
how the earliest environment of the infant affects the growth of its
brain, particularly areas responsible for emotion and emotion regulation. He states that the optimal development of the right hemi-
sphere of the brain, which is growing rapidly in the first 18 months of
life, is literally experience dependent. The requisite experiences are
communicated through touch and particularly through mutual gaze
interactions (Schore, 1996) between infants and their primary caregivers, which both facilitate and express psychobiological attunement (Cohn & Tronick, 1987; Gianino & Tronick, 1988; Tronick, 1989,
2005). These regulatory processes precede and partly determine
caregiver–infant attachment and the individual dyad's attachment
patterns. (For a comprehensive, therapist-friendly guide to understanding this area, I highly recommend Badenoch (2008) Being a

Brain-Wise Therapist; and Schore (2012) The Science and Art of Psychotherapy.)

The coactivation of the infant's and mother's right brains when they are visually engaged with one another triggers high levels of dopamine (an endogenous opiate) and is thereby a source of tremendous pleasure and activation. This "combination of joy and interest motivates attachment bond formation" (Schore, 1996, p. 63). Particularly at this stage of life, affect regulation is dyadic. This implicates two things. First, infants are quite dependent on the adult caregiver to regulate (up or down) their internal state and so are in need of an interested, attuned, and empathically responsive other. Second, as Beebe and Lachman (1994) demonstrate through detailed descriptions of videotaped mother–infant interactions, each partner is connecting with and responding according to the other: baby to mother and mother to baby. It seems that, at an extremely young age, the ventral-vagal complex discussed by Porges (1997, 2001, 2009, 2011) is functioning to help the infant navigate and negotiate the challenges and pleasures of a completely new environment. And, fortunately for the infant, if the mother is in a positive affective state herself, she does not disengage from the infant but, rather, waits for the infant to disengage (Cohn & Tronick, 1987). This has very important implications for how therapists optimally respond to their patients in positive affective states (discussed more at length in Chapter 7).

A major emphasis in Schore's work is the critical role of the orbital prefrontal cortex. This area helps regulate positive and negative affect and is undergoing tremendous growth during the time at which infant attachment patterns are being laid down (Schore, 1994, 1996). Schore describes an early "practicing period" that occurs from roughly 10 to 14 months and parallels an increase in an infant's motoric capacities, ability to represent the self, and, of course, development of the orbital prefrontal cortex. This period is marked by intense hedonic affect (i.e., joyful, exuberant, and expansive) in the baby and a lot of affection, caregiving, and play in the mother, who is delighted by her delightful baby and takes pleasure in her child's new capacities and interests. Schore contends that this period is essential for the growth and development of the prefrontal cortex, which remains critical in the mediation of social and emotional behavior and self-regulation throughout life. He asserts that positive, regulated affective interaction with a familiar and predictable caregiver not only engenders a sense of *safety* but actually enhances learning and the development of new socioemotional and physical capacities through a *curiosity* that has a distinctly positive affective tone to it. Importantly, this is also what is found in adults whose capacities for problem solving and accessing resources are expanded when they are in even mildly positive affect states (Fredrickson & Losada, 2005; Tugade & Fredrickson, 2004).

Emotion Regulation and Resilience

For affective neuroscientists, regulation is not a valueless term. Similarly, affect regulation should also assume a central role in the work of therapists as we seek to support and enhance the resilience of our patients. The value is placed on the capacity to rapidly metabolize negative affect states and return to (genuinely) positive states. Remaining in negative affective states for too long is seen as toxic to brain development and to the ongoing smooth functioning of the central nervous system. In fact, Schore (1996) indicates that the working definition of resilience for infants and their caregivers is the capacity to return to a positive affective state from a negative one. I think that this is, in fact, a good working definition for resilient capacity for people of all ages. Negative affect generally limits one's access to personal and external resources and is associated with fewer behavioral response options compared with positive affect (Fredrickson, 1998; Fredrickson & Branigan, 2005; Fredrickson & Losada, 2005; Tugade & Fredrickson, 2004). So the capacity to repair disrupted states marked by negative affect and to return to coordinated and positive affect states is a critical aspect of resilient capacity that is born in infancy and early toddlerhood.

In summary, the importance of the proper development of the orbitofrontal cortex and its connections to the limbic and motor systems of brain cannot be underestimated. These require at least a "good enough" emotionally resonant and responsive environment to develop properly so that the individual becomes capable of a "relatively fluid switching of internal bodily states in response to changes in the external environment that are appraised to be personally meaningful" (Schore, 1996, p. 73). If these are not well developed, the individual's response capacity is limited, and other parts of the brain may predominate (i.e., the amygdala) in situations that pose challenges, leading to inflexible and, frequently, inappropriate response patterns that are marked, for example, by fear and aggression (Schore, 1994). This is not what one would normally consider resilient.

There are important implications of Schore's work even on clinical interventions with adults, especially if we adhere to the philosophy of interpersonal neurobiology (see below) and the ongoing plasticity of the brain. Together, they suggest that in the development and *healing* of the brain, psychobiological state coordination between individuals, particularly pairs in which one has greater self- and emotion-regulatory capacities, is critical. Second, a major goal and function of these relationships is to rapidly metabolize negative affect and not only to return to positive affect states but also to remain in them, play with them, and elaborate them and all the salutary benefits they proffer. Affective neuroscience and interpersonal neurobiology suggest that the most potent way to do this is through visuoaffective communication, which is primarily a right-brain-mediated phenomenon and includes face-to-face contact, gaze sharing, play, touch, and vocal rhythms that soothe distress and amplify positive affect.

Right-Brain-to-Right-Brain Communication

Interpersonal neurobiology (see Cozolino, 2006; Siegel, 1999, 2003; 2007; Siegel & Hartzell, 2003), a term coined by Dan Siegel (1999), captures the contention of affective neuroscience that one brain influences another brain and that our brains are inherently social organs that are developed through experience. A simple example is the following adapted from Siegel (1999): I am going to write a word. I would like you to pause for a few moments after you read the word to notice what happens inside you as you read the word I write. Be aware of thoughts, feelings, images, physical sensations, memories, and the like after you read the word. Just let yourself notice what happens inside you. The word is: ocean.

Did you see the ocean in your mind's eye? Did you remember the last time you saw it? Did you remember images from pictures, TV, or postcards? Was your memory or association positive or negative? Did feelings accompany your image? Did you feel nostalgic, sad, happy, peaceful? Did you notice any physical sensations, like taking a deep breath, a lightness in your chest, a smile on your face, butterflies in your stomach at the thought of the power of it? Did you have any thoughts? What were they?

The simple point of this exercise is that I had an image/idea in my mind. It was translated into symbols on a page. These symbols translated into images, memories, sensory experiences, thoughts, and feelings in your mind and body. My brain influenced your brain in a fairly significant way without our being with each other in person, and in only a matter of seconds.

Optimal parent–child relating that contributes to secure attachment and optimal brain development should inform our clinical interventions, particularly when that kind of relating did not happen earlier, leading to at least part of the reason the patient may be struggling or suffering in their current life. Right-brain-to-right-brain communication, including eye contact, facial expressions revealing emotion (particularly positive), paraverbal communication that conveys affective resonance (e.g., "aahs," "mmms," tone of voice, pace of speech), is very important. Contingent, caring responsiveness (i.e., empathic responsiveness) helps people develop both self-compassion and to internalize regulation and comfort. Sometimes people need help to articulate their inner experience, what Siegel (2003) calls *reflective dialogue*, which requires the therapist to attend carefully and listen to all aspects of the patient's communication. People often need help to stay with and amplify (the benefits of) positive affects and to regulate and soothe negative affects. The therapist's capacity to repair or receive repair is crucial to the trust of the therapeutic relationship. And her integration of her own attachment history and patterns should allow her to respond empathically and appropriately to people with different attachment styles without abandoning them or intruding on their space or development. The acquisition of all of these relational and self-regulatory skills is foundational to optimal resilient capacity.

Attachment is the primary mode through which interpersonal neurobiology positively or negatively affects the development of the child's brain. In the best circumstances, experience contributes to complexity. The brain is a complex system and is organized in such a way as to move toward maximal complexity (Siegel, 1999), which involves differentiation and integration, as well as the capacity to move back and forth between the two. In fact, Siegel defines healing as the release of these self-organizational tendencies to move toward maximal complexity, thereby freeing the brain's (and the individual's) captivity chaotic or restrictive patterns. (Chapter 7 looks at the importance and impact of complexity, which involves both differentiation and integration and the capacity to toggle back and forth, to emotion processes and how these may affect resilience when discussing the dynamic model of affect.) This sounds very much like the process of restoring resilience when people are able to move from more constricted/resistance-oriented ways of expressing resilience to more expansive/transformance-oriented ways of manifesting resilience. Moreover, the brain is nonlinear, which means that small changes in one area can have quantum effects in another. This is something we see in therapy, when what may seem to us like a small change sets off a cascade of transformation.

And so, optimal development appears to be both dependent and interdependent. Focusing for a moment only on the child, his dependency on the parent makes him extraordinarily vulnerable. Security and safety are his first priority. Once assured, his second priority is exploration and the expansion of his capacities and of his self. Higher levels of mutual positive affect increase the bonds of affection and, if contingent and responsive, deepen the sense of safety and security necessary to fuel exploration and engagement with the world. The caregiver is motivated to respond to the child to diminish his distress, as well as to augment and share in his joy and excitement.

In this way, development is interdependent. While the parent is a critical transformer of the child's experience, she is also changed by the child. Her priorities are shifted; what she attends to and how and where she spends her energy changes (for an excellent review of the changes that take place in the brains of new parents, see Ellison 2006). In order for the child to develop and grow optimally, the parent must be willing not only to be used but also to be stretched and moved beyond boundaries that were once more fixed and comfortable. On a neurobiological level, the *transformational other* is changed by the self. It is impossible not to be.

Change: Inviting It, Marking It, and Expanding It

Even quantum transformation can frequently be broken down into small segments of movement and interchange that effect an overall shift. Understanding the process of change—to the extent that we can understand it—can be extraordinarily useful in helping us recognize when it is happening within ourselves, in another, or in a relationship, as well as in guiding or freeing us to respond in a way that allows the change to unfold. This section reviews several clinically informed discussions of the process of change that prove very relevant to the discovery of and restoration of resilience and transformance. The transcript that follows in the later half of the chapter demonstrates how an approach to finding and restoring resilience is aided by an awareness of change processes and how explicitly acknowledging and processing the person's experience of change (i.e., metaprocessing) deepens and expands the change and growth that can be achieved

We have been talking about change throughout this book. The movement from more resistant/constrictive manifestations of resilience to more transformance/expansive expressions of resilience is an irrefutable change for the better. This section explores the processes of change more explicitly: What conditions invite positive change? What does change look like when it is happening? What tools do we have when change seems to be stuck? How do we catalyze glimmers of possibility into motoric agents of self- and other-expanding change?

Experiential Therapies and Common Facilitators of Change

Hans Welling (2012) has written a compelling article on processes of change for the better in four different types of psychotherapy: emotion focused therapy (Greenberg et al., 1993; Greenberg & Paivio, 1997; Greenberg & Safran, 1987), coherence therapy (Ecker & Hulley, 1996, 2002), AEDP (Fosha, 2000b), and eye movement desensitization and reprocessing (Shapiro, 2001; Shapiro & Forrest, 1997). Welling points out the main common characteristics of these models, which is the patient's processing of emotion, usually negative emotion. What follows in all models is an apparent spontaneous emergence of more positive affective states and perspectives. Welling breaks down this common change process into five components: (1) promoting an experiential stance, (2) accessing hidden or underlying emotion, (3) spontaneous change and nondirectivity, (4) sequential shift from problematic to adaptive emotional states, and (5) symptom change often resulting in immediate improvement. Essentially, all of these models postulate that adaptive affective experiences are present even if unconscious and unprocessed; that resilience, self-righting, and healing are phenomena the therapist can count on; that deep processing of emotions follows a pattern that manifests in more adaptive emotional and cognitive processing; and that increased resilient capacity is the end product of such processing. Welling postulates that all four therapies rely on a principle that "the activation of a negative (problematic) emotional state" will be "followed by the activation of a positive (adaptive) emotional state(s)" (2012, p. 123). He calls this the principle of "transformative emotional sequence." Gendlin referred to this phenomenon as "nothing that feels bad is ever the last step" (1981, p. 26). He points out in many examples how change seems to follow the sequence of maladaptive emotional states being paired with adaptive emotional states in a short period of time.

Ecker, Ticic, and Hulley (2012) postulate that actual memory era-
sure and reconsolidation occur in some of the therapies mentioned
above, including AEDP. They explain that in certain transformational therapies, including their own—which they call coherence
therapy—painful, problematic, and even traumatic emotional learning can be reactivated experientially and, when paired with a powerful and *contrasting* new emotional learning, can be undone. It is
not that the memory no longer exists but, rather, that the emotional
impact and behavioral consequences related to that trauma that continue to be relived (i.e., reenacted) are erased and the new, more
adaptive learning is reconsolidated around the memory.

State Shifts as Markers of Transformation

AEDP seeks to foster new emotional experiences, and therefore it
devotes close attention to markers of change and transformation, to
what is happening affectively, somatically, relationally, and within
the self when change is under way. AEDP identifies state transformations, which are characterized by a qualitative change to a completely different state from the one that preceded it (Fosha, 2002).
States differ along continua that involve emotion (more or less feeling or feelings of a different kind); memory (different memories
are available in different states); cognition (different thoughts are
associated with different states and emotions); soma (the visceral
experience associated with different states, including variations in
vitality); openness versus closedness; level of truthfulness, clarity,
or insight; subjective sense of self (including images of self); intrarelational experience (how different parts of the self feel toward one
another); relational experience (sense of connection with therapist
and imagined others; close vs. distant; feeling understood or safe vs.
not; self-as-compromised vs. self-as-efficacious/open); and for some
people, how spiritually connected they feel.

As discussed in the preceding chapters, the four states of transformation identified by AEDP are (1) stress, distress, and symptoms,
(2) core affective experience, (3) transformational experience, and
(4) core state (see Figure 2.1). Recognizing them and knowing how

to respond to them in a facilitative way are some of the challenges of becoming a resilience-focused affective, experiential clinician. It is also very helpful to be able to recognize the three transformations between these four states that indicate a possible movement from one state to another.

The first state transformation, between States 1 and 2, involves a cocreation of safety. The patient begins to feel safe enough to "drop down" into some kind of affective or relational state. On his way, affects and energy that are different from the more constricted, anxious, or defensive affects of State 1 come forward. Heralding affects signal core affective experiences that the patient may have been defending against or unaware of until that moment. Examples from transcripts in preceding chapters include when the patient says, "This could be calm" (Chapter 3) and, from a tearful and shut-down place, "I don't want to shut down" (Chapter 1). Green signal affects are signs of openness to and curiosity about one's more interior experience, for example, when the patient says, referring to the sinkhole, "I want to look over the edge and see what is down there" (Chapter 4)—the patient is open to a deeper exploration of her own experience, and the therapist follows, encourages, and facilitates.

At the end of a wave of emotional processing and exploration, people have new access to adaptive action tendencies, and this is usually accompanied by postbreakthrough affects of relief, hope, feeling stronger or lighter, and so on. Not infrequently, they sigh or they appear more physically relaxed. These are markers of the second state transformation under way. It is, from our perspective, the place where one sees the unfolding of a more adaptive and fuller resilient capacity. The therapist interested in restoring resilience notices these and brings attention to the subjective, somatic experience of this state transformation and of the difference between then and now. This metaprocessing frequently elicits transformational affects, the affects one experiences in the wake of change and while reflecting on that change.

The transformational affects of State 3 arise in the wake of transformation and change that is felt by the person and that contain reactions to the change itself. They may arise naturally in any therapeutic or natural process in the wake of a powerful emotional experience and one's awareness that the present moment is qualitatively different in some important and good way. In resilience-oriented therapy, we want to take advantage of these naturally occurring healing (and resilience-building) phenomena by focusing on them experientially and amplifying them.

The third state transformation involves the coengendering of secure attachment to other and to self. One settles into a state of calm, flow, or ease and feels at home with the self. This is the ushering in of the core state, which is the optimal state in which to reflect on one's life or a part of one's story (or what one has just been talking about) because compassion toward self and others and acceptance are hallmarks of this state (for a thorough discussion of affective change processes identified by AEDP, see Fosha 2002).

Now Moments and Moments of Meeting

> *The enduring mystery that brings us together time and again in social relationships is that we can never quite know what is on the mind of the other person but that in the best of circumstances we are curious and willing to forgive a great deal if we sense in the other a curiosity about us.*

There is, I think, a temptation to think of change as happening within an individual. We can think of ourselves as clinicians trying to effect a change (or changes) in our patients' symptoms, relationships, sense of self, thoughts, feelings, behaviors, and so forth. But many occasions for change are relational; we are changed in the process as well, and this is associated with some quantum transformation in our patients and in our relationship with them. Our awareness and understanding of the relational piece of our work can be as important or more so than our moment-to-moment focus on the experience of the individual we are working with.

The Boston Change Process Study Group, composed primarily of infant researchers and psychoanalysts, explicated the process of change within relationships by studying closely what happens in the psychotherapeutic environment and by drawing on what they know of the change processes in the infant–caretaker relationship. Speaking about relationships in general, they note (Stern, 1998; Mayes, 2005) that any given relationship is marked by some unique combination of experiences and expectations of coordination, as well as of disruption and how the dyad repairs the disruption. This may have similarities with other relationships the individual is involved in, but each relationship has its own unique patterns or ways of being. They have proposed that all interpersonal relationships are marked by unique expressions of "moving along," followed occasionally by what they call "now moments," less frequently by "moments of meeting," and then returning to "moving along."

The uniqueness of a given relationship is subjectively experienced in the dyad's *implicit relational knowing* (Lyons-Ruth, 1998). As much as we might like to think of ourselves as (and might, in fact, be) equal opportunity therapists, we are at least slightly different in each of our relationships. There are certain predictabilities and perhaps behavioral rules for how the dyad usually functions that operate outside of awareness and yet influence the process. In the process of change, things may happen that alter that implicit relational knowing. Stern (1998) describes the *moving along* phase as the dyad's improvisational, cooperative movement toward some goal. As such, it consists of coordination, mismatches, disruptions, and repairs, as discussed in Chapter 4. Obviously, this process of moving along can be characterized by any number of variations and combinations of coordination, disruption, and repair. For example, the relationship between a parent and a child with disorganized attachment is likely characterized by a preponderance of disruption and very little experience of repair.

At times something happens in relationships that causes disruption. One may become aware of the previous state of implicit relational knowing by its having been disturbed—either positively or negatively. These can be seen and dealt with as positive opportunities for a change, specifically an expansion of the dyad's relational repertoire, or "now moments." They are, to my mind, the relational equivalents to dropping down into core affective experience. Tronick points out that people form relationships with others, in part, to overcome their own inherent limitations. He points out that a dyadic system is often to pool its resources and provide more to each individual than each would have on his own.

Now moments are sudden, unpredictable, and affectively charged and carry the potential for ongoing change if they are responded to genuinely and fully by each member of the pair. "The 'now moment,' as an emergent property, disequilibrates the normal, canonical way of doing business together. It offers a new intersubjective context" (Stern, 1998, p. 304). It is a disruption of the predictable and habitual and thereby creates some level of anxiety for both patient and therapist (or any pair of people) who are now faced with the choice of returning to their heretofore known ways of interacting (from this perspective, now a defensive move) or of allowing this interruption to unfold its possibilities for new ways of knowing one another and interacting, in other words, *new ways of moving along.* We can ignore or deny that new possibilities have entered the fray, or we can welcome the anxiety that accompanies these disruptions as a herald of expanded possibility and see what we can do with it together.

That process of figuring out what the pair can do together with anxiety and possibility is what the Boston Change Process Study Group refers to as "moments of meeting," a term originally introduced by Sander (1988). Here one cannot rely on technique but, rather, must rely on innovation, creativity, openness, and genuineness. Something real, authentic, and particular to the moment must come from each person in order for a moment of meeting to occur, a moment in which the individuals meet at a different level and share an experience they have not yet shared (together). I think of this capacity that resides in a dyad (or larger group of people) as *relational transformance.* It is the activation of each person's orientation toward growth, development, and authentic connection (Fosha, 2008) happening simultaneously and interdependently, each person's openness and risk taking being met, augmented, validated, and nurtured by the other. And this happens, in part, because the system is greater than the sum of its parts. People seem to need to be and to grow in connection with others. And so, relational transformance is the tendency of relationships themselves to draw out our desire to develop, grow, expand, and connect, as well as what happens when this impulse is responded to affirmatively by each individual, resulting in the expanded capacity of each person and of the relationship itself. Achieving that moment of meeting results in what Tronick (1998, 2005) refers to as a *dyadic state of consciousness* or *the dyadic expansion of consciousness*. Basically, each individual, as a self-organizing system, "creates his or her own states of consciousness (states of brain organization), which can be expanded into more coherent and complex states in collaboration with another self-organizing system" (1998, p. 292).

Frequently, after the moment of meeting, there is a pause in which the individuals can be alone in one another's presence, what Sander (1988) calls an "open space." I think of it as a time to digest, to really take in what has happened and to recalibrate. In this space individuals can also be contemplative and mindful of the present moment. When the dyad moves out of this quiet open space they return to their now expanded way of moving along, which involves a different implicit relational knowing. And in therapy, if the therapist practices AEDP, this implicit relational knowing is often made explicit and becomes the focus of the next round of experiential/emotional processing, thus catalyzing a cascade of transformation. To sum up the process of change described by the Boston Change Process Study Group it looks like this:

**Moving Along → Now Moment → Moment of Meeting → Open Space →
(Expanded) Moving Along**

What does this description of relational change processes have to do with building resilience? Tronick's dyadic expansion of consciousness hypothesis (Tronick, 1998) captures it best. As self-organizing systems, we have limitations. Part of being in relation to others, and perhaps part of why relationships are so appetitive to us as human beings, is that they have the capacity to expand our consciousness and thus make us more coherent, more complex systems and therefore, by default, more resilient and adaptive. They also have a unique ability to calm and comfort us, which is part of why we seek them (Porges, 2001, 2011). Relationships, especially at their best, are expansive. This idea is also captured in the concept of the self-at-best (Fosha, 2000b) (see Figure 1.3b).There is openness, communication, and mutual influence in transformance-oriented relationships that permit the emergence and elaboration of the self-at-best. One feels effective and allows oneself to be affected. A dyadic (or polyadic) system is able to gather and use more resources than a monadic self-regulating system. Resilience cannot emerge solely from the individual because our complexity, coherence, and capability are, in part, borrowed, internalized, and integrated. We may be blessed with a well-oiled self-regulatory system (i.e., resilient), but surely it is expanded by and through relationships with others.

Metaprocessing and the Transformational Spiral: Making Implicit Change and Relational Knowing Explicit

One very powerful contributor to lasting change that is unique to AEDP is metaprocessing (Fosha, 2000b), the process of reflecting on, exploring, and expressing the experience of transformation itself, which makes implicit relational knowing (as well as other affective phenomena) explicit. As all clinicians have no doubt heard repeatedly in their offices, the experience of articulating what is felt, remembered, known, and thought to another makes it more real, more deeply felt, better remembered, more completely known, and more clearly understood than if it remains simply implicit and unspoken. Part of what cements and integrates increased resilient capacity is the experiential reflection on the transformed self, including the expanded capacity of the dyad, which is also more resilient in the wake of change. In metaprocessing, the therapist notices the verbal and nonverbal signs of a change having taken place and inquires about or comments on it, asking patients what that is like, how they experience it, and whether or not it brings up anything else for them. This is frequently not limited to one question because as the change is noticed, felt, and processed, there are often multiple rounds of further processing and the deepening of the experience of change for the better (Russell & Fosha, 2008), thus the cascade of transformation or the transformational spiral.

CLINICAL VIGNETTE:
"Connect With Me": Practice With Potential

The following is a vignette that illustrates the microprocess of change in psychotherapy and how it is used to build resilient capacity through the explicit use of the therapeutic relationship. The transcript is taken from a session with Catherine (from chapter 4). The therapist, as always, is focused on what is most affectively and relationally real. The patient begins the session announcing that she is going to visit her mother and still feels surprised that the mother *wants* to see her. This is now a familiar feeling since the mother began a lesbian relationship two years earlier, her first relationship of any kind in the more than twenty years since she divorced the patient's father, when the patient was 10 years old. Prior to this, the relationship with the mother was quite enmeshed. In the first few minutes, she is even more hesitant in her speech and not really connecting to the therapist. It is unclear whether she is searching for how to articulate what she wants to say or is not really connected to what she is saying. I chose this transcript to illustrate the processes of change identified above, particularly relating to the change in relationship and the experiences of transformation that result. This session also captures much of what has been written so far about the "social engagement system" (Porges, 2009, 2010), as well as the kind of right-brain-to-right-brain communication that is initially responsible for the development of the prefrontal cortex in babies (Schore, 1994, 2003) and later helps deepen interpersonal safety (Porges, 2001, 2009, 2011) and allows for the kind of expansion and exploration that secure attachment engenders (i.e., resilient capacity). Finally, it illustrates the kind of empathic responsiveness and work that is so helpful to restoring the receptive affective capacity damaged by prior attachment wounds in many of our patients, as well as situations in which what is affectively real in the moment is what is being expressed or experienced in the therapeutic relationship.

(A couple minutes into the session after talking about surprise that her mother wants to see her . . .)

PT: (**Looking down at floor; long pause**) Mm. It doesn't feel like I am talking about the right thing. [**Heralding affect; something emerging from core affective experience that breaks through what, in this moment, is more superficial or defensive communication. This is also a small "now moment."**]

TP: Mm. Where is that coming from? [**TP following the herald, welcoming it, and going with the now moment.**]

PT: I don't know. It just doesn't feel very connected. I don't know. Like I don't think that there is something else that I am repressing wanting to talk about. Like I could feel myself drifting as I was talking about it.

TP: I was drifting too. [**PT and TP were affectively in sync; TP feeling equally disconnected.**]

PT: Yeah.

TP: So either there is something here that we are both kind of avoiding (**PT laughs**) or it's not really what you want to be talking about. Or there isn't really more you want to say about it.

PT: (**Making good eye contact**) Yeah. Maybe.

TP: This feels very real, though. [**TP marking the shift in felt sense, of having "dropped down" as a dyad into a core relational experience. Also part of a "moment of meeting," TP and PT responding to the now moment of "It doesn't feel like I am talking about the right thing" in an authentic and searching way.**]

PT: Yeah.

TP: You're saying "this doesn't feel right." So where is that coming from? I mean, how do you notice that? [**Experiential focus on heralding affect; now moment.**]

PT: I notice it in my eyes in that they don't feel or they didn't feel very present. Like they felt kind of heavy.

TP: Mm-hmm.

PT: And that I was having problems keeping eye contact with you. But it felt more like drifting away (**making drifting movement with arm**) as opposed to "I have to think about this or I don't want to say this face to face" kind of thing. [**PT aware of the difference between when she is engaged, avoiding/defending, and when her disengagement is due to her focus being very internal.**]

TP: Mm-hmm.

PT: But there's also kind of a (**putting hand to solar plexus**), kind of an energy or something in my stomach that I have been feeling, but what I was saying wasn't really connecting to it. Like it didn't feel related to that.

TP: So do you still notice that energy or something in your stomach?

PT: Yeah.

TP: What's it like right now?

PT: It's like a pressure, but a pressure outward. And (**pause, pointing to chest**) I can feel it a little in my chest as well.

TP: Mm-hmm. And if it could speak? If you ask it, what would it say?

PT: (**Pause, flipping hand over in lap**) Connect with me. [**This is a big "now moment," an evocation and exclamation of a deeply held need wish/desire. In Stern's (1998) typology, it is sudden, unpredictable, and qualitatively different from the moments of relating before. It is destabilizing and creates anxiety in both the TP and PT.**]

TP: Mmm. To me?

PT: Yeah.

TP: (**Big smile**) Mm-hmm. [**TP feels stunned but welcoming of this emergent desire and capacity for deeper connection. This is a now moment that expresses trans-**

formance strivings and is an example of the resilience
potential becoming unbound.]

PT: (**Smiles, starts to laugh quietly**)

TP: What's it like to share that with me? [**Some metaprocessing
of the bit of transformation that has already happened.**]

PT: I don't know. I guess it is a little embarrassing, but kind of
after the fact. It felt good to say it when I did.

TP: It felt good to hear it. [**This and the smile earlier are part
of the moment of meeting; the two welcoming the new
way of relating that has just emerged from the PT.**]

PT: (**Nodding, smiling**)

TP: And I want to share with you. It is funny, the timing. This
morning I was coming and I was reviewing my notes and I was
thinking that I haven't felt as connected to you recently. And
I think part of it was that we had a long and somewhat unexpected break there, so that was a disruption.

PT: Right.

TP: And it feels like maybe we haven't gotten back on track. And
I wasn't sure what that was about, but I felt this morning like
"Okay, I want something different to happen with Catherine."
[**TP elaborating, perhaps somewhat awkwardly, and
talking a lot, but struck by the resonance of both of
their desires to connect more deeply. This is part of the
"moment of meeting" in that it is unique, authentic, and
of the moment. It is facilitated by the TP's comfort with
explicitly using herself and her own affective reactions
to help guide the work.**]

PT: (**Smiling**)

TP: So it is nice that you want to connect with me and I want to
connect with you.

PT: (**Pause**) It surprised me when you smiled. Like it surprised
me when I actually got a reaction out of you (**laughing**). That
it felt more personal instead of just a . . . [**PT frequently has
the fear in relationships of being met with absence or
condemnation. In this moment TP is not concerned about**

directly addressing the projection but, rather, with staying with what is unfolding in the moment; what is new.]

TP: (**Interrupting**) So what's that surprise like?

PT: Um (**pause**). I don't know. It becomes a different feeling. It feels more tentative somehow, which confuses me because it feels like (**holding out hands with palms up toward TP**) "Well wait, this is what I just asked for and I got it." And now I am pulling away from it? I mean I don't know if it necessarily feels like completely pulling away, but just, it's a little like (**holding hands out with palms down and toward TP in tentative stopping gesture**), "Oh!" You know?

TP: Mm-hmm. So what is it like in your body?

PT: But it has changed that pressure. It is not really in my stomach anymore at all. It is (**circling with finger an area in chest/solar plexus**) more in my chest, and I guess it feels more diffuse (**gesturing with both hands moving out from chest**). I mean maybe it is that I asked for it and I got it and maybe it is like "oh, okay" (**eyes opening wider in kind of surprise, head pulls back slightly, small laugh**).

TP: Okay.

PT: "That was good."

TP: So what's that like? So, it feels like you got it (i.e., connection from TP)?

PT: Yeah. I guess.

TP: You are not saying that for my sake?

PT: No (**holding up hands facing each other, with fingers reaching in**). It's not that pressure. Like the pressure is gone. Like the feeling of "Hey, do something" is gone.

TP: Mm-hmm.

PT: (**Laugh**) It amuses me that I couldn't define that as getting what I wanted. It was more like, "Oh, what the hell happened?" (**Still laughing**) But, um.

TP: Uh-huh. So now you are defining it as getting what you wanted? What is that like? [**Return to "moving along" but now with the explicit and implicit awareness of hav-**

ing gotten something desired and new from TP. The relationship, and therefore its way of moving along, is changed and expanded.]

PT: (**Arms rested and hands folded in lap**) It's nice. It is kind of warm.

TP: Mm-hmm.

PT: (**Gazing at TP, then away**)

TP: Where did you just go?

PT: (**Looking back at TP**) I guess I kind of feel like, "Okay well now what do I do with it now that I have it?" kind of feeling. **[Anxiety arises in the face of core affective experiences of authentic connection and intersubjective moments of pleasure.]**

TP: So you kind of went back up into your head and started worrying about it. [**Naming the anxiety/defense pattern**.]

PT: Yeah (**resuming good eye contact**).

TP: (**Slowly, gently**) If you let yourself go back to the warmth, where do you notice that?

PT: (**PT looking away, pausing, then looking back up at TP**) It is throughout my chest (**gesturing across chest**), and my breathing feels easier.

TP: Uh-huh. Is there anything else there with the warmth? Are you aware of anything else or just that?

PT: I guess I feel like my eyes want something more. [**As PT relaxes into good feeling around connection, there emerges the desire for something more; connection is appetitive when anxiety is removed; we are back into State 2 again.**]

TP: Mmm.

PT: Like I guess I feel like I want to conceal that from you (**pause, looking at TP in a long mutual gaze**). [**Despite the desire to hide, PT is led by the desire to connect and reveals herself and a very new level of vulnerability by allowing herself to gaze into the eyes of the TP; this is another, profound "now moment."**]

Mutual Gaze, Mutual Vulnerability: Using and Being Used

In these subtle, quiet, powerful moments, half of the last 20 years of research and theorizing on the brain, interpersonal neurobiology, emotion theory, and the role of others in the healing process is borne out and simultaneously integrated. As Catherine allows herself to feel and express what is affectively real for her (primary vs. secondary emotion) (Bridges, 2006; Fosha, 2000b, 2002, 2005; Greenberg & Safran, 1987), that is, her desire for deeper connection with the therapist, she wavers between allowing its full expression and thereby her need for recognition (Benjamin, 1990) and regulation by the therapist (Gianino & Tronick, 1988; Tronick, 1998, 2005), and her usual defense of overrelying on her own self-regulatory capacities, which will necessitate withdrawal (Porges, 1997, 2001, 2009, 2011). As she allows herself to gaze at the therapist, she is interpersonally regulated (Siegel, 1999, 2003; Schore, 1994, 1996, 2000; Tronick, 1998, 2005), and she experiences the safety, expressed as a sense of warmth, that our "social engagement system" and capacity for symbiotic regulation have wired us to feel in order to be able to "use" others to help us. As she reveals more of herself, deeper safety is needed, and as it is recognized and received, she unveils more in the transformance-oriented, resilience-engendering process of solidifying and expanding from safe attachments (Ainsworth et al., 1978; Main, 1983, 2000). Importantly, this development requires the willingness of the therapist to be vulnerable and to be used, to make herself available in an authentic relational way. This powerful restoration of her resilient capacity and the redirecting of her resilience potential away from conservation and toward the expansion of transformance continue for the rest of the session, step by step.

> *TP*: So what happened in that moment when you didn't conceal that from me, just now? Was I reading that right?
> *PT*: (**Pause**) It was a little uncomfortable.
> *TP*: Mm-hmm.
> *PT*: But. And, actually a little pulled back. Like I was able to let you see some of it, but not all.

TP: Mm-hmm.

PT: (**Pause, now more intense gaze at TP**) I guess it. I don't know. I guess my head starts talking and there is a responsibility to have to define it, and say (**adopting deeper voice and more harsh tone**), "Okay, well if I am going to show you that I want something then I have to be able to tell you exactly what it is or I can't ask for it."

TP: Mm. Mm-hmm.

PT: Or I don't know. That I immediately feel on the spot to say "this is it." That to feel unsure about it feels . . . (**looking for word**).

TP: Not safe?

PT: Yeah, or like (**again with deeper voice and harsh tone**), "Well don't bother me with this!"

TP: (**Soft, clear, empathic tone, slow pace**) Well, I think we have a sense of where that comes from, right, and I am just wondering, 'cause I am really willing, if you could imagine just putting that part of you aside (**PT nods**), that kind of censoring voice that says you have to be very clear and definitive . . .

PT: Right. [**TP avoiding getting distracted by dynamic exploration in favor of moment-to-moment processing of experience.**]

TP: And just kind of put that part aside. Because I am willing to just kind of play here and figure it out with you and put my head aside. [**Another moment of meeting; TP's invitation and spontaneous use of the word "play" are responses to the more right-brain-to-right-brain communication that the PT's gaze seems to be asking for.**]

PT: Mm-hmm.

TP: And just make a lot of space for something that feels a little tentative and a little undefined, and that's fine. It feels *very* real to me.

This new addition of gazing to the relational knowing of the dyad is so important. It is such a vulnerable state for the patient, and yet in the here and now it is experienced in relative safety. It also renders the therapist quite vulnerable; something is being taken from or seen in her over which she has no control, except to look away and break the contact. At the moment that it was happening, I had an embodied memory of nursing my son when he was barely coming to life after a few weeks of postbirth sleeping, trying to make his way to six pounds. As I nursed him, he gazed intently and intensely into my eyes, literally and figuratively drinking me in. All I knew then, as with my patient, was that I had to allow myself to be vulnerable to that and to remain in the gaze until each had had enough.

This gaze is an element of what Porges (2001, 2009, 2011) describes as the social engagement system, or the ventral-vagal response, our highest and most evolved form of coping with stress. Unlike our less evolved responses to stress (i.e., fight, flight, freeze), which rely entirely on self-regulation, the ventral-vagal response, which involves gaze, vocalization, facial communication, and modulation of heart-beat, is dyadic in that it involves self- and other-directed regulatory behavior (Gianino & Tronick, 1988). It accomplishes the goal of regulating emotional states while simultaneously interacting with others and the world (Tronick, 1989). Here and in the rest of the session, much of this dyadic regulation and communication is accomplished through mutual gaze. Unlike the popular, particularly American, purported wisdom that strength lies in self-sufficiency, resilience also lies in the capacity to use others to complement our own limited self-regulatory capacities. In this session, the patient is exercising her ventral-vagal system in a way that she never has before, and the therapist must allow herself to be used to that end.

(Continuing where we left off . . .)

TP: And just make a lot of space for something that feels a little tentative and a little undefined and that's fine. It feels *very* real to me.

PT: (**Nodding**) Mm-hmm. Yeah.

TP: This desire to connect. It may be fraught with all kinds of other things, but it feels very real.

PT: Yeah.

TP: (**Smiling**) And very welcome.

PT: (**Big smile, face flushing**) Well that's good (**looking down, then back up at TP**).

TP: What happened inside just then?

PT: (**Pause, deep breath, looking down**) It was kind of a (**bringing hand up from lap above shoulder**) like a surge of happiness to hear that. [**Receptive affective experience; PT able to take in TP's delighting in her and reciprocal desire to connect.**]

TP: Mm. Mm-hmm. What's that like? What's the happiness like? [**TP focusing experientially on the deeply positive affects that have emerged as markers of transformation and as fuel for further transformation and increased resilience. (See Chapter 7).**]

PT: (**Hand to chest**) It's a warmth.

TP: Mm-hmm. And it's kind of in here (**hand to chest**)?

PT: Yeah (**pause, alternating gazing at TP and then looking away a few times**). It makes me realize or it makes me wonder if you're seeing my other face, my nonmasked face, the unhidden face I guess.

TP: Mm-hmm.

PT: What I have been talking about in group (therapy) like the difference of letting the walls down. I mean I think they're usually down certainly more here all the time, you know, but um . . .

TP: Mm-hmm.

PT: I guess it feels connected to that.

TP: Sure. That softness versus the harshness or the hardness, whatever the feedback from the group was.

PT: Yeah (**pause, mutual gaze**).

TP: I think I am seeing that.

PT: (**Smiling**)

TP: It's very nice (**pause**). What's that like for you to imagine that you're letting it down more with me, that you're letting me see that more, even than usual, this softer unhidden side of you. Or maybe you mean "usually hidden"? [**Metaprocessing the**

transformation; thus, also making the new implicit relational knowing explicit.]

PT: Right, um. I don't know. There definitely seems to be a lot of energy around it (**gesturing to chest**). Um (**pause**).

TP: Mm-hmm.

PT: I'd even say some excitement with it. [**Vitality affects.**]

TP: Mm-hmm. How do you notice that?

PT: It's kind of a (**bringing hand to chest**), I don't know, a higher feeling here. It feels like everything is just kind of slowly coming up (**smile**).

TP: What is the smile about?

PT: (**Smile disappears, and PT looks pensive**)

TP: (**In playful tone**) You don't have to get rid of it!

PT: (**Laughing, moving in chair**)

TP: I just wanted to know what was coming up. It seemed like you were thinking something was funny, but maybe it was just kind of a joyful feeling inside? [**Minor repair and attempt to return to coordinated state.**]

PT: Um. Yeah, or I guess kind of. I guess I was more liking the idea of, like getting close to something or something is happening. Or that whatever is usually so hidden away is coming up.

TP: Or out.

PT: Yeah.

TP: And that feels exciting?

PT: Yeah. But I guess it feels hard to say. I thought it, and it took a while to actually say it.

TP: So what is it like now to say it?

PT: I don't know. It is still a little guarded I guess, or . . . it is not that it is fear, necessarily. Like I don't feel scared of it or telling you.

TP: Mm-hmm.

PT: I don't know. Maybe it is the habitual "Wait, is that what you really want to say?" Maybe it is the automatic censoring, or . . .

TP: It's also new what is happening here, it seems to me.

[Reframing caution as part of transformation: tremulous affects—the kind of nervousness that is not fear and is

**not real inhibition but is part of many new experiences
for most people.]**

PT: Yeah.

TP: It's not that we've never, we've certainly had many moments
of connection, but this feels very alive and it feels very new,
and it feels like you are pretty consciously taking another step
with me.

PT: Mm-hmm.

TP: And pretty consciously revealing more, and letting me see
more.

PT: (**Nodding and gazing at TP**) Right. (**Looking away**) I don't
know. It kind of reminds me. I made the connection with the
same feeling when things are going really, really well at work.

TP: Mm.

PT: When I feel really on top of things and sure of myself, I guess.

TP: Mm-hmm. Wow.

PT: But obviously in a very different, like in a personal realm,
which is definitely new (**laughing**) to connect those two
feelings. [**PT describing experience of self-at-best, now
emerging within an interpersonal-emotional context.**]

TP: Wow. So what is that like?

PT: Um.

TP: To have this sense of yourself as being strong and effective,
but interpersonally, and very open.

PT: Yeah, um, I guess it is kind of intoxicating. It is kind of, it feels
like it is filling up (**moving hands across shoulders and
out**). [**More transformational affects: mastery/joy.**]

TP: It is funny that you say that 'cause I had a similar association
when you were talking about the energy coming up, and you
did this with your fingers, and I had this image of champagne
bubbles.

PT: Yeah! Yeah, yeah, yeah. Kind of a bubble, definitely.

TP: And it is not even ten o'clock in the morning!

PT: (**Laughing**) Exactly. What a way to start the day! (**Gazes at
TP and then away**)

TP: (**Pause to make space**) Tell me, if you can, what happens in these little moments when you really look at me and let me look in your eyes. You don't have to define it. [**TP now experientially exploring the gaze itself.**]

PT: Mm-hmm.

TP: But just tell me what is going on inside.

PT: I think there is kind of a pause, like almost (**pause, stopping to gaze at TP**). I don't know. I guess that I am waiting for either some sort of sign from you or some, I guess some feeling in me that is like the reverse that doesn't happen. But it is like, "Okay, where is it?" kind of feeling (**holding gaze with TP**).

TP: (**Slowly, gently**) So, you are just really checking me out (**PT nods**) and really checking in with your own internal experience while you are doing that, making sure everything is okay. [**PT is feeling and dealing while relating.**]

PT: Yeah.

TP: And how is it?

PT: It's kind of, it is okay, but I feel poised for it not to be. Like I don't trust it to last (**gazing at TP, looking away, and then resuming gaze**).

TP: Any reactions to hearing yourself say that?

PT: It is a little sad to hear. And I kind of realize that that is what I am waiting for. That I am waiting for that sadness or that fear, or . . . I can say to myself, "Okay well it is really new and something to learn to trust" (**resuming gaze**).

Perhaps we have trained our patients well to be on the lookout for pathology—their own, specifically—or psychotherapy attracts people who are quite sensitive to and aware of their own neurotic tendencies. Or perhaps as people we are inclined to cling to our old habits when we feel the tremulousness of change. Whatever its origin, the emergence of self-doubt and the propensity to drop into despairing states about the self in light of the emergence of something new are robust phenomena. Perhaps more than others, psychodynamically trained clinicians need to be careful with our own similar fascination and our willingness to follow the patient when they go into hopeless states in the middle of a transformational process. In moments such as these, when yellow signal affects are clear, this proclivity is essentially a distraction, a temptation to give into what is known and familiar rather than to stay in uncharted waters and with the discomfort they elicit. Fortunately, here, the patient begins to self-correct, and the therapist supports that correction and maintains the focus on the new, emergent, transformative experience and all it has to offer, discomfort included.

> *TP*: Mm-hmm. And what's that like? [**Invitation to stay with the new.**]
>
> *PT*: It is reassuring, I guess and it also [**accepting the invitation**] if I just let myself stay, as opposed to running away to think about it, I kind of realize that those bad things aren't there. It reminds me of jumping into that hole and not really finding anything. [**PT referencing earlier work with frightened and frightening parts of self of Chapter 4.**]
>
> *TP*: Right. Mm-hmm. And what's that like when you let go of those fearful thoughts and what you realize, if I am understanding you, is that there isn't anything bad? It isn't scary?
>
> *PT*: Yeah.
>
> *TP*: What's that like for you?
>
> *PT*: It's kind of *amazing* in the full sense of the word; like "wow, really? Okay." [**Transformational affects: the realization affects.**]
>
> *TP*: Wow. Uh-huh.
>
> *PT*: It is kind of freeing, I guess.
>
> *TP*: Can you stay with that? Just let yourself take that in? It sounds *wonderful.*
>
> *PT*: Mm-hmm (**PT gazing at TP for a long time**). It feels like there is all this (**hand across chest and out toward shoulder**) room, you know. There's all this space of like, "Oh, what do I do with all of this?" (**laughing**). [**Core state phenomena: sense of openness/space.**]
>
> *TP*: Uh-huh (**delighted tone**). It's like a new four-bedroom house or something.
>
> *PT*: Right, exactly.

TP: And you don't have enough furniture for it yet.

PT: Yeah, I could spread out a little.

TP: (**Delighted**) You get to go shopping.

PT: Exactly (**big smile**). Buy something new (**gazing at TP**).

In part because of moments like these in sessions, AEDP has recently added another category of transformational affects called the realization affects, affectionately called the "wow!" affects. It captures our clinical experience that people frequently access deep feelings of awe, amazement, wonder, compassion, and even humility in the wake of the experience of transformation and the new understanding that brings. While compassion is also a hallmark of core state, when it first arises it is both deeply felt and very present as the overriding emotional experience, rather than part of an overall state of being present, calm, centered, and so on.

> *TP*: (**Long pause during gaze**) How are you experiencing me right now, just as you're kind of aware of this space opening up in yourself, and you have continued to put aside the fearful thoughts and be present here with me in a very open, vulnerable way?
>
> *PT*: (**Pause**) I guess I feel like you're (**long pause**). I guess I am getting too caught up in the words. I guess I feel like you're very caring . . .
>
> *TP*: Mm-hmm.
>
> *PT*: Um, and receptive, but maybe a little neutral. Or just a little careful. That there are times when I feel more like you really are responding to me, with the smiling or whatever, but that there's definitely, I don't know, like a "don't scare her" stillness that is going on. [**Another now moment. PT is about to shake things up again. This is also a very clear moment of dyadic affect regulation. Now that she has allowed herself to be regulated by the TP and to relax, she notices the TP and gives feedback that permits a further deepening of and risk taking in their relationship.**]
>
> *TP*: Don't scare you? Uh-huh.

PT: Yeah. It's like, "Okay, I am here and I am not threatening."

TP: So what's it like for you to experience me in that way? That is very interesting 'cause I think that is probably right on. That's very perceptive of you. [**Dyadic expansion of consciousness. TP is now challenged to let go of more protective layers of what has been their implicit relational knowing.**]

PT: I appreciate it. I need it! But it does feel a little (**pause**), I guess "less real" comes to mind, but I don't know if that is really true.

TP: Like you are ready for more? [**TP speaking to PT's developing resilient capacity and transformance strivings.**]

PT: Yeah, well (**rolling eyes, looking dubious, but smiling**), I don't know, kind of.

TP: Uh-huh.

PT: Like at the very beginning when you actually smiled when I said, I don't even remember, and I was like "oh, wait" or when I just said I want a connection.

TP: Right.

PT: And you had an immediate response to that.

TP: Mm-hmm.

PT: And I had to be like, "Okay, wait, do I really want this or not?"

TP: Right.

PT: I guess I feel like you are doing the right thing instead of just reacting . . .

TP: (**Soft tone, slow**) Mmm. I am sorry about that [**TP attempting to repair disruption, or disjuncture.**]

PT: (**Laughing**)

TP: No really, because I have felt *so* connected to you and *so* excited. But you are picking up on my being careful about not overwhelming you so that you run away.

PT: Yeah.

TP: I think part of you is saying to me, "It's okay, I can handle more."

PT: Right.

TP: But the other part of you is saying, "I am not sure about that."

[TP naming what she had been experiencing throughout

the session, which was yellow signal affects: green then some red, openness and then some reservation or fear, approach then withdrawal.]

PT: Yeah, that's definitely how it feels. It feels like it might have been overwhelming, but yeah, that I am, most of me appreciates, but yeah, there is a little part that's like, "But wait, I want more of that."

TP: Mm-hmm. So what do you want? (**Pause**) I think this is wonderful that you are saying, and it's funny, every time you say that, it really invites me in more. I really feel invited in more. I really want to know what you want. It feels like it gives me permission.

PT: Yeah (**pause**). I guess what comes to mind is that I want more feedback. But, something like, "When you say that it seems like . . . you're pulling away when you say that."

TP: Mm-hmm.

PT: I guess I want to see more of my effect on you, in you, as opposed to the "Okay, I am here and you can be however you want to be" kind of feeling.

True Dyadic Affect Regulation: The Therapist's Changing Role as the Patient Becomes More Resilient

The transformational other needs to be affected by the self. And when the process of transformation involves a focus on the therapeutic relationship explicitly, as it does here, the patient's self needs to have a real sense of having an impact on the other in order for the fullness of that transformation to happen. While this can at times be very challenging for the therapist (it is easier to hide, as I was doing in some ways above by being "careful"), it is also very liberating. The vulnerability on the part of the therapist to allow herself to be affected and, more, to make that explicit helps deepen the relational security of the patient and avoids the patient slipping into a sad solipsism. As the importance of this relates to Catherine, in particular, it echoes an unmet need in her relationships with both parents. Her father was too self-involved and insecure to allow her to be a separate self with different ideas and feelings. He aggressively took over to the point that she developed a deep and lasting mistrust of herself and her own perceptions, intentions, values, desires, and so forth. Her mother, who had intentions to be loving and supportive, was often an "as if" self, was enmeshed with her daughter, and often responded in a manner that felt supportive but like she was "doing the right thing." Their relationship often did not feel very "real" to Catherine, but it was the only thing she had to depend on. And so, her passionate push for more and deeper connection, her vigilance about the therapist responding to her in an authentic and connected way, is a wonderful assertion of self, an expression of her deep resilience, and an awareness of her true and trustworthy desires.

TP: That feels really nice.

PT: Good, it feels good to say (**pause, gazing at TP**). And a little like, "Oh my God, what have I done?" (**laugh**).

TP: (**Laugh**) What does it feel like you have done?

PT: It's a little like, "What if she takes me up on it?" [**More tremulous affects.**]

TP: (**Somewhat playfully**) Well, I probably am going to take you up on it. It feels very good. The whole, it's all felt very good. I think your feedback to me in these last couple of minutes is absolutely wonderful supervision.

PT: (**Smiling**)

TP: You know, really and exactly, what I need. 'Cause I think you have really grown. And the stuff you have been doing in the group is just making it possible for you to do more of this. And I just feel really welcoming of it. And I think what you are saying to me is "I can do more, I can do more."

PT: Yeah.

TP: And because you can do more, I can do more. [**TP explicit about the impact of PT on her and on their relationship.**]

PT: Mm-hmm. That feels right.

TP: It's like I have to catch up to you.

PT: (**Laugh**) Right, yeah.

TP: What's it like to hear me say that? [**Metaprocessing.**]

PT: It's good. Like it feels like, "Oh, okay, there are other possibilities." Like we can go so much further. [**This is transformance
in full swing; the sense of freedom, possibility, safe vulnerability, optimism, and hopefulness. It gives her fuel
for her life and for her continued healing.**]

The next week Catherine came in reporting excited anticipation, but
also, with a laugh, "performance anxiety." Despite that, she described
her experience of the previous session in the following way: "It felt
like something new. And it felt like moving towards where I wanted
to be. You know that it was, I don't know. It was like, 'okay that's how
I want to feel. That's the connection that I want. That's the truth that
I want.' Kind of awake, in-the-moment feeling." She went on to say
how much she appreciated the equity in the therapeutic relationship.
She revealed that part of the relief that followed being able to ask
for more, related to her constant wondering about what is "really"
going on inside other people. This she subsequently linked to her
mother, who tried to do many of the "right" things but was cloaked in
so much false self that was evident to Catherine, but not something
to be acknowledged. What she owned more deeply in this session
was her deep desire to connect to other people, a desire that a few
months later led to her to pursue having a baby on her own, which
she later abandoned in favor of pursuing more friendships and the
possibility of a romantic partnership.

I presented this transcript because I think it demonstrates how
therapists oriented toward restoring resilience might notice, feel,
and listen to the pulse of change that occurs in their patients every
day. As people feel safe, they reveal more of themselves, they take
more risks, they dare to be more vulnerable. And at each level of
vulnerability their neuroception, or subconscious system of threat
detection (Porges, 2009), evaluates whether or not it is safe to remain
there and to possibly explore further. Much as the newly toddling
baby looks to his mother when he is just about to step into snow for
the first time or pet a strange animal, we look to each other for clues
about our safety and, specifically, our safety with one another. Our
patients do that with us all the time, consciously and unconsciously,

implicitly and explicitly, even when we think they are mostly working things out on their own. The more attentive we are to what is already resilient in them, the more attentive they become to it, and the more aware they become of the sacrifices made for the sake of their current resilient capacity. As they feel seen, cared for, and understood, their own self-compassion deepens, and the figure and ground shift in their vision. Mindful of the limits imposed and the sacrifices made, they become interested in and moved by the power of the resilience potential itself, and specifically its transformance strivings—the propulsive force of change that beats inside of them all of the time. This force is not fearful. It is not fettered. It knows what it desires and of what it feels capable. It is always on the lookout for people and environments in which to reveal itself (Fosha, 2009), and we should always be on the lookout for it when it makes its sometimes fleeting, but terribly vital, appearance.

Summary

This chapter focused on occasions of change, whether they arise as glimmers of transformance from the patient or are facilitated by the therapist. We looked at different ways of understanding and recognizing change as it is happening. This change is in the direction of building a more resilient self. Affective neuroscience and interpersonal neurobiology emphasize the importance of emotion regulation and right-brain-to-right-brain communication to the building up of resilience and complexity, especially in the capacity to rapidly return to positive affect states after negative affect states have been induced. This capacity is relationally emblematic of secure attachment relationships and should also mark the resilience-engendering therapeutic relationship. Becoming attentive to and aware of what the Boston Change Process Study Group calls "now moments" is a way of recognizing and seizing moments of potential change and responding to them in creative and authentic ways that further invite the patient and the dyad into new, expanded (i.e., more resilient) ways of being and relating. Metaprocessing, a technique unique to AEDP, catalyzes the natural change and healing moments of therapy and deepens them by focusing affectively, experientially, somatically, and existentially on how the patient experiences small and big moments of transformation, thus creating not just a moment but a spiral of transformation.

Finally, we looked at a transcript of resilience as promise, in which the patient goes back and forth between trusting transformance strivings for greater authenticity, self-revelation, and connection and hiding from them. She is very much a self-in-transition accompanied by the therapist as transformational other, who is reading and responding to her verbal and nonverbal (right-brain) cues in order to help elaborate that part of her that wants to be herself and herself in connection. In that context, we looked at the importance of mutual gaze, how vulnerable an experience that can be for the therapist and patient alike, and the fact that the nature of dyadic affect regulation changes as the patient becomes more resilient and the dyad goes through what Tronick calls a dyadic expansion of consciousness.

Part 4

RESILIENCE AS TRANSFORMANCE/ FLOURISHING

CHAPTER 6

Freedom Is Frightening

Trembling and Savoring in the Wake of Transformation

Every time I want to make this movement I almost faint;
the very same moment I admire absolutely, I am seized
with a great anxiety.

-Kierkegaard (1983, p. 48)

In the last chapter, the patient left us with the statement that "there are other possibilities . . . we can go so much further." This is the statement of someone whose resilience is being restored. She is disposed toward ongoing development, growth, and health. Rather than her resilience potential expressing itself as constriction, self-protection, or resistance, she is open, connected to others, and safely vulnerable and feels capable and interpersonally effective. Her resilient capacity has increased and is increasingly more fitting and adaptive to her environment, which is, generally speaking, welcoming of her. Of course, this transformation from resistance to transformance is not a once-and-for-all kind of thing. It happens over and over in life and even in a given session. But the more it happens and the more powerfully it happens, the more deeply resilient a person becomes and the more positive experiences of self, other, and the world they have to draw upon when life again becomes difficult, as it inevitably does.

Everything in this book up until this point has been about the transition: the self struggling to move forward, to let go, to face life in its painfulness and beauty, to become vulnerable, to develop more currently adaptive defenses, and to cultivate healthier relationships. This chapter is about the *arrival*, exploring more of what *transformance strivings* look like when they are unencumbered by excessive fear, doubt, or resistance. It also discusses the importance of positive emotions in the process of resilience, of healing, of being well, and of flourishing that is elaborated in Chapter 7. Related to that, we will look at the *capacity to savor* and its role in that ephemeral "good life" that all generations and people seek in their own ways.

This chapter also examines that tender time in the wake of powerful and meaningful change, how people may react to it, and the importance of recognizing it as a transitional space rather than a regression. There is an "open space" (to use a term from the Boston Change Process Study Group [Lyons-Ruth, Bruschweiler-Stern, Harrison, Morgan, Nahum, & Sander, 2001; Stern, 1998, 2007; Mayes, 2005; Tronick, 1998]), a pregnant pause in which the possibility of meaningful and lasting integration is very present, but so too is the possibility of fear, and even retreat. The therapist as the transformational other in such contexts needs to be comfortable with these possibilities and able and motivated to facilitate the ongoing transformance motivations of the patient, normalizing fear, validating choice, savoring the already transformed state, and celebrating the possibility of the new.

In that context, this chapter looks at how powerful transformation can be quite frightening. A case study illustrates one man's experience of that and his therapist's response. We look at the role of recognition and intersubjectivity in restoring resilience and the use of open space in those two processes. Case examples and transcripts of sessions demonstrate the full flowering of transformance as expressed in the experience of having "arrived" and the experience of savoring and gratitude. The chapter ends with a brief discussion of the importance of desire—listening for, helping elaborate, and following it in the process of transformation.

Freedom Is Frightening

Becoming free of misery and unnecessary suffering or struggle is presumably the whole point of the psychotherapeutic endeavor. And certainly, if patients are willing and we are even marginally effective, they achieve a reduction in symptoms, an increase in productivity or clarity, more satisfaction in their relationships and work, and they know themselves better—something we value a priori. This is certainly an important kind of freedom. But the capacity to be happy, to flourish, to self-actualize, and to savor transcends the freedom from misery, and not everyone ventures that far. The challenge of surrendering to the fullness of oneself, of letting go of the limitations we wittingly and unwittingly impose on ourselves, is beautifully revealed in a session between "Dennis" and Diana Fosha (Fosha, 2009b). The following are my own thoughts on what transpired between the two of them, what we can learn from it clinically and theoretically, and what it has to say about evolved and ever more complex manifestations of the resilience potential, as well as our habitual or reflexive response of fear to that kind of expansiveness.

In Fosha's account of her work with Dennis, the patient is experiencing and articulating an existential struggle, one that many of us experience at turning points in life. It illustrates the reaches of the resilience potential in the form of transformance. Having moved beyond survival and "bouncing back," when the right conditions exist, the part of ourselves that works always on behalf of the self is freed to explore the boundlessness of the self. I am not referring to the "get everything you want just by believing you are capable of it" schemes that tempt us in myriad forms in our culture but, rather, a more spiritual, deeply personal process of transformation that ushers in not only personal happiness but also compassion, wisdom, surrender, and humility—those qualities that make us more humanely human. Having discovered a solid and solidly good self, we become more capable of letting that self go into a deeper sense of unity with the world and others. As Kierkegaard put it, "That which is suspended is not relinquished but is preserved in the higher" (1983, p. 54).

CASE STUDY:
"I Am An Old Dog and This Is a New Trick"

Fosha's (2009a) patient Dennis is in his second round of treatment. A divorced father of two and a successful professional, he has overcome by this point in the work both his depression and his substance abuse, and he also has processed much of his early-life trauma. In a period of much progress in his life, he nevertheless comes to this session not knowing what to talk about, which is unusual for him. He feels as if he has plateaued and that perhaps his therapeutic work is done. This is not an uncommon exchange in a therapy that has been going reasonably well. Most therapists start to wonder in these moments if the pause is caused by defense, by a need to review what has happened in light of original goals for the treatment, or by the possibility of termination. Here, however, the therapist remains open, curious, and not compelled to define or direct, and the patient's plateau now becomes a very pregnant pause in the work. She allows for an open space to explore the vague sense of plateau and of accomplishment. Provided the space, the patient recognizes his own resistance to the optimism he feels in the wake of multiple and important life changes.

The therapist's stance is one of *radical curiosity*," as my colleague Steven Shapiro calls it. There is no judgment. She is not trying to change, reframe, pathologize, or glorify what the patient feels. She offers some of her sense of things but then gives back the reins to the patient, several times explicitly stating her curiosity and her openness to what is emerging in him. I think it is not just her curiosity but her faith in the process and her trust that what arises in him is meaningful and important and has something to tell them that allows him, over and over, to surrender himself to the process of unfolding this "resistance."

I think of this as an example of relational transformance: the overarching motivational force, operating in relationships, that strives toward genuine contact, optimal relatedness, transparency, authenticity, and intimacy. It manifests in the coordinated state but also underlies relational partners' attempts to understand one another and to repair disruptions and their willingness to expand their selves in relation to one another. It operates in secure dyads but is also latent and waiting in insecure dyads.

What this session demonstrates that I think is relevant to a depth-oriented, resilience approach is an instance of two complete minds struggling to come in contact with one another, one needing recognition in order for the self to be better known to the self, and the other struggling to recognize and to actively communicate not simply what she understands (when it is finally fully formed) but what she is witnessing, what she is experiencing, and what she is understanding as she goes. The self is in transition from a more conservative, self-protective to a more transformance-guided way of being in the world and in relation to oneself. And the therapist is a transformational other not because she knows how this is going to go or even what the patient needs to do but because she allows herself to be open to the unfolding of this, to trust the process, to trust what is authentically coming from the patient, even as it is difficult and amorphous. As it relates to relational transformance, it is evident in this session that the therapist, too, is quite vulnerable, at times "vibrating with uncertainty," as she describes her patient. In the hopes of a deeper connection between him and her and between him and himself, she surrenders: rather than pushing an agenda or hiding behind silence, she accompanies him, reflects him back to himself—and not simply her cool detached "observations" but also her subjective experience of him in any given moment. She is with him—she is present and engaged in a palpable way. She uses herself to help him find his way. This is a fundamentally intersubjective moment in which the patient's awareness of the therapist's affective syntony and interest, as well as her openness to exploration and tentative, but accurate, articulation of what she is experiencing with him, helps him recognize himself. That further stimulates his curiosity to understand the avoidance, the fear, and the comfort with misery he recognizes in himself in light of that feeling of optimism and the hope and joy that he is "standing on the edge" of.

As the patient is free to explore the resistance to the new, to his own optimism, he recognizes his attachment to the self that was not yet transformed. He states, quite boldly and with alarming honesty, "You know, uh . . . I am really very accustomed to my life's miseries" (Fosha, 2009a, p. 43). He speaks about what he was able to glimpse in the process of transformation that involved the "dredging up" of old things related to his family. He describes that glimpse at possibility as being "searing": "It's almost like I can't quite look at it squarely.... Even when I tell you that it's searing, I sort of feel like I'm standing on the edge of something and I can only look sideways at it" (p. 44). Whether this man considers himself religious, spiritual, or not, one can argue that he is having a spiritual experience and that he is not quite sure what to do with it or how to respond to it.

This is important to our exploration here because his articulation of what makes it difficult to embrace the good things of life provides words for an experience probably all of us have at some point. Certainly, in my own clinical practice, I have seen it many times. We resist the good; we cling to what we know or feel in control of versus what we do not. This is not to say that we are not capable of that kind of embrace or that we do not deeply, deeply want it. Rather, sometimes it is hard, and we need to be accompanied in the challenge of embracing life and joy as much as we need to be accompanied and reassured when we are in the midst of struggle. As the self is transitioning to ever healthier, more integrated, and more joyful manifestations of self, the transformational other can help to explore resistance to that joy, or the fears connected to living a fuller life.

Is he defensive in saying, "I can't quite look at it squarely . . . I can only look at it sideways"? Or is this a very common human response to something that feels larger than ourselves, even if the only thing that is larger is the self we are becoming? It seems that some amount of fear or tremulousness may be part of "taking in" or integrating the impact of profound transformation. I think this is also where humility comes into play, where our sense of smallness is not riddled with shame because we simultaneously feel surrounded by a connection to benevolence, or love, or hope, or a larger sense of meaning or purpose. It is the kind of humility, the kind of feeling that is expressed in bowing one's head not in humiliation but in consciousness of the full presence of the moment, of the other, of the truth, or of the true self.

Because these moments of transformation involve tremulousness and fear, we can retreat from them. We can avoid them and what they may ask of us or promise to us. Kierkegaard wrote, "Every time I want to make this movement, I almost faint; the very same moment I admire absolutely, I am seized with great anxiety" (1983, p. 48). We can always go back to the familiar—people often do.

Thus, the role of the transformational other at these times, as a witnessing, validating, regulating presence, is so important. Freedom is frightening, but people need to know that it is still okay to keep moving, to be free. This kind of transition, specifically that which involves metaprocessing momentous transformation of the self, goes beyond letting go into the feeling of the moment, about a relationship, concerning a situation. It is letting go into one's essence, into one's source, one's resilience potential itself, into that "light. . . . that most frightens us" (Williamson, 1992). It is about being innervated and animated by our transformance strivings, by hope, joy, curiosity, and courage. It is about allowing the full flourishing of the self unencumbered by excessive doubt, unnecessary shame, restrictive fear, or paralyzing passivity or lethargy—all habits built up over time to protect us from something that is no longer, in fact, a threat.

Dennis is eventually only aware of a feeling of discomfort, and the therapist encourages him to "stay there" and to allow himself to be aware that she is there with him, waiting, open, curious, trusting. He describes something being on the edge of his vision and then becomes aware of the ways in which he avoids seeking out what this is in his life through various kinds of mindless busyness. The therapist responds to this important insight with some playfulness about his "being in big trouble" now that the he has outed himself and his defenses. He responds playfully with a very apt association to a cartoon of a dog on a high wire who says, "I just realized this is fun, but I am an old dog and this is a new trick." It may be the safety or the relief of this playful exchange that allows for the breakthrough. Everything clicks into place: what emerges is an extraordinarily coherent and poignant understanding, as he realizes that what is on the edge of his awareness is "who I am supposed to be, the person who I was always meant to be, who I just can't seem to get to." He is realizing that he is frightened by all the possibility he contains within him. And now, in saying and knowing this, he is in contact with the essence of his resilience potential and with his own trans-formance strivings in a very pure way.

The impact of play. It cannot be known how this part of the session would have unfolded had the therapist not been playful and joked with the patient, but I would wager that it was this playfulness that allowed for the subsequent breakthrough in the patient's awareness and affect. They sit together with the discomfort, and the patient begins to realize that he fills his time with busyness to avoid something. This is a now moment. The therapist, who is not afraid of what is coming up, has a big reaction to this insight, this moment of recognition, and responds in an authentic, creative, and playful way: "You're in big trouble." This is a moment of meeting. She offers back to him what might have felt heavy or overwhelming in a humorous way and in so doing may have made it more palatable, less frightening. He has just outed himself and his defenses, and she is playfully ominous: "trouble." He responds in kind with his own memory of an apt and funny cartoon. They both laugh heartily, and in the next moment he realizes (he has a breakthrough of the unconscious) that he has been avoiding the person he is supposed to be. That is a pretty big breakthrough!

Joking and laughter are primary manifestations of adult play (Panksepp, 1998). Panksepp (1998, 2009) includes playfulness as one of seven basic emotional systems, which requires no input from the neocortex. He notes that play centers are rich in opioids and located near ascending dopamine systems. Playfulness is inter-rupted by fear and isolation, and Panksepp notes that play is pos-sible only when confidence and affiliation are present or restored after disruption: "Playfulness is probably an experience-expectant process that brings young animals to the perimeter of their social knowledge, to psychic places where they must learn about what they can or cannot do to each other" (2009, p. 16). I wonder if the therapist's playfulness in this context allowed the patient to realize what he could do *with* her: perhaps this is not so frightening, perhaps he can do this with her.

It also seems probable that this moment introduced shared positive affect between the two that allowed the patient to have a broader sense of his own resourcefulness. Fredrickson's broaden and build theory of positive emotion (Fredrickson, 1998; Fredrickson & Branigan, 2005), discussed more in Chapter 7, suggests that positive affect expands people's problem-solving skills and their awareness in general, as opposed to fear or anger, which tend to narrow our focus and limit our problem-solving ability. The release of opioids in the brain during play episodes (Panksepp, 1998) may have been just enough for Dennis to feel less afraid of what was on the edge of his vision and more open to the intensely positive feelings that came in the wake of this breakthrough (see below).

Elevation, awe, beauty, and being moved. As patient and therapist are able to stay with what feels like fear around the sense of possibility, Dennis realizes that he could take off the rest of his misery as if it were an exoskeleton, and this brings tears. What started out feeling like fear he realizes is "searing" because it is uncontainably happy. The transformational affects that AEDP calls *mastery affects*, specifically that of joy, flood in now in abundance, and the patient is literally moved. His eyes are filled with tears, but they are open wide as if in a state of wonder. His arms open at the idea of taking off the skeleton (the protection of the misery) and putting it aside, and he mimics doing precisely that (Chapter 7 provides more detail on the importance of positive affect to the psychotherapeutic process). These moments are also examples of *recognition affects*, the experience of being struck by an important and emotionally relevant and resonant awareness. I have found that people often experience some sense of wonder, awe, amazement, and even beauty or the sublime in such moments of recognition.

This experience not only is a marker that healing is happening but also fuels ongoing healing. It provides energy for the continual process of transformation, and because it is so emotional, it can leave a potent memory of hope and transformation to draw upon later. This kind of emotional experience and energy is creative, is welcoming, is open but discerning; it moves us to do something, even if that something is simply receiving in a nondefended way. Feeling moved and grateful, but also awe, compassion, desire, the sense of possibility and potential—these fuel us for life-enhancing experiences, and they coexist with, but can be covered by, forces of boredom, withdrawal, stagnation, resistance, and the like.

In some later moments of moved reflection, Dennis has an association to the movie *Cocoon*, in which aliens are looking for places for their shells to hatch beings of sheer light. This is the image and analogy that goes with his feeling moved to let go of the "shell" of his misery and to embrace the possibility of happiness. In fact, he contrasts the rather simple awareness that he could just be happy instead of holding happiness for a future contingent on so many external things being just right. He is realistically aware of the difficulty, in fact, of letting go of misery but is deeply moved by the experiential sense of the sheer possibility of it. The therapist goes back to an earlier point and shares again her own feeling of being moved by his seeing, at the edge of his vision, "the person (he) is meant to be," and the patient is once again moved to tears. "It just feels very beautiful," he says as he begins to sob, and he is left speechless for a time in the wake of this. The therapist stays with him in a very present, dyadically coordinated way. These are "tears of possibility" as opposed to "tears of sadness," according to the patient. It is another wave of transformational affects.

The emotional experience of beauty, awe, and wonder, as transformational affects, occur in the wake of something being changed or transformed in the self. We are uplifted and moved, our cynicism has a moment of reprieve, our worldview is suddenly opened in some important way, our minds or hearts are expanded, our sense of self is enlarged, or the relationship of our selves to the world is elaborated in some important way. We are more permeable.

Johnathan Haidt and his colleagues have argued that certain positive emotions are elicited by witnessing others act from their best, most social, and compassionate selves (Algoe & Haidt, 2009; Algoe, Haidt, & Gable, 2008; Haidt, 2000, 2003). Specifically, he writes about *elevation*, being the opposite of disgust and a "warm, uplifting feeling that people experience when they see unexpected acts of human goodness, kindness, and compassion" (Haidt, 2000, pp. 1–2). It is interesting that Dennis seems to be elevated or uplifted in seeing "at the edge of (his) vision" the image of the self he is meant to be. It is like he is witnessing a better, more whole self (i.e., a being of pure light). In Haidt's research, the feeling of elevation was found to be different than feelings of happiness, in that people who feel elevated are more likely to describe warm, pleasant, or tingling feelings in their chest, and such experiences were associated with prosocial, affiliative feelings of wanting to help others or to become better people themselves (Haidt, 2003).

Following this last round of tears, the patient is calm, reflective, and solidly in core state. He feels a warmth in his heart and has an image of savoring a pear, both satisfying hunger and quenching thirst. And he reports a sense that something permanently changed in these many minutes of exploring this uncharted territory of abandoning misery and embracing joy.

The Importance of Open Space

The Boston Change Process Study Group's concept of "open space" between the therapist and the patient (see chapter 5) is a space in which each partner takes a few moments to be alone with himself in the presence of the other, as if metabolizing what has happened and what may therefore be possible going forward (Sander, 1988; Stern, 1998). This is the pause before the return to being with each other in the now expanded implicit relational knowing of the dyad. Something similar happens in the self in relation to itself following transformative or restorative experiences, or moments of meeting oneself. One needs to pause, to recognize what has happened, how things are different, and how the self is different, perhaps to grieve what was not able to be and to dream of what might come. In some ways this is a vulnerable time. If handled with tenderness, care, curiosity, exploration, and support, it can be a very meaningful time of recognition, recollecting, savoring, gratitude, and integration.

One of the things that is evident in the session discussed above is how much space the therapist provides the patient and encourages him to give to himself. It is not agenda driven; she is not looking to fix anything or even to know anything with certainty. There are multiple now moments in the session between the patient and therapist and between the patient and himself. These are followed by many moments of meeting in which each responds authentically and creatively (including playfully) to the other and to the moment itself. It is very clear that the therapist trusts the patient, wants him to trust himself, and trusts his intrapsychic unfolding and the relational unfolding between the two of them. At the end of the session he tells her how powerful it was for her to encourage them to be uncomfortable together and for him to be patient with his own frustration and unknowing.

To my mind, the risk of any model of psychotherapy is that of losing the capacity or willingness to really listen and to try to understand with depth what another is saying. Our maps are incredibly useful, but they are not the landscape itself. As Stephen Mitchell (2002) astutely points out, the *other* is always a mystery to us in some way or at some level, no matter how much we do understand, no matter how keenly we see the other, no matter how intimately we know the other. In the open space between therapist and patient, as their relationship with one another takes on new contours and complexities and resolves confusions, there is a deep respect for this mystery that keeps us open to one another. Allowing for this also helps the patient to learn to remain open to and trust in the mystery of the self and its unfolding over the course of his lifetime.

Open space in the wake of or the midst of things shifting is not the same as a more passive open-endedness. To provide too much space around defense or anxiety threatens to leave the patient too alone, either working too hard by himself or not working at all. Allowing for open space is most productive when it is reserved for breathing together in the wake of change or transformation or for powerful witnessing or accompanying as someone is in the midst of what might be a painful or confusing, but bearable, transition. Anxiety, whether general or specifically in response to intimacy, threatens to rob many people and dyads of this lovely, open space. The more comfortable the therapist is in just being, and in being present, the more reliably she can foster the dyad making use of such productive openness. Ultimately, open space used or provided well is reverent.

Identification and Elaboration: Recognition and Intersubjectivity in Restoring Resilience

Is it possible that deep down we long to give this up, to "come clean" as part of an even more general longing to be known, recognized? Might this longing also be joined by a corresponding wish to know and recognize the other?

Transitional affects are those often brief affects in which the patient is aware of something different emerging, of some deeper affect coming up, of some awareness coming into play. It is important that the therapist recognize these moments because they can be fleeting, and people can readily return to what is more comfortable and perhaps defensive. The transitional affects include heralding affects (see Figure 2.1), which are glimmers of core affective experience (the grit teeth of anger, the small tear of sadness, the sense of clarity about something that has been shrouded in confusion), and green signal affects, which express openness to experience, curiosity, safety and a readiness to shift to deeper work. When patients experience these transitional affects, they are not yet fully immersed in a core affective experience—they are only on the edge of it, as Dennis was on the edge of an authentic self state for much of the session described above. But what is happening in these moments is very important. They are recognizing something within the self, and even if they are frightened or confused by it or their habit is always to turn away from it, they sense that it is something important, something real.

Fosha (2009b) makes the distinction between emotion and recognition. Emotion involves accommodation, expansion, and the awareness of difference. Recognition, on the other hand, involves the assimilation of the self, the fitting together of two apparently disparate parts (whether self and other, self and self, self and experience, etc). Recognition presumes some kind of similarity that is not entirely foreign, that is, recognizable. If something that is new is to be accepted, worked with, and integrated, there has to be some response to it as possibly having to do with the self. Insistent "not me" experiences are the exact opposite of the process of recognition. The dialectic between recognition and emotion is constant in the process of transformation, driven by transformance strivings, cumulatively building resilient capacity, and is marked, appropriately, by a sense of aliveness, or *vitality affects* (Stern, 1985), and the release of tension. The work with Dennis was a perfect example of this dialectic between recognition and emotion as patient and therapist continue to stay with vague feelings of resistance and discomfort, which contain within them the sense of something important. There was something that was making him uncomfortable and against which he was resisting. The therapist encouraged his own capacity to step outside of the discomfort and resistance, to observe them and to be curious about them, rather than be ruled by them or afraid of them and therefore needing to defend.

Jessica Benjamin argues that recognition is part of the emergence of the capacity for intersubjectivity: "Intersubjective theory postulates that the other must be recognized as another subject in order for the self to fully experience his or her subjectivity in the other's presence. This means, first, that we have a need for recognition and second, that we have a capacity to recognize others in return— mutual recognition" (1990, p. 35). It is exactly what is missing in relationships when one or both of the pair are narcissistic and limited in their capacity to see and experience the other as a truly separate other, with a different mind, thoughts, feelings, and reactions. An intrinsic part of this mutual recognition is pleasure, evidenced in infant–mother research (e.g., Beebe & Lachman, 1994; Gianino & Tronick, 1988; Trevarthen, 2005; Tronick, 1989, 2003, 2005; Tronick & Cohen, 1969), in love relationships, and even in benign encounters with strangers. The development of intersubjectivity involves the discovery that "there are other minds out there" (Benjamin, 1990, p. 37) and that those other minds can share our feelings but also may disagree. Benjamin continues, "The need for recognition entails this fundamental paradox: In the very moment of realizing our own independent will, we are dependent on another to recognize it" (p. 39). Benjamin does not discuss the logical corollary, but from this perspective, it also makes sense that in the experience of someone else recognizing what is ours, we are freed to see it more clearly ourselves. This, I think, is the "click" of two pieces coming together (Fosha, 2009, p. 178) that had until that moment been inchoate and relatively formless but now are clear, articulable, and experienced as part of the self.

These moments of recognition—of self by self, self by other, other by self—are immutable aspects of the change process, of the unfolding that happens in so many instances of therapy going right. I want to underscore how this process of recognition and the vitality affects that accompany them are precisely the markers of the self-in-transition, who is being helped to identify and elaborate that which is already present but inchoate, that which is emerging but needs direction, safety, encouragement, and recognition by the transformational other. In the *Velveteen Rabbit*, the little boy relates to the rabbit and loves the rabbit as if it is real, and it is in part that recognition that allows the velveteen rabbit to become real.

The Triumph of Arriving: The Full Flowering
of Transformance

We are not in the realm of invention here. We are in the
realm of mining what is there and learning how to best
access it.

Healing is not simply the receipt and integration of some exogenous
corrective experience but, rather, or also, the realignment of one's
mode of being from resistance to transformance, from conservation
and safety to expansion and freedom. It is a signal switch and a track
change. One starts to use something that has been there but has
been dormant or distorted and therefore unable to serve one's needs
for expansion, exploration, and the elaboration of one's true self.

Looking again at the map of resilience first introduced in Chapter 1, our focus in this chapter is phenomena in the middle and to
the right of Figure 1.5. Throughout this book, we have looked at
moments of transition, at little and big steps away from resilience
expressed as pathology or resistance-driven functioning toward
resilience expressed in more adaptive, transformance-oriented ways.
The next sections focus on what happens in the wake of healing,
what healing looks like, and how to support, deepen, solidify and
expand it and its effects.

The patient, Fiona, is a creative writer and teacher. She had come
for treatment a few years earlier, having done some previous psychoanalytic work that left both her and the therapist frustrated. While
we had a productive and emotionally meaningful first session, she
returned the following week to challenge me with all of her negative
feelings, suspicions, and judgments of me. I soon learned that these
were judgments to which she frequently subjected herself. Positive
experiences, of her self in particular, were highly suspect. She suffered with some social fears and awkwardness that stemmed from
her certainty that others were judging her harshly and some related
performance anxiety around presenting and teaching, despite rou-
tinely receiving glowing praise from her students. She is a very warm,

vivacious, quick-minded, and large-hearted person who essentially feared she was a fraud and that she would be discovered for the very mediocre, possibly dim-witted person she believed herself to be.

In the three or so years we worked together prior to this session, she made great strides in her artistic and teaching careers despite the sometimes crippling anxiety she faced. She slowly let go of denial and processed a lot of feelings toward her parents, who had completely failed to ever be transformational others for anything authentic, unique, and emerging about her. She was saddled with tremendous self-doubt and an aching void, which she called "the pain." She turned to her parents less and less when in need of support or when desirous of sharing an accomplishment and, despite her doubts about their sincerity, turned to friends (including her very supportive husband) and colleagues who believed in her and recognized her talent and hard work.

In the following session, she speaks about having a long meeting with her new boss, by whom she is quite intimidated. In her usual way, she started to overprepare, believing that her knowledge and scholarship were insufficient and that she would be discovered by her boss to be someone with little to offer and undeserving of a position in an intellectually rigorous environment. This somatically rooted anxiety surfaced for her in almost all professional situations. At a certain point in the meeting, she decides to let go of the projected images of how she should be and decides instead to "be herself": to be open and to speak without editing herself. Her boss is open and somewhat vulnerable with her as well, expressing real interest in and encouragement of her and her work. To Fiona's surprise, she is very receptive to her thoughts and ideas. We had a session within hours of that meeting, and the following is what transpired.

CLINICAL VIGNETTE:
"I Realized How Really Grounded I Really Am"—
Resilience as Transformance/Flourishing

PT: It's totally freeing. It's like a whole history of suffering just falling off my shoulders . . . All I feel right now is great. Possibility. I talked a lot. I had a lot to say . . . I felt like "I belong

here" . . . I would want to keep this person (me) in the front . . .
It's powerful and exciting, and you can propel yourself into the
world. [**Postbreakthrough affects of relief and lightness
and transformational affects: mastery (pride and joy)
and the realization affects.**]

TP: Where do you notice that in your body? [**Somatic-experien-
tial focus on transformed state.**]

PT: It's like I've gained height . . . It's like a slinky that's no longer
coiled. [**Rich, somatically based images are indicative of
deep emotional processing, as well as integration.**]

TP: What happens when you stay with that? [**Expanding exploration of deeply transformative experience.**]

PT: I just feel very awake. I like who I am. (**Pause**) Just the word
"possibility."

TP: Mmm. Sounds wonderful! [**TP joining and resonating with
deeply positive experience of PT.**]

PT: Yeah. And it is so interesting to be in this body. I have this
complete flip from what it was before this lunch where I was
a complete fear-ridden body. [**Continuing with her own
metaprocessing.**] I am aware of the exhaustion I felt, how
much suffering I take into my body when I am not in this
place. It's a totally different psyche. Now I am like "Yeah! I like
myself." [**PT experientially aware of physical and psychological difference between self-at-worst and self-at-best.
Awareness of contrast is also indicative of healing.**]

TP: What would you want to say to the former self from this
place? [**Working with the self-at-worst from the vantage
point of the self-at-best; using the contrast to solidify the transformed state. There is so much history
and experience with the former self, we want to work
actively with the more resourced self in order to retrain
neural pathways and solidify these gains**.]

PT: I want to think about it. (**Pause, then speaking to old
self**) "You so underestimate your power, how you are perceived . . . You are a quiet, thoughtful person. You are unaware
of how you radiate that energy . . . There is so much to you!" I

almost have to say to this self, "You are not seeing you. As vulnerable as it may be and as insightful as you think you are, you are not seeing you" . . . Just on this basic level I got the feeling that she (**referring to her boss**) was enjoying me. And I was enjoying myself. You know how when you're your favorite self, you are not usually wrong? [**The integrated self does not have to exclude parts of the self.**]

Several important phenomena evident in this part of the transcript are relevant to our discussion and understanding of healing and of flourishing. First, the power, the fittedness, the integration involved in her arriving at this place of recognition of self by self provides so much of the energy for deep healing and for moving forward and continuing a spiral of healing and transformation that cannot be achieved when understanding is not experiential or emotional. Second, the integrated, whole, essential, core self does not have to exclude parts of the self. She does not have to dismiss or denigrate her more frightened or diminutive self from this vantage point. Rather, the smaller, frightened self can enjoy the expanded self and can relax. Another patient, in an integrated self state, described himself as feeling "capable" (i.e., self-at-best) and "adult" and from this vantage point recognized that the fear-ridden younger part of him was able to "relax" and "go on vacation" and finally "be a kid again." The expanded self can offer compassion, encouragement, and a wiser perspective to the younger, constrained, or compromised self. The integrated self is de facto compassionate and accepting.

Finally, there is a difference between simply recognizing and receiving positive feedback and the felt sense of being oneself and recognizing the positive reactions that one engenders in others. They both may feel good but differently and to different degrees. The latter feels unambiguously good, easy, natural, relieving (i.e., "I don't have to work so hard") and is affirming. It is accompanied by a sense of relaxed confidence. The former usually feels good but is limited by how much of the positive feedback we recognize as belonging to us. It is easy to partially or fully dismiss this feedback from an other based on a fear or conviction that one cannot be one's real or full self and still be received positively. It's the old "if X *really* knew me, X wouldn't be saying this about me." Fiona's core self recognized something right, true, and real about how her boss was recognizing her, which allowed her to really take it in and be changed by the experience. This is what I mean when I say that while we are trying to help people get to core state (State 4), core state also emerges or reveals itself in small ways to encourage us.

(Continuing where we left off . . .)

TP: And it seems it started from you taking this risk and, on several occasions, deciding to just be yourself.

PT: Yeah. (**Pause, thinking**) This is the thing that really stays with me. At the end of the meeting, she said, "I have one plea." And I thought, "Oh, here she goes." But, instead, she said, "I have these drawings. You seem like someone who does a lot. So could you let me know about openings or shows and maybe we could go together?" . . . So, I was like, "What the fuck?! This is really messing me up!" How do you go from my fears to this power switch? . . . And (her), "Can you let me ride on your coattails?" I can hardly believe it. Can you?

TP: Yes, I can, in fact. Everyone feels this with you. [**TP validating power of her true self that is regularly responded to in highly positive ways by others.**]

PT: . . . She was essentially saying, "We're in the same league." It's the total opposite of my expectations. I am feeling really happy as I am talking to you because I think I am reporting this accurately. [**This comment highlights the importance of the truth sense to experiences of self-at-best and core state.**]

TP: What's this happiness like? [**Experiential focus on affect of happiness; metaprocessing the transformational affect of joy (mastery affects).**]

PT: Light. I feel unburdened . . . I can just go on with my day. It's very light and awake. It makes me want to paint. I don't know how to explain that. I am a painter and I want to paint. [**This is a combination of postbreakthrough affects, mastery affects of joy (State 3), and core state (State 4). There is something about these states that elicits, facilitates, or is associated with the release of play instincts and creativity, just one aspect of the benefits of intense positive affects.**]

TP: Tell me more about that desire and affirmation.

PT: Just as I was talking, I realized how really grounded I really am. It feels like, "This is the real thing!" And I heard that inside and I was like, "This is the truth. All your struggling is about these things that are really important to you." It kind of really encouraged me to go with it. In some ways it maybe helped clarify some things.

TP: Tell me more.

PT: About the conflict between wanting to be talented, but not wanting to be an academic.

TP: Tell me more. It feels okay to not be an academic?

PT: I am not there yet. I think I felt this pull to paint . . . Like someone just gave me this gift . . . and it felt so nourishing. And I just had the feeling from Seline (boss) that maybe she's a frustrated intellectual. There's something there that felt kind of starved. There's a big difference between being the one who is in the moment creating and the one who is watching that person create. And I almost felt like—I used to think, "How can be you an artist and in the academy?"—And I feel like I did it just then. It felt very natural. [**Integration of parts that have previously been experienced as being in conflict. This is also an aspect of core state experience.**] And I was making her laugh a lot!

TP: Hold onto this . . . [**TP encouraging savoring.**]

PT: (**Deep breath**) You know as old as that other stuff feels (e.g. the anxieties about the self), this feels just as old. [**More evidence of the resilience potential; people remember glimpses of it earlier in life when they can fully feel it later. There is a sense that it has "always been there."**]

TP: Tell me more.

PT: I told you about a feeling I had when I was a kid. On my own sometimes, I had this feeling that I had this potential, a certain power and capability that were just there, that were innate. **[Present experience of resilient, embodied, empowered self-at-best, opens memory of early similar self experiences as a child.]**

TP: What is it like for you to reconnect to that other young part of yourself? **[Again we are in territory of discovery and rediscovery, and this is when the opportunity for integration is ripest.]**

PT: It's so hopeful. This is so old in some ways, and I am seeing it actualized. It is here. It is real. When I was young it was more of an out-of-body experience, imagining myself as if I were totally one and illuminated. Wow, it is very real! Not only "you're okay" but "you're gifted, you're successful. There could even be more. It's happening and you're doing it." **[PT marveling at this transformed state. This is an example of the realization affects. It also exemplifies how dreams and daydreams are manifestations of resilience potential and how the living out of a dream, hope, or fantasy often involves the restoration of resilience.]**

TP: Right. Right. It is you! Refound. It is in the moment. It's really great. I am so glad we got to process it right afterward.

In the words of Marianne Williamson, quoted at the start of the introduction to this book, Fiona is "powerful beyond measure." This is a peak moment, of course, but peak moments last longer and nurture us more deeply if they are privileged, elaborated, deepened, and integrated. They do for the self what a long fun date with your spouse or partner, or a heart-to-heart talk with your friend, or an afternoon of play with your children does for those respective relationships. They are restorative, grounding, motivating, and transformative.

If transformance is the force that underlies our healthy strivings toward maximal vitality, genuine contact, and authenticity, then flourishing is the state that results from transformance strivings being unleashed and met with the accomplishments of our goals, the fulfillment of our desires, the discovery of our true selves, the deep connections made with others, and the sense of meaningfulness that accompanies all of this. When people have the experience of having arrived, of actualizing some potential, there is very often the paradoxical sense that what they are experiencing is both old and new. Fiona says poignantly, "You know as old as that other stuff feels (the anxieties about the self), this feels just as old." There is a recognition that this state, while also new, has existed in some form previously—either as an actual memory or as an intuited potential. I think this paradoxical sense of one's experience being both old and new has something to do with desire, which I return to below.

Savoring, Gratitude, and the Practice of Presence

Humans have ordained savoring and the slowing down required to allow for it by imagining that God must have stopped to savor the wonder and goodness of God's own creation. At the end of each day of creation, according to the story of Genesis in the Old Testament, God reflected on what God created that day and said, "It is good." One can imagine God's sense of satisfaction and pleasure in what God was doing. Such satisfaction, presumably, allowed God to "rest" on the seventh day, finding sufficient for the moment all God had done.

Savoring is a conscious, reflective, mindful appreciation of experiences of pleasure, fulfillment, and connection. Bryant and Veroff, in their book *Savoring: A New Model of Positive Experience* (2007), describe it as the "positive counterpart to coping" with stress (p. 2). In other words, it is people's capacity to enjoy positive experiences, and they argue, and I agree, that it is the critical piece of subjective well-being, mental health, and wellness that is not captured simply by looking at how people cope with stress and whether or not they exhibit symptoms. It has to do with an active process of enjoyment and, as we would say in AEDP, "taking in good stuff" *and* being aware of what that process is like. To simply have a pleasurable experience without some kind of attention to it, mindfulness about it, or appreciation of it per se is not savoring but "merely" enjoyment or pleasure.

In psychotherapeutic language, savoring is the metaprocessing of pleasurable experiences. What is the experience of happiness like? What is the experience of joy or pride like? What is the experience of connection like? And what happens when one stays with those experiences, luxuriating in them and letting them wash over the self? How much more does the pleasurable experience deepen? Or does something else interfere with it? How do we understand the interference, and what do we do with that when it occurs? In an affect-oriented experiential therapy, facilitating savoring requires a very careful balance between the experience of pleasure and the reflection on it. Pure experience is not savoring, and too much reflection and attempts to articulate the experience in language threaten to intellectualize what might otherwise be a focused, embodied experience of pleasure, fulfillment, or meaning. Savoring requires balance between experience and reflection.

Savoring requires some level of the surrender of the sense of pressure and responsibility we all carry. If we do not allow ourselves savoring experiences, they either do not happen or we circumscribe or strangle them. God might have said, at the end of a long day of creation, "This is good. Now, moving on. What is on the agenda for tomorrow—darkness and light?" So it is interesting that the authors and editors of the Old Testament included that God *rested* at the end of all this work, thereby ordaining rest, slowing down, satisfaction, restoration, and presence, human experiences that seem all too uncommon in our technological fast-paced world that prizes busyness as a status symbol. Being slowed down and present is the only kind of mindset in which we can really savor, and it is truly conducive to gratitude.

Savoring also requires attention and focus. Bryant and Veroff contend that "focused attending gives positive stimuli greater emotional power, gives people greater access to their feelings in response to these stimuli, and establishes a more reliable way to recall and relive a positive experience later. We suggest that focused attending makes a positive experience more distinctive, more vivid, and more easily and fully savored" (2007, p. 69). This is evident in the transcript that follows. Frequently people do not allow themselves to savor positive experiences in the moment or the moments following. And so, inviting people to slow down, notice their feelings, and savor the experience and the feelings associated with them helps people realize all the benefits named above. Many people have at least as much if not more defense around positive affect as they do around negative affect. The sense of lightness, freedom, and possibility that comes with taking in very positive experiences can be quite frightening, especially to people who have grown so accustomed, and even identified with, a more protective joy- and soul-crushing approach to life and their own selves. Bryant and Veroff speculate, "Perhaps it is because savoring is so rewarding that men's and women's puritanical souls rise up in protest" (2007, p. 10).

Savoring by oneself may elicit one kind of reservation, but savoring something about the self in the context of a relationship with another who is savoring it about you at the same time can bring up all other kinds of hesitations on the part of both patient and therapist. It is a very vulnerable thing to do. And yet, that kind of delighting in the self by an other is such a natural part of secure, healthy attachment relationships between parent and child, which contributes to a sense of goodness and solidity of the self, which in turn helps buffer the child against failures and humiliations. "It is . . . not about relishing the perfection in life, but finding hope, meaning, joy, satisfaction in a broken world or a wounded self" (Bryant & Veroff, 2007, p. 135).

As present as one needs to be to savor, one also needs to have a bit of distance and be cognitively engaged. Immersed in a state of ecstasy, not much is left to savor. This is an important point for us as therapists in that it suggests the need to allow enough space for people to firs have their experience and then to reflect on it. Therapists who are new to metaprocessing transformational experience often make one of two predictable errors: they either forget to do it in moments where it might deepen the transformational experience, or they are so overeager that the metaprocessing may disrupt the original transformational experience itself. This gets back to a point made earlier in the chapter about the importance of allowing for open space.

There is a difference, too, between savoring that focuses more on the self and the self's thoughts, feelings, sensations, and urges or desires and savoring whose object is someone or something outside the self. Bryant and Veroff (2007) refer to these as *self-focused* and *world-focused* savoring. They are important for clinicians because they tend to elicit different positive emotional responses. World-focused savoring tends to elicit gratitude and awe, depending on one's level of cognitive reflection, whereas self-focused savoring tends to elicit pride and physical pleasure. Gratitude is one of the healing affects that result from the experience of something coming together, of being healed or helped in some way. We have seen instances of this throughout the book. Awe is one of the realization affects that results from taking in something very big or experienced as beyond oneself. And pride is one of the mastery affects that results from feeling expanded and more effective in the world. All of these are transformational affects. Encouraging savoring is another way to metaprocess and to open space for deeply transformational affective experience. And savoring itself may also result from metaprocessing. Something may come up in the course of processing some transformational experience that the dyad (or the person himself) may elect to pause around, really be present to, and take in all that an experience feels like and means to a person. In one session with a male patient who simultaneously found the courage to leave a job he had outgrown and had the experience of feeling seen, held, and "beloved," we both metaprocessed and savored this profound healing experience for the entire session. Frequently, during our metaprocessing, he would become aware of yet another piece of this experience that was meaningful or healing for him, and he would stop and cry or just breathe it in (see Russell & Fosha, 2008).

There are many naturally occurring savoring strategies that people instinctively engage in to deepen and prolong good feelings. Things like "counting blessings," comparing, focusing attention on a pleasurable event or experience, recalling happy experiences in memory, sharing positive experiences with others, and allowing for absorption into an experience are all ways that people savor and attempt to prolong savoring (Bryant & Veroff, 2007). Importantly, pessimists, and many of the patients we see in our office, are less likely to engage in savoring strategies and, in fact, employ ways of thinking that tend to mitigate the impact of positive events and diminish one's related positive feelings. This is especially important for psychodynamic psychotherapists to understand. Most of us were trained to think of naturally occurring savoring strategies as defensive ways in which people refuse to deal with negative experiences.

As will be discussed more in Chapter 7, there is evidence that people who are happy have as much access to negative emotions as do unhappy people, but the difference is that they have *more* access to positive feelings. I infer from this that we clinicians should be more wary of what Bryant and Veroff call "killjoy thinking" that defensively minimizes positive experiences and the positive feelings associated with them.

CLINICAL VIGNETTE:
"It Makes Everything So Much More Pleasurable"—
Resilience as Transformance

The following is a transcript of a session with Rita, a young woman in her thirties. Very bright and capable, she has a history of being extraordinarily accommodating in relationships and deflecting, deferring, and denying her own needs. Abandoned as a child by one parent, she spent much of her early childhood with her mother and stepfather. Both of them were self-involved and self-preoccupied to the point of serious neglect of almost all of her emotional needs, and many of her practical needs as well. The parental relationship, additionally, was more than a little tumultuous and eventually ended in divorce. She was forced to grow up and do things for herself far earlier than most and has little experience in really being taken care of by others despite the fact of being very well liked personally and very well respected professionally. She is recently involved in a very loving relationship with a man who is pretty solid and sane—not her usual choice. She comes in talking about feeling pretty good about life in general, and in particular about her current experience of mental health and excitement about this relationship.

PT: I think for me it is like trusting myself that I have made a good decision so that I can build on the decisions I have already made. I had the thought the other day that everything I need is pretty much within my grasp. Like I just have to rearrange it; I have to shape it. And that is a weird feeling because I've always felt like I am anxiously chasing something I don't have.

TP: Mm-hmm.

PT: And now I don't have to do that. Everything is there.

TP: So what is that like? [**Experiential focus on the positive sense of real possibility and even abundance.**]

PT: (**Looking up, big sigh**) It is really relieving. It is very exciting. It is kind of scary because it's kind of how I am with arts and crafts projects. Like I will do an arts and crafts project that I did not plan . . . I am a little afraid that I will not make the best of what I have and just like rush and botch it in some way, do a good enough job, but not as well as it really could be if I were thoughtful. Like with this relationship with this woman where I will be working next year. Historically I would have barreled into that relationship and just done the best I could and in my mind thought, "Well, I can make it work . . . she'll like me because I will do this and that . . ." Now, I feel like the stakes are too high. This is my career. It matters to me. [**PT describes the difference between flying by the seat of her pants and feeling solid and taking herself seriously. Earlier in the treatment, the therapist reflected back to her that she sometimes seems to think of herself and treat herself as if she were vapor rather than a real flesh-and-blood person. This was an extremely helpful metaphor for her.**]

TP: Good!

PT: She is a really difficult woman. She is going to trigger stuff in

me. I want to use it as a learning opportunity where I can grow.
I do think we have things to offer each other, and I don't want
to get into avoidable conflicts with her. I have other things I
want to put my energy toward.

TP: Mm-hmm.

PT: And that is huge to be able to be thinking ahead to that. I
feel proud of myself. [**Transformational affects: mastery
affects (pride).**]

TP: Good.

PT: And even just to say with my (current) job, that there were
all these endings that I would like to talk about—just the fact
that I wanted to talk about that; that I recognized that . . .
(contrasting with how in the past she would not know what she
was feeling). In the past I would feel kind of filled up and over-
stimulated and not reflect on it . . . I can *feel* why these things
are important. [**More reflecting on contrast between
transformed self and earlier self states that were less
grounded, resilient, mindful.**]

TP: I feel like so much of what we are talking about today is your
experience of becoming solid. As you referenced my having
said at some point that you see yourself as a vapor, it feels like
so much of what we are talking about today is really focusing
in on what it is like to feel real, to feel solid.

PT: (**Welling with tears, nodding**) Yeah.

TP: And how that is changing so many things for you.

PT: Yeah. It is really a great metaphor, actually because it feels
like I literally feel physiologically different in my body. Like I
feel heavier in a good way. Like when I walk, I feel more solid
in myself (**hands open, palms facing in toward chest**). Like
when I played soccer in college, I remember feeling this physiological sort of transformation, like feeling more confident . . .
I remember feeling a lot more power in my body . . . Like doing
this feels a little like when I was in college. It feels physical,
like the molecules are more tightly connected, like you would
say in chemistry. [**PT elaborating experience of feeling
embodied and real.**]

TP: More bonded.

PT: (**Sigh**) Yeah. It makes everything so much more pleasurable, to feel solid.

TP: Tell me more. [**TP wanting to make more space for ongoing exploration of this transformation and her experience of it.**]

PT: I feel like I can enjoy the little things more. Like last night . . . (boyfriend designed a new drink with mint). He was making the drink and I was just smelling the mint.

TP: Hmm.

PT: And I noticed that I was able to just completely enjoy that. And I just felt this like exuberance (**tears welling**) about it. I am so glad that I have that back. I could enjoy a lot of things in my childhood and even in my twenties. But I feel like my time with John (former boyfriend) and the last two years, it has been a struggle to just enjoy something more directly. I feel like as I become more solid I feel like I can just enjoy something.

TP: Wow. So tell me about the mint and the drink and what was it like for you [**TP eliciting specificity to make the experience more affectively real in this moment in order to elaborate it and draw from it more transformational experience.**]

PT: It was just like, like holding that bunch of mint. It was cool to feel a plant.

TP: Mm-hmm.

PT: It had that light kind of feeling, light, fresh, healthy, bushy kind of texture. And the smell was really strong. It is a purifying, energizing kind of flavor. I smelled it and it was that kind of sharp smell.

TP: Mmm. Kind of waking you up in a way?

PT: Yeah (**smiling**). So that was so nice. And Matt was making dinner for all of his friends and for me. And he is just like so cute, cooking, happy making his food. And I was just like he is like that—just fresh and clean and has that sort of invigorating wholesome feeling to him (**wiping tears**).

TP: (**Smiling**) So you were able to savor both of them, the mint and Matt.

PT: (**Nodding**) Yeah.

TP: And the whole experience, just being really present, really enjoying.

PT: Yeah. I mean I wasn't present for the whole night just because I was a little anxious after my meeting with the new boss and feeling like, "Oh my god, there are so many things to worry about."

TP: But just for those few moments [**TP not distracted by the exception because that is not the point in this moment.**]

PT: Yeah. It was kind of neat. I keep seeing new sides to him that I didn't notice before, and it opens up more desire and love that I have for him. [**Being present and savoring the good things deepens desire, connection, and love.**]

TP: Wow.

PT: And it is just more. It is just amazing. He's just amazing. [**Transformational affects: realization affects; PT is in the middle of a cascade of transformation in part because TP keeps creating the platform for more.**] It is really nice. He was like, "I want to give you your present!" [**PT describes a present the boyfriend made that was a very personal reflection of her and took a lot of work and thought. She starts to really cry.**]

TP: (**Hand to heart**) That is so touching. Oh my gosh. [**TP self-disclosure of being moved/touched.**]

PT: (**Still through tears**) Yeah . . . (**more description of details of the gift**). It was so sweet (**tears**). He just gave it to me last night. It is going to take me a little while . . .

TP: Uh huh. [**Recognizing the impact of such a gift.**]

PT: . . . to internalize that. [**This is a frequent characteristic of powerful transformational affects, especially of the healing affects: people recognize that it may take some time to absorb the enormity of them and of the meaning of the event or exchange for the person (see also Russell & Fosha, 2008).**]

TP: To absorb it. Uh-huh. So what is it like just talking about it now, the extent to which you are absorbing it now? What do you feel? [**Experiential focus on feeling loved and known in a very deep way in the moment.**]

PT: It's so hard. It's almost like it is so good I can't feel it. For a minute I was like, "Is this creepy? Is he obsessed with me?" He has listened to all of my stories, remembered them all, and made a painting out of them. Like is he like crazy? Of course, that is my bad thought. [**It is not uncommon to defend against overwhelmingly positive, deeply transformative experiences in the way the PT is describing and, gratefully, recognizes as such.**]

TP: That is the part that needs to regulate how good this is and "let me get a little distance from it." [**TP reframing as a defense needed to regulate intense positive affect vs. a "bad" thought.**]

PT: But it is just so wonderful. Like he is so wonderful. I just sit there and look at him and say, "I don't know what to do with you, like you really are this sweet." I still just feel shocked. I mean I feel excited and really happy when I think about what an amazing partner he really is. [**PT able to tolerate the intense and unambiguously good feeling.**]

TP: So what is that like the excitement and the happiness behind the shock or mixed in with the shock? What are those pieces like for you? He really is your partner, not someone else's partner. And he didn't make that gift for anybody else. He didn't paint that painting for anybody else. He wasn't listening to anybody else's stories as attentively as he was listening to yours. [**TP upping the ante; pressuring with empathy and drawing in the specifics and placing the full platter in front of her.**]

PT: I don't know. It is great. It is really great. It feels (**sigh**) exciting and happy and really like I can let go on this new adventure of being happy. Almost like I have been on the ride of "anxious and obsessive" for the last two years and I got off that ride and I can get on the "be happy" ride and see what that is like. It is new, and I love new things. And it is new to be with someone as healthy as him.

Listening to and Nurturing Desire: The Wellspring of Flow, Creativity and a Meaningful Life

May you have the courage to listen to the voice of
desire that disturbs you when you have settled for
something safe.

In the earlier transcript, one of the things that appears to have been most satisfying and exciting for Fiona, was the fulfillment of a long-held, privately nurtured desire: "'How can you be an artist and in the academy?'—And I feel like I did it just then. It felt very natural." Something has come full circle for her—a longing, a wish, a need, a fantasy, an image of how she wanted her life to be, of who she wanted to be. Part of what got her through teaching anxiety, delivering papers, and the insecurity and boredom of meetings was a deep desire to be, to become the person she felt in that moment with her boss: an artist in the academy. That is a powerful force worth paying attention to. Many desires are expressions of transformance, so it is important to listen to them as such and not simply as passive wishes. This is an arena in which we can be transformational others, helping to identify and elaborate the deepest wishes of a person's heart and mind. Often people need help to take themselves seriously and to have the courage to listen to and be led by deep desires or the stirrings of heart and soul.

This is speculation, but perhaps the whole cycle starts with some kind of recognition that something seen as outside the self is attractive and resonant. Attraction, unhindered by unnecessary self-doubt, fear, or envy, fuels desire. As long as that desire is allowed to blossom and is not squashed by repressive forces, it fuels seeking and motivation for its own fulfillment. As its fulfillment or actualization become more possible, excitement and other positive affects provide more energy to the system and perhaps even more clarity about how to proceed. There is a feeling of a "propulsive force" at work within the self, as one of my patients very helpfully put it. When actualized or realized, the sense of truth, rightness, familiarity, of something having been known peripherally now being known integrally, is deeply satisfying, self-affirming, and affirming of the recognition and desire that prompted this whole endeavor. There is now an opportunity for savoring, the intentional and mindful, affectively charged mining of all that an experience is worth. As Fiona says, "This is the real thing!"

One of the things that is evident in the transcript is Rita's awareness of and clarity about her desires. She says "I want" several times and also articulates what she does not want. In this context, such desires emerge as part of the adaptive action tendencies that come with experiences of joy and connection and also with embodied experiences of the self. They are a culmination of her hard work and healthy experiences. At other times, however, desire may be the only marker of the true self we have to go on.

In my opinion, desire is an extremely important, vastly underappreciated clinical phenomenon at the beginning of the transformational spiral. It is barely mentioned in the research literature. And modern psychotherapists talk about it almost exclusively in the context of sexuality. But desire expresses the self's wishes and dreams while it fuels the search for their fulfillment. It moves us––literally. And if we have created lives of control, constraint, and safety, its emergence into consciousness or the public sphere can be deeply threatening. Therefore, when it does emerge in our patients, it is critically important to pay attention to and focus on it. I believe the content of desire is less important than the experience of it and how it moves or intimidates the self.

At a seminar on couples therapy and sexuality I attended a few years ago, the facilitator emphasized two points. The first is that avoidance of sexual intimacy leads to more avoidance, creating a cycle of disconnection that has potentially disastrous consequences for some. The flip side of that, and his second point, was that desire begets desire. Allowing ourselves a little, even simply creating the circumstances that might elicit desire in us or our partners, begets more desire. This is very different from our common notion of desire being "satiated." Perhaps even the satisfaction of desire begets more desire, as in any positive feedback loop or reward system. *The expectation that our desires can or might be fulfilled—which is hope—allows us the freedom to desire.*

Part of what is so deeply satisfying for Fiona is the experience of the fulfillment of a long-held desire, the actualization of a potential she had sensed but never fully lived in. In this moment, two parts of her, which she frequently experiences as counterposing, come together and coexist, and it feels "natural." These aspects of her self do not have to counter one another, and the experience of holding and being both feels "like the truth." This is integration par excellence. Its actualization was preconceived only by her desire and imagination.

In a lovely and deeply satisfying book titled *A Healing Conversation: How Healing Happens* (2006), Neville Symington explores more precisely what is healing about a conversation between two (or more) people. He notes that symbolism and language are ways in which we attempt to make inchoate experience communicable to another and also more graspable to ourselves. Slowing down enough to really study the process, he notices, that the process of symbolization or the production of language (before it is produced) is, in itself, a creative act. One is engaged in the act of creation, of making something *more* (more understandable, more complex, more universal or shared, etc.) than it was a moment before. Moreover, I would say, one is engaged in the process of transformation, in making something *different* than it was a moment before. Symington writes that "every action, emanating from a desire inside, that ends in an external epiphany elaborates the act into something more fulsome and developed. It is like a small seed that remains dry and impenetrable while it lies upon a stone in the sun, but when it is thrust into damp soil it sprouts into a plant with beautiful blue flowers. All this magnificence was the seed but invisible, impenetrable; but when it is planted into this favourable environment, the largeness and variety congealed within that small hard seed becomes accessible and visible to the senses" (p. 10).

This is where I think our role as clinicians is so important. To be able to attend with heart and mind deeply enough, with a radical curiosity and an expansive compassion to hear the stirrings of a soul, the desires of a heart, the wonderings of a mind, is a gift we can give because we are focused on the gift that is wanting to be received from the depths of our patients. Sadly, people have become cynical about their own desires. I wonder if that is sometimes because their deeper desires have been masked by desires that are proscribed for them by significant others or by our culture, media, and advertising. Sometimes people do not really know how to listen to themselves or, if they do, do not really know how to trust what they hear.

Leaning on Symington's words above, a transformance-oriented life, a life of expanding resilient capacity, a creative life must start with desire. If that desire is not heard and heeded, so much potential can be wasted or dehydrated. Mihaly Csikszentmihalyi, psychology's voice for creativity, notes that "to have a good life, it is not enough to remove what is wrong from it. We also need a positive goal, otherwise why keep going? Creativity is one answer to that question: It provides one of the most exciting models for living" (1996, p. 11). And, in a nod to the importance of innate resilience and the essential role of support, he adds: "Each of us is born with two contradictory sets of instructions: a conservative tendency, made up of instincts for self-preservation, self-aggrandizement, and saving energy, and an expansive tendency made up of instincts for exploring, for enjoying novelty and risk—the curiosity that leads to creativity belongs to this set. . . . But whereas the first tendency requires little encouragement or support from outside to motivate behavior, the second can wilt if it is not cultivated" (p. 11). The second needs transformational others!

Summary

This chapter has focused on the mixed reactions people can have to arriving, to finally being happy or feeling freed from long-carried burdens. On the one hand, it is what they have been aiming, wishing, and working for. On the other, they often feel unprepared, and the sense of expansion, possibility, freedom, and joy can feel overwhelming and even frightening. People can resist that which they have been yearning for, not so much because they do not want it as because they suddenly feel unprepared to have it. As people make this transition from a more constricted, self-preservation way of being resilient to a more expansive, transformance expression of resilience in the face of life's challenges, they often need help relocating the strength they have and validation that this transition can be frightening but is well worth making.

In that context, we discussed the importance of allowing for open space in the therapeutic relationship, which requires the therapist trust in the change process itself. The impact of play or playfulness in the therapeutic relationship was also looked at as a way to help metabolize and digest experiences that at first seem too big to take in. We looked at the importance of recognition and the experience of being deeply seen by a real other (intersubjectivity) and how that therapist other can help identify and elaborate the changes happening in the self, as we have discussed throughout the book. We looked at two transcripts of moments of arriving. One focused on the joy, fullness, healthy pride, and a sense of recognizing this new self as not being entirely new. The second focused on the intentional slowing down and taking in deeply positive experiences in the process of savoring. Finally, we looked at how the expansive experience of desire is often an important expression of transformance strivings and how the fulfillment of desires frequently connects people to early transformance strivings that they were never able to fully own until the present. The hopefulness of the experience of desire is often an important precursor to action and creativity, more positive affects that some patients may need help embracing. The need for both therapist and patient to become more comfortable with positive affect is the main focus of Chapter 7.

CHAPTER 7

Fully Human, Fully Alive
Resilience as Transformance and Flourishing

So much of the psychotherapeutic process involves traversing, transitioning, transforming—crossing over from one place, one state to another. Whatever language we use, whether it is moving from self-at-worst to self-at-best, processing feelings to completion, character transformation, building of the self, symptom reduction, behavioral modification, integration of parts, or resolution of trauma, it is all suggestive of effecting change. Our work as therapists, whether we think of ourselves as analysts, clinicians, facilitators, allies to the healthy self, or midwives, involves attending, listening, intuiting, formulating, working, facilitating, pressuring, and waiting for those transitions to happen. However we define the process of our work and our own roles within that, when a patient comes in reporting a significant and desirable change, we all experience some level of satisfaction, some affirmation of the purpose and meaning of the work, some reassurance of our own contributions, and some relief, pleasure, and joy in witnessing someone we care about having arrived, experiencing happiness, and having access to the kind of vitality that is required to live life fully.

This chapter explores the positive side of psychology that is often more evident when people heal: happiness, joy, or contentment. Happiness, in fact, is an often overlooked component of a healthy life, at

261

least among mental health professionals. In my mid-twenties, I told my analyst at the time that I was not concerned about being happy; I wanted my life, rather, to be "meaningful." Fortunately, his dilated eyes told me I should give that intention some more thought. The state of happiness, by which I mean a range of positive experiences from contentment and pleasure to ecstatic joy, can be fleeting or it can be more chronic, a fortunate person's baseline. In the first case, it is something we want to draw upon and explore in an effort to expand it and to provide some stability to a person who is overly bur- dened. In the second, a happy state of mind has multiple benefits, not the least of which is happiness as an end in itself. Other benefits this chapter explores, by no means an exhaustive list, include a broader perspective on problems and problem solving, greater resilience to pain, myriad health benefits, a capacity for play and creativity, access to meaningful friendship and support networks, and the kind of emotional complexity that marks mature and transformance-en- dowed resilience. With that comes a deeper and broader compassion for self and others that makes life more sustainable and meaningful at the same time.

Happiness, however, is but one manifestation of a life fully lived. This kind of life also includes pain, struggle, or suffering. Mental and emotional health and mature resilience do not depend on and should not be defined as the lack of struggle, suffering, or pain. Rather, resilience that manifests as transformance is characterized by acceptance and the willingness to roll with the difficulties of life even when they are painful, because one is buffered by enough access to positive affect (e.g., happiness), positive relationships, and positive and meaningful engagement in the world. Happiness or joy is an important counterweight to the struggles of life and the nega- tive emotions they tend to elicit in us. Healthy, *mature resilience* is grounded and undergirded by hope. This flowering of mature resilience and many of the attendant positive emotional states of mind that facilitate, mark, and flow from it is another subject of this chapter.

In addition to positive emotions and mature resilience, this chap- ter continues the exploration of resilience in the forms of transformance and flourishing, when a person's healing has resulted in a "transfer to adaptive pathways," in the words of resilience researcher Gil Noam (Lawrence, 1996). It distinguishes between transformance and flourishing, looks at the role of positive emotion in a healthy life, and explores some of what makes people happy and why it is important for clinicians to understand happiness and what it means to our patients. We will look at the relationship between emotional complexity and resilience and explore the idea that painful experiences might bear the fruit of beautiful consequences and that, in some cases, that fruit may not have been born, that joy may not have been fully realized had the struggle not been endured.

Positive Emotion and Flourishing: Good Feelings in the Course of Growth and Transformation

Affect regulation . . . also involves an amplification, and intensification of positive emotion, a condition necessary for more complex self-organization. Attachment is not just the re-establishment of security after a dysregulating experience and a stressful negative state; it is also the interactive amplification of positive affects, as in play states.

Happiness is perhaps the most obvious and colloquially understood instance of positive affect, which, more broadly, is a category of affects that subjectively feel good and lean toward contentment-joy or interest-curiosity (Darwin, 1872; Damasio, 1999; Nathanson, 1992). This section looks specifically at happiness but first focuses on more general positive affective states, what we know about them, and why they are important to clinicians. If positive affect is simply a passing phenomenon that breaks the monotony of difficulty and struggle, then as clinicians and scientists we should pay it little attention. But if, in fact, it is associated with and even leads to changes in cognition, mood, and behavior, it compels us to understand it better and to use it strategically in our work with people who are so often beleaguered by anxiety, tension, fear, depression, stagnation, and the like.

Before delving into some of what is known about the effect of positive affect on functioning, it is important to reiterate, in case it is not clear already, that what I am advocating is not a simple prescription to change one's thoughts, attitudes, or behaviors, and voilà, feeling better is the result (although I believe there is some validity to that perspective). Rather, I am interested in the role of positive affect in the integration of a life. It buffers us against stress. It makes accessible aspects of consciousness and memory that are not accessible in negative or even neutral affect states. It makes bearable the pains of life and our own failures or wounds. It thrusts us into the future. It protects our health and relationships and contributes to increased overall well-being. Given its salutary effects, we should know something about how to harness it. Perhaps most basically, we have to learn to (1) recognize it when it emerges in our patients organically, (2) work with it to solidify those states of mind, and (3) use it to facilitate healing, health, and resilience in our patients.

One of the most important and interesting things to come out of recent research on happiness is that happiness is not simply an outcome but may also be a very powerful predictor of success and satisfaction in life. If that is the case, then limiting ourselves as clinicians to the notion that removing the bad stuff will make room for happiness (which does not always happen) not only is practically problematic but also ignores a whole other pathway toward mental health and well-being. That is, there are real short- and long-term benefits to augmenting happiness and positive affect and to focusing on removing not only defenses against pain, grief, anger, and other subjectively aversive affective experiences but also defenses against joy, intimacy, pride, contentment, and hope. I have come to appreciate that no matter how much we consciously want these good things and good feelings in life, when we find ourselves on the brink of having them, most of us betray, in one way or another, our own reluctance, suspicion, fear, disbelief, cynicism, or capacity to undo (see Chapter 6). Similarly, as therapists, as much as we want our patients to have these positive experiences, when they come into our office beaming with them, we often do not know what to do and find ourselves strangely uncomfortable and at sea. "What do we do now? Should we be thinking about termination?"

This is one of the reasons the work of infant researchers and affective neuroscientists has been so important. In addition to the more recent contributions of positive psychologists, they have helped elevate the topic of positive affect to something worthy of our discussion and understanding. Pathology usually involves a deficit of it. In contrast, secure dyads are marked by a return to coordinated states after only brief periods of shared negative affect (Beebe & Lachman, 1994; Tronick, 1989, 1998, 2005; Tronick & Cohen, 1969). Schore talks about the "positively charged curiosity" that provides not only the safety but also the fuel for exploration in secure dyads (2003, p. 144). Russell and Fosha (2008) have proposed that this positively charged curiosity is a marker of health throughout the life span. The "practicing" phase of infancy from approximately 10–16 months, marked by intense positive affect, has been shown to be very important to the development of the prefrontal cortex (Schore, 1994; Mahler, Pine, & Bergman, 1975), and a similar phenomenon appears to be equally important in the facilitation of healing in patients in psychotherapy (Russell & Fosha, 2008).

There is a consistent finding in resilience research that risk and disadvantage (i.e., factors that predict problematic adjustment and functioning, like poverty, single-parent families, or mental health or substance abuse issues in the family to name a few) are cumulative and that as they increase, so too does the need for positive inputs and resources to counterbalance the weight of what Garmezy calls "cumulative risk" (1987, p. 167). In restoring resilience, we want to help people develop what we could call "cumulative resources." This helps people transition to more open, safely vulnerable, currently adaptive expressions of resilience in response to stress or adversity.

The Broaden and Build Theory of Positive Emotions

Barbara Fredrickson's broaden and build theory of positive emotion elaborates the function of positive affect. She and her colleagues contend that positive emotions have the effect of widening our scope of attention (especially compared with negative emotion), improving problem-solving capacities and behavioral flexibility, increasing cognitive flexibility, and even undoing the effects of negative emotions on the heart (Fredrickson, 1998; Fredrickson & Branigan, 2005; Fredrickson & Losada, 2005; Fredrickson, Mancuso, Branigan, & Tugade, 2000). In fact, Cohn, Fredrickson, Brown, Mickels and Conway contend that "positive emotions are evolved adaptations that function to build lasting resources" (2009, p. 361). Whereas the adaptiveness of negative emotions is in helping us survive, the adaptiveness of positive emotions is helping us grow and thrive. This may even be seen in animals. Panksepp's research suggests that "during play, animals are especially prone to behave in flexible and creative ways" (1998, p. 297).

These researchers also remind us of the myriad studies showing that resilient people (as defined by researchers) are no less likely to experience negative emotions than are their less resilient peers. Rather, what differentiates them is that they have *more access* to positive emotions. So, the idea that resilient people are happy-go-lucky folks with their heads in the clouds, unable or unwilling to feel negative or uncomfortable feelings, is simply not supported by the research.

In fact, Cohn et al. (2009) looked directly at the relationship between daily affect (positive and negative) and ego resilience, defined as a person's ability to adapt to changing environments (Block & Block, 1980; Block & Kremen, 1996). In a study of approximately one hundred university students, they explored the relationship between daily positive and negative emotions, ego resilience, and life satisfaction. They found, in this nondepressed group, that positive and negative emotions did not correlate on any day or in the aggregate. Positive emotions, however, predicted both ego resilience and life satisfaction, as well as increases in these measures over the course of the month. One of the main findings of this longitudinal study was a predictive relationship between positive emotions and ego resilience over time. Specifically, the presence of positive emotions over the course of the month predicted an increase in ego resilience over the same period of time. Similarly, an increase in ego resilience was associated with an increase in life satisfaction over time above and beyond any effect of positive emotions alone, which did not have a direct impact on overall life satisfaction. The authors conclude, in keeping with the broaden and build theory, that it is the momentary, quotidian experience of positive affect that increases ego resilience (adaptability and resourcefulness), which in turn ultimately increases life satisfaction.

Another important finding of Cohn et al.'s (2009) study, and one that is consistent with other studies (see the discussion of work by Zautra and colleagues below), is that daily positive emotion is a better predictor of increases in ego resilience over time when the level of negative emotion is high than it is when the level of negative emotion is low. In other words, *the power of positive affect is more powerful when negative affect is high.* While they were not working with clinical populations for whom the experience of daily negative emotion can be very high, this suggests the importance of helping people more prone to regular negative affect to access and enhance the experience of positive affect. This can be done during therapy or outside of the office on a regular, even daily basis. There are now many websites that offer positive psychology exercises that anyone can do for free. The one started by Martin Seligman and other researchers in positive psychology is called "authentic happiness."

Seligman, Rashid, and Parks (2006) wanted to examine the impact of web-based positive psychology interventions on groups of people, including those who were clinically depressed. All interventions were aimed at increasing positive affect, character strengths, and sense of meaning or purpose in life. Subscribers to their website took questionnaires to assess, among other things, their level of depression. Fifty of them scored in a range indicating severe depression. Those people did the Three Blessings exercise, in which they wrote down three things that went well each day and why they went well. Two weeks later, 94 percent of them were less depressed. Of course, such people were probably motivated because they signed up on a site called "authentichappiness.com." But they were probably no more motivated than those who get themselves into therapy. The authors speculate that this result is due to a retraining of attention, memory, and expectations toward the positive and away from the negative, which is the affective and cognitive bent of someone who is depressed. I wonder if it is also due to an increase in mindfulness, self-reflective capacity, and perspective taking (i.e., differentiating) that may have resulted from the second part of the task, which is to speculate about *why* something good happened.

In a larger group of six hundred volunteers, those who did one of the positive psychology exercises daily for a week were significantly less depressed over the course of the week than the placebo group that simply wrote an essay about themselves at their best. For those subgroups that focused on the three blessings and on their strengths, these gains lasted 6 months. More striking still are the findings of their study comparing weekly individual "positive psychotherapy" (PPT) with treatment as usual (TAU; with eclectic doctoral-level psychologists) and with TAU plus medication for depression (TAU-MED). On a fourfold measure of depression remission, 68 percent of the PPT group were deemed to have remitted over the course of 14 weeks, whereas only 11 percent of the TAU group and 8 percent of the TAUMED group were deemed to have remitted.

I think of patients I have seen and people I have known who have experienced deep depression. They are wounded and scarred by such experiences even if they learned some things along the way. Frequently, they are left not trusting their emotions and being terribly frightened by sadness. The unrelentingness of that despair, hopelessness, void, or pain remains something to be feared and avoided at all costs. What if their experiences had been dotted with moments of pleasure, appreciation, contentment, hope, gratitude, or a sense of meaning or purpose? The nature of depression itself is that it essentially robs people of these affects in their naturally occurring state. What the research suggests is that if those feelings can be intentionally called up or induced, even if at only moderate levels, people can begin to feel better and become more resilient even as they are still making a difficult journey. It seems that, like social support, which was studied extensively in the 1970s and 1980s (e.g., Cohen & McKay, 1984), positive affect serves to buffer people against the negative impact of stress.

Positive emotions, therefore, seem to do what secure attachment does for the child: they allow and even encourage exploration and the seeking of experience. This is fascinating. It raises the question of how we have thought about what is operating in secure attachment that engenders exploration. Attachment researchers and clinicians who apply attachment theory to their clinical work traditionally define the potent factor as "safety." The child feels "safe" to explore the environment once the contact with the caregiver has been reestablished. The patient is willing to explore previously warded off emotion because of a sense of safety with the therapist. But what does this mean? How is this safety achieved? Is it possible that, as with infants and their caregivers, safety is a by-product of pleasant experiences and their related positive emotions and the pleasure in reconnection after a disruption?

Interestingly, but perhaps not surprisingly, Fredrickson has described the trajectory of positive emotions as an upward spiral. It is the same image AEDP gravitated toward to refer to the process of healing, initially as the "cascade of transformation" and later as the "transformational spiral." Positive emotion begets more positive emotion, and it liberates and builds resources and the self's capacity to work on behalf of the self. If the effect of positive emotion is to increase and expand behavioral and cognitive resources and to diminish the impact of negative emotions, then it is an essential element of restoring resilience. I imagine it as, rather than a straight spiral, a cone-shaped spiral directed upward and outward; the former reflects the affective valence, and the latter reflects the expanding capacities of the self. Similarly, I imagine the downward spiral of depression as the same cone-shaped spiral, only one starts from the top and as one goes down the spiral of mood, so too do one's thoughts and behaviors become more restricted, repetitive, and oppressive.

Psychodynamically and experientially oriented therapists trust in the self-righting power of depth and darkness. Suggesting that one can be really healed without traversing the darkness, the bottom, the pain, the grief, and so forth, is anathema and possibly even ridiculous to such therapists. We trust that if it does not kill a person, the trial of facing trauma, darkness, pain, and internal conflict will make one more resilient in the end—most of the time. But what if one stood the chance of becoming even more resilient or of becoming resilient more quickly simply by making conscious choices to experience and savor positive affect even while traversing the darkness? If the darkness can occasionally be relieved by a little light, the pain by a laugh, the grief by an experience of comfort, doesn't that make the journey more bearable and the sojourner more resilient?

Whether it is theoretical, based on the research, or ideally some combination of both, the idea that resilience involves having access to positive emotion no matter the stress or no matter the level of negative emotion is very compatible with the idea proffered in this book that resilience is the self's differentiation from that which is aversive to it. The negative, the traumatic, the overwhelming is not the only thing going—it is not forgotten or irrelevant, but it is not wholly defining. There is some space between the self and what is happening or what has happened to the self that can have access to other self experiences, more positive emotions, adaptive ways of functioning, and supportive relational connections.

Positive Affect and Constructing Reality:
Building Receptive Affective Capacity

> *What we are suggesting is that mood plays a role in what comes to mind.*

Many people, though certainly not all, who present for psychotherapy have difficulty taking in and making use of positive experiences and emotions. They have either internalized so many negative messages or so many prohibitions against feeling something good about themselves that their instinct is to spit this medicine out when they are presented with it. Working with positive affect in therapy often involves pressuring with empathy and actively helping people to relinquish defenses against the positive and to develop their receptive affective capacity for positive experiences and positive reflections of self.

A whole series of changes occur in people when they are induced into positive affect states. Isen, Shalker, Clark, and Karp (1978) found that people who received free gifts were more positive in their evaluations of things they owned than people who did not. They also found that those who were told they "succeeded" at a task (which presumably induces positive affect) subsequently recalled more words from a list they were asked to remember than those who were told they had "failed," and they recalled significantly more positively valenced words. In other words, in a positive affect state, their memory was better in general and, more specifically, better able to retrieve information that had positive associations.

This is evident in psychotherapy as well. There have been many times in my own work and in work I have seen of my colleagues and supervisees in which the positive affective state—usually associated with taking in something good from the therapist or from someone else—unhinges long-forgotten memories of experiences and people in the past that elicited similar (sometimes precisely so) good feelings. For example, the patient I mentioned in chapter 1, when she was able to take in something good about herself, about my feelings for her, or someone else's obviously positive feelings of love, affection, admiration, or tenderness, would regularly go back to memories and a felt sense of her grandmother, who was the one consistently uncompromised and unquestioningly loving person in her life by whom she felt really seen and understood. This often righted her when she was tempted to despair about herself, her life, or her future, and it helped sustain her and eventually became more and more a part of how she consciously experienced and treated herself. When positive experiences in the present find a foothold in the past, they are harder to dispute or defend against. And people can land and feel restored.

Positive experiences shape our sense of self and, in turn, influence our subsequent behavior, feelings, and information seeking. More relevant to clinicians than the retrieval of positively valenced words is the finding that experiences of success make people more open to receiving both positive and negative evaluations of themselves on subjectively relevant life goals and values. Trope and Pomerantz (1998) found that people who had just experienced failure were more interested in positive feedback about relevant life goals and assets than they were in negative feedback. Those who had just experienced a success were equally open to both positive and negative feedback about important life goals and personal assets. In the face of failure and accompanying negative affect, people may be more in need of positive feedback to maintain or increase self-esteem and less open to negative feedback even if it is presumably important information from which they can learn something. People who have experienced success and the accompanying positive affect seek both types of feedback. They can accept the positive, but they are also more capable of metabolizing the negative. In other words, they are more flexible—that sounds like resilience! In contrast, people who are depressed take longer to remember pleasant experiences and relatively little time to remember unpleasant ones.

This kind of research supports the clinical prescription of accessing the self-at-best to work with the self-at-worst. As discussed in Chapters 1 and 3, accessing the self-at-best first brings a more resourced, integrated self into the healing process. The self-at-best, by definition, has access to his or her own feelings and self states, usually has more compassion for the self, frequently has access to some positive affects, and is therefore more capable of looking at and dealing with problems at hand than the more conservation-oriented, reactive, defensive self-at-worst, who is just trying to get by and is not particularly capable of taking on more. This was beautifully illustrated in Michael Bridges's (2006) article contrasting the treatment outcome of three different patients discussed at length in Chapter 4. The first two patients did not benefit as much from the treatment as did the third because they were either defending against what they really felt and so relying on venting and complaining, or trying to maintain some kind of control over very powerful feelings that might have been transformational had the patient felt safe enough to fully express them. The third, in contrast, moved through intense states of grief following the experience of intense embodied positive feelings. I think it is very likely that she was able to have such a profound breakthrough of unprocessed grief and experience such relief from the session, as well as such good outcome in the overall treatment, because she was both buoyed and made more flexible and open by the experience of intense positive affects, much like the people in the above research who were more flexible, open, and appreciative and had better memories following experiences of success or induced positive affect.

What Good Is Happiness? The Benefits of Frequent Positive Emotion

Defining happiness as the "frequent experience of positive emotions over time," Lyubomirsky, King, and Diener (2005) conducted a meta-analysis of 293 studies, comprising more than 275,000 participants focusing on the relationship of happiness (or some close cousin of it) to myriad outcome measures. In cross-sectional analyses, which can only yield correlational and not causational information, they found that happy people, or those high in subjective well-being, were more successful in work and relationships, and they were healthier. Specifically, they secured jobs more readily, were better evaluated by supervisors, showed better performance and productivity, and handled management work better. Their work tended to have more autonomy, meaning, and variety than their less happy peers, and they were more satisfied with their work. Moreover, people who work for happy bosses are also happier and healthier and report their work environments to be warm and positive. They also tend to make slightly more money and are more likely to do tasks that go beyond the requirements of their job for the sake of the organization.

Socially, happy people volunteer more of their time. They tend to have more friends or companions they can rely on and are more satisfied with their friends and in their social activities. They also experience less jealousy of others than their less happy peers. One of the strongest and most consistent findings regarding relationships and happiness is that married people are happier than any other group. Among them, individuals who are happy tend to have fulfilling, satisfying marriages. As with happy bosses, marital satisfaction is associated with an individual's happiness. It seems that happiness is contagious; happy people may make other people happy as well.

In terms of their health, it almost goes without saying that people who are frequently happy report fewer symptoms of psychopathology and are much less likely to report histories with substance abuse. Regarding physical health, a plethora of studies suggest that even when severely ill, people who are happier fare better on physical outcomes, experience less pain, have fewer absences from work due to illness, and have a better overall quality of life (Lyubomirsky et al., 2005). In fact, the study of physical pain provides a very good example of the role of positive affect in mitigating the impact of chronic stress and accompanying negative affect, as we will see below.

Thus, the assessment, exploration, and nurturing of positive affective experiences and positive self states are essential parts of restoring resilience. It is not pursued to the exclusion of depth, complexity, pathology, or pain. But nor should it be treated simply as by-product of good therapy under the assumption that people naturally make good and sufficient use of positive feelings and experiences. Most do not, as Baumeister et al.'s (2001) work on the human proclivity toward the negative so compellingly makes clear. Their study cites the human tendency to notice more, pay more attention to, and give more weight to a broad range of negative psychological phenomena such as negative affects, negative feedback, negative events, and problems in relationships. Unfortunately, the list goes on and on!

Mature Resilience and Emotional Complexity

The capacity to maintain and preserve the boundaries between positive and negative emotional states may represent one potential pathway underlying flexible adaptation.

Having established a foundational relationship between positive affect and processes that promote resilient adaptation, this section looks more closely at the complexity of that relationship. The relationship between positive affect and resilience is not straightforward.

While we have seen that in most cases, looking at large samples and broad ranges of people, positive and negative affect are mostly independent of each other (Watson & Clark, 1992), when researchers look at people at increasing levels of stress and, in particular, the stress of pain, there frequently is an inverse relationship between positive and negative affects (Zautra, Smith, Affleck, & Tennen, 2001). The more negative affect they feel, the less positive affect they have access to. Zautra and colleagues (Zautra, Johnson & Davis, 1985; Zautra, Potter, & Reich, 1997; Zautra, Reich, Davis, Nicolson, & Potter, 2000; Zautra et al., 2001) have done extensive research on people suffering with chronic pain. In their dynamic model of affect, Zautra et al. have proposed that "the relationship between negative and positive emotions changes as a function of ongoing events, and may vary between persons as well" (2001, pp. 786–787). The theory predicts that negative and positive affects become less differentiated, and therefore more (inversely) correlated, when people are under stress. Practically speaking, that means that during times of stress, people's awareness of their own emotions is significantly reduced, and this, in part, is what contributes to people's greater vulnerability to negative affect when in pain. During pain episodes, people's ability to attend to complexity, including that of their own emotions, is reduced, and they are more likely to adopt simpler descriptions of their affective experience. This is evident in the thought processes of people who are depressed as well, and is in keeping with Fredrickson's broaden and build theory of positive emotion described above, which postulates that people experiencing positive affect have more access to a broader range of thoughts, behaviors, and problem-solving strategies.

In one study of 175 women with rheumatoid arthritis or osteoarthritis over the course of 12–20 weeks, Zautra et al. (2001) found that while weekly positive affect was generally related to decreases in negative affect and increases in pain were associated with increases in negative affect, there was less of an increase in negative affect during episodes of greater pain when positive affect was also high. In other words, positive affect did mitigate the impact of negative affect when people were experiencing severe pain. Another study by

Zautra et al. (2005) found that chronic pain sufferers showed less rise in negative affect during weeks of higher interpersonal stress when they reported more positive affect during that week. So, as stress or pain increases, positive affect seems to protect people from too much negative affect and its sequelae. It appears to help regulate their mood. So how is it that some people, and not others, are able to have enough protective positive affect in the face of increased pain or interpersonal distress? To answer that they are more resilient gets us into a tautological knot. We need to understand better the nature of that kind of resilience in this context.

A clue to answering this is perhaps one of the most interesting, important, and clinically relevant findings of Zautra's work. Zautra et al. (2001) measured what they called "mood clarity," using a subscale of the Trait Meta-Mood Scale (Salovey, Mayer, Goldman, Turvey, & Palfai, 1995). Mood clarity is defined as the capacity to differentiate different mood or affect states within the self. Those who were high in mood clarity did not show changes in positive affect associated with changes in negative affect during pain episodes. Those who were less able to distinguish their own affect states were much more vulnerable to decreases in positive affect when there were increases in negative affect associated with intensifying pain. As is also true in regard to stress (Ong, Bergeman, Bisconti, & Wallace, 2006), as pain increases, positive affect plays an increasingly important role in regulating negative affect. But if people are not skilled at differentiating or sensitive to their various affective states, they may not be able to access more positive affective states that can be truly protective. Again, in general, positive and negative affect are not necessarily related, but the dynamic model of affect suggests, based on the research, that under conditions of stress or pain, negative and positive affect do show an increasingly inverse relationship, and the need to access positive affect is even more crucial. This research, by implication, also supports the use of affect-oriented or emotion-focused therapeutic approaches to help people differentiate their various affective experiences, which is foundational to the approach to restoring resilience proposed in this book.

Ong et al. (2006) in their study of people ranging from 62 to 80 years of age found that while daily negative emotion scores were higher on days when stress was higher, daily positive emotion interacted with stress to weaken its influence on negative emotion. In other words, positive emotion buffers the impact of stress on negative emotion. Moreover, while the effect of one day's stress on the next day's negative affect was significant and positive (i.e., today's high stress predicts tomorrow's high level of negative affect), when they factored in the first day's positive emotion, the relationship between one day's stress and the next day's negative emotion disappeared, suggesting that emotional recovery is due, in part, to access to positive affect. Another study showed that patients with pain who had experienced more positive affect had less catastrophic thinking about their pain the next day (Ong, Zautra, & Reid, 2010). They also found that trait resilience (as measured by Block & Kremen's [1996] Ego Resilience Scale) moderated the relationship between daily stress and negative emotion. In other words, those higher in trait resilience were less likely to suffer with too much negative emotion in response to stress. Finally, they found that resilience moderated the relationship between stress and the next day's negative emotion. Those who were more resilient recovered more quickly. But, importantly, this was no longer the case when they added positive emotion to the equation, suggesting that what helps highly resilient people recover faster is the greater extent to which they can access positive emotion.

While pain and stress are not necessarily the same thing, these kinds of results suggest the increasingly important role of positive affect when people are under stress or even in emotional pain—precisely when it is hardest to come by because, as the broaden and build theory suggests, negative affect constricts our range of focus and awareness. So, therapeutic interventions that privilege helping people to access and differentiate affect and, more precisely, privilege the emergence and elaboration of positive affective experiences should directly contribute to increasingly adaptive expressions of resilience.

CLINICAL VIGNETTE:

"I Feel a Lot More Myself . . . I Am a Complicated Man"—

Resilience as Transformance and Flourishing

The patient, Jack, is a divorced man with a history of and ongoing infidelity about which he feels some shame. He has a deep need for affirmation from women, especially those he finds attractive, and a deep rage at them for making him feel so small and emasculated. He began having rape fantasies in college, and although the frequency, intensity, and objects of them changed, they continued in some way to the time of this session. Both his past depression and rejection by any number of valued women have plummeted him into experiences he has described as "a black hole." A lot of work and healing around these issues preceded (and followed) this session in which he is in a very different state. In this session, he has just returned from a business trip, announcing how much more comfortable he was in interactions with women, strangers and acquaintances alike. He both feels good and is reflective about his experience. He starts out in self-at-best with minimal defenses and low levels of inhibitory affect, which do not ultimately interfere with his connection to himself or with what he is trying to communicate about it to the therapist. He starts to speak about his experience in the past tense, but the dialogue quickly shifts to his in-the-moment feelings about his trip and himself.

The therapist is aware of the importance of his opening statements about himself and wants him to elaborate on these and his experiential awareness of what this kind of truth and acceptance is like in his body; in other words, she wants to help him deepen his experience of these very positive affects. She bypasses defenses that come up that would interrupt a fuller experience of himself in this way and actively attempts to help deepen his "good" feelings (i.e., transformational affects) and his immersion in core state; that place of naturalness, ease, and acceptance that is evident throughout this dialogue. I chose this segment for two main reasons. First, it illustrates how the transformational process is deepened by the therapist's active focus on the positive and her helping the patient to take it in and metabolize it. Second, the patient is fully in touch with his own transformance strivings, and his articulation of his own resilience conveys this, as well as his relationship to the complexity of his self, which is a sign of mature, transformance-oriented resilient capacity.

> *PT*: It was natural . . . It was also natural to talk with this young woman . . . I think, reflecting . . . coming full circle to our discussion last Tuesday, I think the way these women felt, I never felt natural until recently because of all these bottled up emotions. I didn't feel natural. I didn't feel myself. I couldn't even fake feeling myself. [**Core state is marked by a sense of naturalness, ease, calm. It is also an ideal space from which to reflect and to knit together a coherent, cohesive narrative of the patient's life and experience. Here, Jack's changed recent experience and groundedness allows him greater insight into himself and others.**]
>
> *TP*: Wow.
>
> *PT*: And now (**raising hands, looking around**), I feel a lot more myself. I don't mean this in a, uh, pat-on-the-back type of thing or a derogatory way, but I am a complicated man, just like most men are.
>
> *TP*: Mm-hmm.
>
> *PT*: There are good aspects to me, there are not such good aspects of me. You know, I'd like to think I am much more accepting of myself than I have been in a long time. [**Self-acceptance and self-compassion are hallmarks of core state as they are of restored resilience.**]
>
> *TP*: (**Smiling**) I'd like to agree with you.
>
> *PT*: (**Small laugh**). Well, thank you. And that is making me feel more comfortable with who I am.
>
> *TP*: Yeah. Yeah.
>
> *PT*: And maybe that is what these women sense; that, instead of trying to force something, instead of trying to gain a woman's approval, instead of trying to force a friendship . . . [**PT constructing a coherent narrative in core state; making better sense of women and his experience of himself with women.**]

TP: Mm-hmm. (**A moment later**) Wow. Jack, you are just doing some amazing integrating and processing. This is so . . .

PT: (**Shy laughter interrupting**). Well, thanks. (**Stuttering**) I've been thinking it over for a little while.

TP: (**Somewhat playfully, but insistently**) You know what I am saying is true, don't you? [**Pressuring with empathy.**]

PT: I don't know. You know, uh, I don't know the scale; you do.

TP: Who cares about the scale? (**Clearly excited and playful, but serious**) What are you feeling as you're saying this to me?

PT: (**Big smile, good eye contact**) Embarrassed. Well, I feel embarrassed right now, but I feel good about it! (**face shifting to more assertive but pleasant expression**). I feel good about it. It *is* okay . . .

TP: It's amazing.

PT: It sounds good. Of course, I'll probably leave here and run into some situation with a woman . . . [**Defense against the positive.**]

TP: (**Interrupting**) Jack, what comes up for you when I say, "It's amazing"? Because I think you know it. You feel how good this feels; this kind of freedom that comes from seeing yourself more clearly, . . . relaxing, how you may have carried anger in the past and not being at ease with yourself and what they were picking up on . . . How much more relaxed they are with you . . . [**Pressuring with empathy; mirroring; summarizing and integrating PT's own words to encourage him to take in the whole of it.**]

PT: Or trying too hard. [**PT joining by elaborating.**]

TP: . . . recognizing your boundaries and your limits . . . who you are responsible for and to and who are you not . . . I mean this is great stuff. [**TP also in core state. Big picture and smaller details are all quite clear and she is gathering them up in a whole and feeding it back to him to really take in.**]

PT: (**Appearing touched**) It is great stuff. And I feel good about it.

TP: Mm-hmm.

PT: I feel good about seeing your face so enthusiastic about it. I didn't think it was that big of a step, but from the look in your face it seems bigger than I realized. But, sometimes when you make incremental progress, sooner or later you realize what a distance you've gone (**smiling**).

TP: Right . . . It's *really* big.

PT: Even though it just seems like the last step was such a small one.

This is dyadic affect regulation. But, rather than downregulating negative or distressing affect, the dyad is upregulating positive, empowering experiences like the "practicing phase" in late infancy (Schore, 1994; Mahler et al., 1975; Russell & Fosha, 2008). The tone of the session is celebratory. The therapist and patient are coconstructing the patient's narrative, not just intellectually but emotionally. The therapist's understanding of the change in light of his history, her own affective response to it, which reflects her excitement about his progress, and his own experience of transformation are incredibly important pieces of information for him. The response of the therapist allows him to see himself and the transformation even more clearly, and it gives him permission to own it emotionally and to feel proud of it and hopeful. A flatter or more neutral response on her part might have interfered with his expansion into this spiral of transformation that is evident below.

(A few moments later . . .)

PT: I feel okay. (**Pause**) I think I told you a couple of weeks ago that when I say I feel okay, I kinda look over my shoulder to see if where there is a black cloud coming up. Do you remember that?

TP: (**Nodding**)

PT: I just said to myself, when I said that I feel okay, "You know, I can handle the black clouds." [**Explicit acknowledgement of feeling more resilient.**]

TP: Wow.

PT: I don't know. Maybe you are catching me on a high, I don't know.

TP: Don't be so quick to dismiss it, Jack. I think that comes up as a little bit of a defense because it is new, you know? What is coming out, everything you are saying about being more grounded, feeling more yourself, knowing more what your boundaries are and what other people's boundaries are, feeling like you are less threatening and you're also less threatened. It's like what you said before that maybe it seems bigger to me because for you it feels like every little incidental step, but I wonder if that consciously you really are recognizing that things feel *quite* different. And when things are different, we tend to do a little pinching of ourselves, like, "Is this real?" And I think it *is* real. I don't think it is just catching you on a high. It doesn't mean you are always going to feel this great . . . this confident. I think this is like a new you that is being knitted together. [**TP providing psychoeducation in the wake of experiential transformation rather than before it; explaining that this tremulousness and doubt is often what we feel in the wake of transformation.**]

PT: I thank you. I feel that way too. [**Defense bypassed; he is able to take it in**] I'm not sure . . . I feel like I am exploring a new territory. [**Transformational affects: realization affects and tremulous affects; State 3.**] It feels good. (**pause**) . . . I recognize that there are times when I have to have my guard up. There are times when I can have my guard down. I don't know. The last few weeks I have felt . . . You know, I haven't taken Lexapro in 3 weeks?

TP: Oh? I didn't know.

PT: Part of me feels I don't need it now . . . I feel better. I feel more focused.

TP: So when you say to me right now what you have said a few times, just focusing on right now, . . . when you say it feels really good, what's the good feeling? What's it like in your body? How do you notice it? What's it like right now? [**TP experientially, somatically grounding and exploring the good feelings to allow them to be as precise and clear as possible in order for them to bear the most fruit. "Good" is vague, just as** is "bad," and as we help people to differentiate negative affective states, it is just as important for them to learn to differentiate positive affective states.]

PT: It's like (**looking up and to the left, then leaning forward and looking at TP in eyes; motioning from chest with hand**). I don't feel in control of my life because I know that there are things about my life that I can't control. But as much as I can control my life, since I know myself so much better now, since I am more in touch with who I am, both good and bad, I feel, I don't know; it sounds silly, more grown up. I feel, "Hah, here's Jack X (**PT says his full name**). That's how I feel." [**Senses of groundedness, clarity, acceptance, self-compassion, self-recognition are hallmarks of core state.**]

TP: Wow.

PT: I feel like (**motioning gently with hands coming out and down from chest to rest on legs**) "here's Jack X (**PT says his full name**)." [**True-self experience; core state.**]

TP: It's a true sense of who you are.

PT: I guess. Yeah. I mean warts and all. I have some warts and parts of me that are hopefully not so warty. God knows I have things to work on . . . But I really feel, I don't know, kinda relaxed. That's how I feel, relaxed. [**Feeling relaxed and at ease are other markers of core state.**]

TP: Mm-hmm.

PT: You know, this is who I am. Bad things can happen to me. I can overcome a lot of them . . . (**speaks about soldiers in hospital recovering from lost limbs**). You sit back and you think to yourself . . . I can handle my mistakes. [**A statement of mature resilience; transformance-oriented resilient capacity.**]

TP: It's wonderful, Jack.

PT: Well thanks, Eileen.

Part of what allows the therapist here to be so genuinely appreciative and enthusiastic about Jack's transformation and solid, positive, mature sense of himself is that she has traveled a long and sometimes

difficult journey with him. She holds the memory of how he first presented, his depression and anxiety, his ironic naivety, his damaged
sense of self, his distorted, negative, and black-and-white view of
women, his violent fantasies and accompanying sense of entitlement,
and the traumatic early attachments and experiences with women
that, in part, gave rise to such conflicts. For him to arrive in such a
place, even if he cannot hold it permanently, even if he "regresses,"
as he does, is cause for celebration because it is the arrival to a new
platform, to a greater level of complexity, acceptance, and understanding and sense of resilience that are now part of the self in a way
that they had not been before. There is more to build on and there
is more to build with. This is a self-at-best experience that can be
drawn on in the future. This is the kind of experience that makes
one's past pain and struggle bearable. There are also experiences,
rarer for sure, that make one's past pain or struggle seem necessary.

The Hero's Journey From Mourning to Dancing

There is a part of me that does not want to write this section, a kind
of resistant part of me that does not want to "give" anything to our
sufferings and struggles by acknowledging that sometimes they are
the reason for our particular strengths as they are often also the
reason for our particular vulnerabilities. I am not fond of platitudes
like "whatever doesn't kill you makes you stronger," or those of the
more religious type: "God never gives you what you can't handle."
On a daily basis clinicians are too close to people getting much more
than they can really handle. And even if they are not dead, we know
many who are certainly not stronger than they might have been in
the absence of whatever adversity they have had to endure.

But I think the positive changes in the self that occur in the wake
of and perhaps as a result of enduring hardship, adversity, or suffering are a human phenomenon that has to be acknowledged in a
book about resilience and particularly on the subject of healing and
transformation. People sometimes are able to transform suffering
into strength, to turn their "mourning to dancing" (Psalm 30:11)

(Bonanno, 2004). With enough healing and perspective, they may be moved to realize that without a certain adversity, they would not know certain beauties, they would not have certain strengths, they would not be resilient in the way they are, they would not have the depth of compassion that they do. This does not happen for everyone, and it should not be pressured or expected or pushed, thereby setting someone up for failure if they cannot find a way of transforming their understanding of their adversity into something positive. But for those for whom it does happen, it is an expression of deep healing, and it contributes to healing. It is an example of the realization affects of the transformational affects, in AEDP terminology.

A young woman patient, Alison, who had suffered with some depression and at times paralyzing anxiety since she was in adolescence, spoke about her relationship with this place of pain and fear where she can go. She spoke about how her sister, whose personality was much "tougher" and who seemed less easily rocked by negative events in her life, did not understand depression. But she observed that she also did not experience a ready gratitude for the good things in her life. Alison was deeply moved by good people in her life, moments of joy and connection, advancements in her life, and other people's successes. She had a gift for not taking too much for granted, and she knew this allowed her to savor the sweetness of life more than many people. She attributed this to her struggles with depression and anxiety. She came to live in a somewhat paradoxical relationship to her suffering. She would never wish it on herself or others, but she also found ways of feeling grateful for the perspective it gave her.

This capacity to partly embrace our pain may be part of the process of integration for some. This is something that usually happens (if it happens) gradually as people move through the practical and emotional fallout from trauma. It is core state (State 4) phenomena and very different from the more defensive move to "create meaning" in an effort to feel more in control. It is usually mixed with feelings of gratitude and a sense and demeanor of humility. Embodied, emotionally informed meaning making is a very important part of healing from trauma. As mentioned in Chapter 4, Jonathan Shay in his book on combat trauma in Vietnam uses the ancient Greek word *themis*

to denote a culture's definition and shared understanding of what is
right and wrong: "the moral order, convention, normative expectations, ethics, and commonly understood social values" (1994, p. 5).
These are shattered by trauma. They are not just challenged; they
simply cannot hold up against someone's lived experience. Janoff-Bulman (1992) talks about the same phenomenon in her research on sur-
vivors of horrific trauma. This work has been influential in the clinical
world, helping us understand that certain traumatic reactions like
self-blame are really efforts to restore earlier held assumptions and
articles of faith (e.g., "I am in control," "I am worthy," or "the world is
a benevolent place"). The meaning people can make of suffering or
trauma when they are already healing is usually very different from
the meaning they make of it while they are still experiencing it, if
they are consciously making meaning of it at all.

Post Traumatic Growth

Tedeschi and Calhoun (Calhoun & Tedeschi, 2001, 2006; McLean et
al., 2011; Tedeschi et. al., 1998) have nominated something they call
posttraumatic growth (PTG). By this they are referring to positive
changes that result not from the trauma itself but from efforts to
cope with trauma in its aftermath. People evincing PTG are changed
through their struggle with adversity or trauma. PTG is marked by
the fact that changes happen in the wake of trauma but not during
lower levels of stress; people experience positive changes as an outcome or result of coping with the trauma versus a way of coping in
and of itself. The label PTG requires that basic assumptions about
life have been shattered by the trauma in a way that lower levels of
stress would not have done.

Similar to how resilience has been discussed throughout this
book, Calhoun and Tedeschi (2001) point out that the presence of
PTG does not necessarily indicate the absence of pain or distress
and that PTG can be limited to certain areas of life. Rather, people evincing PTG are able to see and articulate positive and negative
aspects of their experience of loss or trauma. This is concordant with

---

STRENGTH FROM PAIN: LIVING LIFE AFTER DEATH

In chapter 1, I introduced "Jacob," the man who was repeatedly sexually abused by multiple men as he entered adolescence. In the same conversation with his therapist mentioned there, in which he talks about the impact of two old friends remembering and reflecting back to him what a good and kind boy he was even then, he says that he had already written the ending of his own story. He tells his therapist that he was convinced that the abuse would be "the destruction of my life." In realizing that he was stronger than he ever imagined himself to be, he has a "crazy" thought: that he could almost feel a little gratitude toward the man who abused him, "that despite everything he didn't destroy me . . . it had the potential and all the markings to destroy me . . . And it made me stronger." He spoke about how he thought of himself always as a "weak, despicable, ugly, withered person. And so I just kept reinforcing that. And of course, how would I think any differently until I started allowing truthful things to enter that place?" As they are ending the session, the therapist says to him affectionately and playfully, "Congratulations, you are a much better story." And without missing a beat, Jacob responds with a warm and genuine smile, "See me on the bestseller list!"

---

the findings on emotional complexity discussed earlier in this chapter and the findings that as pain or distress increase, the effect of positive affect on regulating negative affect also increases. Positive experiences and emotions are more necessary. Perhaps the active meaning making in people experiencing PTG helps regulate the ongoing distress affect. Alternatively, perhaps people who can differentiate positive and negative affect can use some positive affect to engage in more hope-inspired meaning making.

On Flourishing, Transformance, and Being Complex

The discussion of resilience takes as a premise that someone has suffered something many would consider highly aversive if not traumatic. We do not talk about resilience in the context of unremarkable, normal development. Adjusting to adverse, neglectful, depriving, or abusive environments has often involved making adaptations or compromises that may have resulted in the loss of other possibilities (e.g., freedom to be oneself, pursue one's interests, or sustain healthy relationships) at least for a period of time. Restored health must then have something to do with the capacity for greater fluidity and the letting go of old, habitual, or rigid ways of meeting life and its challenges. Real, lasting resilience has something to do with a capacity for happiness and joy, with our own desire and capacity to grow and to be open, and with fluidity—with being able to be truly present to the life we are living, "warts and all."

While flourishing, as it is beginning to be used in the research literature, is synonymous with the presence of "mental health" and not simply the absence of mental illness (Keyes, 2002), I think it is still a term that is weighted by our colloquial use of it, thus suggesting a state of unencumbered vitality for life, a fluid capacity to respond to challenge without getting knocked over, a number of areas of a high degree of satisfaction in life, and usually success, prosperity, or both. While Merriam-Webster's online dictionary defines *flourish* as "to grow well; to be healthy," it also includes definitions relating to success and prosperity and "to grow luxuriantly" or to thrive. The former, I think, is consistent with the view of mature resilience I am offering here in that I do not think growing well and being healthy are equal to having no areas of lack of health or struggle. It may be purely semantic, but when we are borrowing nonpsychological terms to define psychological realities or states, I think it is important to be precise about what we mean. Resilience can sometimes manifest as flourishing, as health, growing well, being basically free of psychopathology, and so forth. It can also manifest as thriving, but to the extent that flourishing and thriving are sometimes used interchangeably, I want to avoid saying that this is the goal—not because it is not a worthy goal, but simply because it leans too much on circumstance and fortune. Resilience as transformation includes but is not limited to flourishing or thriving. Overly prizing flourishing, as we overly prize such attributes as youth, wealth, strength, and thinness, threatens to turn a venerable goal into a golden calf. Resilience cannot and should not be equated with flourishing. Rather, because life deals its blows, most people do not stay in states of flourishing or thriving. on a constant basis. And while people certainly contribute to their own states of flourishing, there is also a piece of chance, randomness, or luck that nothing is currently happening to them (e.g., the loss of a loved one, fire in one's home, a traumatic experience, serious illness, or severe financial hardship) to disrupt such a positive state. So, it seems to me that if we are aiming for our patients to be and remain in states of flourishing, we, and our patients, might be quite defeated.

Rather, I think the goal of resilience-oriented work is helping people move through life in touch with the forces of transformance and being able to embrace and perhaps be grateful for the times of flourishing or thriving. This relates more to the process than the product. A person who is in touch with his own transformance strivings is not in denial about life's difficulties or their impact on himself. In the face of adversity, challenge, or even trauma, he can be honest with himself and trusted others about what is going on. He might ask himself questions such as, "I wonder if there is something to learn from this very difficult situation." "Whom can I reach out to now for some extra support?" "What can I do to take care of myself when I am feeling like this?" "How can I be engaged in order to keep some perspective?"

What this perspective suggests is that health and restored resilience are certainly possible in the context of ongoing adversity, suffering, or mental illness. A colleague of mine shared a story of what she and her family endured when her son became very ill for a protracted period of time. They were all under considerable stress. Were they flourishing at the time? No. Were they resilient? Yes, absolutely. Did they know that? No, their subjective experience was that they were getting through, surviving. It was only after it was all over that she could look back and marvel at how they got through all of that as well as they did, that they were as resilient as they were. They accepted what was happening. They did what needed to be done. They leaned into the support available to them. And they strung together enough moments of joy, laughter, or reprieve to give them sufficient energy to keep going. While we would, of course, want for our patients (and ourselves) to experience lasting states of flourishing, that does not have to be the standard against which we measure restored resilience. Rather, the bottom line must be some sense of hopefulness, of security in the self and its capacity to handle life's difficulties and the ability and willingness to seek the help of others when these difficulties are overwhelming. One of the things that can very often happen in people who have survived against great odds is a sense of being able to get through—the pit does not have to be bottomless even if it is black and deep.

Pulling It Together: The Case for a Truly Integrative Approach to Restoring Resilience

Certain personal strengths are highly predictive of or associated with happiness, flourishing, and emotional well-being. These strengths include capacities for gratitude, hope, vitality, curiosity, and love (Corliss, 2013). As psychotherapists we are in a position to help our patients lean into, develop, and use those strengths for their own health and wellness. It is not enough to simply quietly recognize people's strengths from the start. It is far more powerful to share our observations and reactions, knowing the likelihood that we may have to work with patients around their discomfort or disbelief in receiving that from us or from others. Moreover, we can encourage people to use those strengths and to observe with them what happens inside and with others when they do.

This focus on encouraging the development of health and positive habits is a gift of positive psychology (Seligman, 2002; Seligman & Csikszentmihalyi, 2000). This is hardly incompatible with working deeply on relational issues, blocks, resistance, and problematic ways of seeing self and others. Because the removal of pathology does not always evolve into the adoption of health or vitality, positive psychology can provide people with experiments and experiences of themselves that provide energy, a different perspective, and the kinds of emotional experiences (e.g., gratitude or hope) that balance or mitigate the weight of grief, depression, isolation, anxiety, and the impact of stress. We cannot be aware of that to which we do not attend. Many of us have to learn to pay attention to the positive. In fact, Baumeister et al.'s (2001) work suggests we *all* need to learn to reorient to the positive, as the call of the negative to our human minds is evolutionarily more compelling. Once reoriented, it is so much easier to absorb and benefit from that which is good, rewarding, affirming, and healthy in life, in ourselves, and in others. Greater satisfaction and fulfillment are natural products of such an orientation.

Part of what a depth-oriented approach offers is a compassionate and informed understanding about why certain intentional activities or changes of thought do not make enough of an impact on a person and may, in fact, leave them feeling ashamed for not having been converted by what may, for some, be overly concrete approaches. There is a deep understanding and appreciation of the impact of our experience on the development of our psyche, the complexity of the psyche itself, our sense of self, our sense of safety and trust in relationships, our hopes and fears, our capacity to achieve or to fulfill our potential. For many, some historical "stuff" needs some processing and integrating before they are really free to make use of more straightforward, in-the-moment techniques to increase happiness or life satisfaction.

Positive psychology has been a necessary apposition along the arc of a pendulum, but it is a swing back from something that was also necessary. Keeping people in asylums, blaming their character, and claiming that theirs or their parents' sin is the cause of their mental or emotional struggles were not particularly enlightened or humane responses to people's suffering. Some started to get curious about what caused these difficulties to begin with. And this was not just idle curiosity or morbid voyeurism but, rather, sprang from the belief, or at least a hope, that if you could get to the root of the problem, it could be cured and people could be restored to life. That is a very beautiful and humane impulse and conviction. During that first swing of the pendulum, early psychologists and psychiatrists wrestled with the possibility that maybe madness makes sense if you follow the thread far back enough. Maybe light could be found in this darkness. Maybe what appears mysterious is somehow knowable. Maybe order could be found in chaos.

It is not only psychoanalysts that shoulder the blame for the heavy or pathology-oriented focus of psychology and psychotherapeutic approaches. The *Diagnostic and Statistical Manual of Mental Disorders*, the so-called bible of our profession, is a compendium of symptoms, problematic behaviors, thoughts, feelings, and internal maps. Our competence is at least partly assessed by how well we know clusters of symptoms, what they represent diagnostically, what possible medications might ameliorate some of these, and what treatment might be done to remove the symptoms and help people back to baseline. All of us, with the possible exception of humanistic psychotherapists, were firmly planted on the pathology-oriented end of the pendulum's arc.

But now the pendulum has swung again, and positive psychology is on the rise as the next "new" movement in psychology. We have a lot to learn from it. But I think it is important for all psychotherapists, both those who are clinging to the earlier way of seeing and doing things and those who have thrown out the old and are clinging to the new, to remember that this is just another stop along the pendulum's wide and varied arc. Gravity eventually steadies us and brings us back down to earth. It centers us. And I think that it is that center, where the two halves of this pendulum's arc are integrated, that has a very deep truth to offer us.

An older woman, one of my first patients on my second externship when I was still quite young, taught me something important—even though I did not want to hear it at the time. She challenged me to give her something concrete to do. She was so frustrated with how I wanted to listen to her and have her tell me her story. She was very depressed and desperate to feel better. Some part of her knew she needed to be doing something more for herself to help lift her out of her depression. I was insulted and probably self-righteous about how "not so simple" it was. But that was partly a cover for the fact that I did not know what to tell her to do. I was being trained for the long haul, for the deep, dark work, in the belief that people do not and cannot make changes until the thorn and all its splinters are removed and that when that happened, they would presumably, magically know what to do. When I look back I think she might have been more willing to do that "deep" kind of work with me if I knew something to offer her to help buoy her in the meantime.

But I also worked with a few patients in a mode more directly drawn from cognitive-behavioral therapy. Several of them could not engage the work of keeping track of negative thoughts, trying to replace them with more positive or adaptive thoughts. They needed to talk and be heard and had lots of feelings to sort through but often needed help expressing them. They had not contacted whatever life energy they had inside to be able to do something differently on their own behalf. I have referred people for more focused, active, behavioral work on issues that remain sticky after a lot of processing, and I have had patients who have come to me having done more task- or goal-oriented psychotherapy because they feel there is a lot of unprocessed emotion or internal conflict standing in the way of their being able to make use of the other work.

The point here is that we need to consider seriously the benefits of integrating models of psychotherapy or of integrative models that already draw on the strengths of varied established approaches to psychotherapy. It may take more time to master different approaches and find a way of effectively integrating them, but that is okay. Ours is a field that still values experience, time, trial and error, and wisdom. As therapists, unless we get burned out, we can count on being better and better at this whole endeavor as we age.

Positive psychology and researchers interested in happiness per se outline at least four different kinds of happiness: (1) hedonia (pursuit of pleasure), (2) eudaimonia (derived from fulfilling one's potential and a sense of meaning), (3) optimism (belief in the probability of good things happening), and (4) vitality (enthusiasm, positive energy toward life) (Corliss, 2013). In a culture saturated with hedonistic messages about life's values (and our own within it), it is really important to be reminded that there are other, perhaps more enduring sources and types of happiness that have nothing to do with immediate need gratification, whether sexual, appetitive, or material. As I was writing this chapter, and this section in particular, I was eating lunch at a local cafe. An employee came along to wipe the counter near me and throw away a few things. He was an older man who moved somewhat slowly. He greeted me and asked me how I was doing. I told him that I was fine and asked how he was doing. And he said, spraying the table with a lovely smile, "Enjoying the moment." I laughed to myself at the appropriateness of this exchange at this moment, and said, "Good. That's a great way to be." And he, in a less qualified reply, said knowingly, "It's the only way to be."

The Transformational Spiral: From Languishing to Transformance and Flourishing— The Optimal Trajectory of the Resilience Potential

Facilitating the emergence and elaboration of the resilience potential into increasingly healthy, more complex and flexible manifestations of resilient capacity involves a journey of transformation and healing. The microprocess of that journey in the therapeutic encounter often feels like a cascade or spiral, one moment of transformation preceding and facilitating another. One aspect of healing and transformation (e.g., mourning-the-self) processed by the dyad allows for another aspect of healing and transformation (e.g., healing affects) to be consciously felt and integrated. This spiral of transformation is characterized by an acquisition of new experiences, not simply the rehashing of what has already been known. The process starts with letting go into deep emotional processing that had been feared to be too painful or too overwhelming. That letting go is almost always unburdening even when it is quite painful. Part of this process, by itself, releases adaptive action tendencies and leads to new connections and bodily felt insights that additionally deepen the healing process. This is nothing new. And it is where most psychotherapies, including most experiential therapies, stop.

But reflecting on one's own passage through the complex of feelings, as well as the transformed state that is now the consequence of that passage, ushers in new experiences. There is the experi-

ence of the self—affective, cognitive, somatic, present, and historical, as different, changed, transformed in some way—*now, in this
moment*. And this transformational experience of self, as we have
seen throughout the transcripts of this book, usually includes some
variation on themes of relief, lightness, strength, absence of tension
or fear, ease of breath, greater sense of connection to self and others, strength, solidity, and hope. By continuing to intentionally bring
our attention and focus to these transformed states—in other words,
by savoring them—a new cycle in the process of transformational
change is initiated. Rather than letting go, excavating, unwinding,
unraveling, unbinding, we are now in the phase of building up, of
resurrecting what had been there at some point, even if only in
nascent form, and restoring it to what it should have been, what it
was meant to be, much like Michelangelo's *David* created by "restoring" the block of granite to the beautiful form that was always there.
This is a very active process of construction and requires a different
focus, a different energy, a different interest than our earlier work of
deconstruction or excavation. The patient is different, and so is the
therapist. The work of actively restoring processes of health, wellness, and flourishing looks and feels different. In the process, the
therapist learns more about what wholeness looks like and what is
possible in the therapeutic endeavor.

An analogy of an archaeologist comes to mind when I think of this
process and the shift it requires of us as therapists who are attempting to facilitate it and are passionate about restoring resilience to our
patients. An archeologist engages in a process of searching, seeking,
and eventual discovery. His hunches about some important buried
historical treasure lead him to do the heavy, but careful work of dig-
ging and sorting. As he discovers and sorts, he starts to put pieces
together in his mind, making sense of the whole as it once was. New
discoveries lead to more questions, which lead to more research, dig-
ging, sorting, and so on. When enough of that work has been done,
sometimes he is interested enough to rebuild in a way that comports
with how he understood this treasure to have been before it was buried or lost. There is something that is thrilling to him in this process
of restoration, and it allows those of us with less vivid and histori-

cally minded imaginations to see what he is seeing and to experience a past reality in a way that, more or less accurately, reflects how it really was and what its originators intended it to be.

And so it is with restoring resilience. We are mining for gold, and the gold is there. It may be brighter or bigger or more brilliant in some than in others, but it is there nonetheless. And therapy that focuses from the beginning on finding *that* as its starting point holds the promise of facilitating healing on two fronts simultaneously: reducing psychopathology and its fallout and enhancing and elaborating strengths and capacities that already exist but require recognition and nurturance. This kind of two-pronged approach instantiates hope in the patient from the beginning of the work and sustains both patient and therapist to remain deeply engaged for the sometimes difficult emotional journey. The essence of resilience, which is the differentiation of the self from that which is aversive to it, is what becomes clear and consciously felt in the experience of healing and transformation. Healed, people are able to see themselves and even their pathology and pain with compassion and even awe. What we see only glimmers of in the beginning, we see cascading in the end. What is hard to hold onto at the start becomes a recursive process of repair, change, and the freeing expansion of the self's capacities as one's resilience is restored and the courage to be fully human and fully alive is finally embodied.

Summary

This chapter has focused on the role of positive emotion in the process of healing and restoring resilience. We discussed the broaden and build theory of positive emotion and the many benefits of happiness in the realms of physical, emotional, relational, and vocational health. Clinically, we looked at how many people may need help taking in and making use of positive affects (receptive affective capacity), especially as negative experiences and their accompanying emotions are more evolutionarily compelling to us as human beings. We also reviewed the dynamic model of affect and the relationship of emotional complexity to what I call mature resilience, which involves being connected to transformance strivings even when life is difficult. Flourishing and thriving, while worthy goals, should not be the gold standard of mature resilience because they usually require that life not be particularly demanding. And because we are talking about resilience and not simply optimal functioning, mature resilience involves being connected to and actively dealing with the challenges of life. We looked at how the process of finding one's way in the wake of trauma can even result in transformation and growth, something called posttraumatic growth. Finally, a case was made for an integrative approach to restoring resilience, one that respects the story of the life and the interior complexity of the person, helps patients process what has not been processed (memories, emotions, relational states, and the like), and actively encourages and helps elaborate positive emotions and other eruptions of the resilience potential and transformance strivings.

Until this point, this book has focused almost entirely on the experience of the patient in the process of restoring resilience. But this kind of work that is emotionally rich, relationally engaged, focused on finding glimmers of resilience, strength, and hope from the beginning of treatment turns out to be healthy and often resilience building for the therapist as well. The next and final chapter of this book will explore the reflections and experiences of therapists who are doing this kind of work and the cycle of hope that is engaged and is invigorating and restorative for the therapist.

CHAPTER 8

The Resilient Clinician:

How Resilience-Oriented Work Transforms the Therapist

The decision to improve the mental health of others is a choice to improve ourselves in the process.

It seems necessary, in writing a book about working with resilience, to devote a few pages to exploring therapist growth and restored resilience as well. Much of the metapsychology described in this book requires, in practice, a certain orientation toward the world, self, and others that is generally positive, basically hopeful, forgiving, and curious. Such an orientation is hard to achieve or maintain if we therapists are inundated with our own personal problems or stress and thus struggling just to survive, with too little mental energy left over to devote to thriving. The reality of how our personal lives, with all their struggles and joy, affect our work in a particular and particularly intimate way leads naturally to the question of how we might take care of ourselves in order to be able to do the work. Others are more qualified than I to offer strategies and suggestions about self-care.

And so while the following is not explicitly about caretaking, it is still a divergence from the rest of the book. The voice is different, more personal. While I offer the stories of patient in foregoing pages, the main focus is on what it is like for you, for me, for us to do this kind of work. Of course, there is research to support what is stated below, but the emphasis here is more on the art rather than the science of psychotherapy, more on the persons who are part of the exchange than on what the exchange looks like between those persons. And because we therapists are half of the transformational dyad, our own experience with growth, healing, and increased resilience deserves more than a passing mention.

It is in that spirit that I attempt to explore how the work of therapy—its philosophy, orientation, and interventions—has recursive, positive effects on therapists that maintain or increase therapist resilience both professionally and even personally. To that end, this chapter does several things. First, I share some of my own experiences, which made this work feel "right" to me. Second, I introduce a patient whose adaptation to life was to sometimes hide her own true resilient capacity and how her experiences in therapy earlier in her life reinforced that hiding. Third, I offer some reflections on therapist resilience by therapists trained in AEDP. And, finally, I tie this all together with a bit of research on how the use of our own affect and the deep offering of our selves as therapists contributes to our own well-being and resilience.

Personal Reflections

Many times over the years, friends, acquaintances, and especially patients have either casually remarked or seriously asked, "How can you sit around all day and listen to people's problems?" I am sure every therapist has been asked this many times. The questioner usually then adds that it would make her crazy to do this work, or she would not be able to be in this kind of role. It is true that some days are just plain rough. Sometimes our patients' despair is contagious, or more often, at least in my experience, on those rough days I have entered some new story of a patient's trauma through my imagination and it has left its mark on my mind, soul, and body. Especially in hearing stories of abuse or violence, I am left to ponder the depravity of humanity, the undaunted and sadistic cruelty that we can visit upon others when we are frightened by them, feel superior to them, or objectify or vilify them—in short, when we dehumanize them. Entering that awareness seems to me to be part of being or becoming a good therapist. As my patients have taught me over the years, if you do not enter people's pain, your capacity to help them is impaired.

But neither can we stay in that pain or become overwhelmed ourselves, at least not for long. We have to find our ground, our own footing. We need to gird ourselves with whatever or whomever gives us hope, strength, faith, courage. One possible source of that hope or strength may be the admiration we feel for our own patients in witnessing their stories and in deeply appreciating how they have gotten themselves through against incredible odds.

Perhaps like many of you reading this book, I am not undone by "sitting and listening to people's problems all day," because that is not ultimately what it feels like to me. Most of the time, I am honestly and truly awed by what people have come through and how their desire for healing resides right next to the invitation to despair, even when it looks like the latter is stronger. It also stimulates me to explore different ways for that healing to occur and to be intensely curious about the phenomenon of resilience as an existential reality and as a personal reality that manifests in countless ways. Except on the worst days, I do not see just a "pile of problems" in front of me, and that is what makes doing this work more of a privilege, than a burden.

As a fledgling psychologist, I worked at Bellevue Hospital in New York City with people, mostly men, with serious substance abuse disorders. Most of them were also homeless, and many were also struggling with comorbid psychiatric disorders. Their lives were replete with trauma, and for the most part, only a small portion of that was due to the consequences of drinking or drugs. Most of them started out in family environments that were extremely neglectful, abusive, substance abusing, or rife with the heaviness of loss. Their substance abuse usually began at an early age as a way to cope with or obliter-

ate emotional pain, and by the time I was seeing them in psychotherapy, several of them had been abusing substances for as long as or
longer than I had been alive.

I was pretty naïve in many ways. I had vaguely heard or read that
one shouldn't do depth-oriented or emotion-focused psychotherapy
with substance abusers because they were too "fragile" to be able to
tolerate the feelings that would come up. But, honestly, I did not know
how to do anything other than depth-oriented, feeling-focused work.
I had no real skills in cognitive behavioral therapy and no training in
motivational enhancement techniques, and discussions of relapse prevention, as useful as they were, only took us so far. What really interested me was my patients, their lives and stories, and the fact that
they were trying, and trying hard, every day, to be sober for the first
time in their lives and to rebuild a life that was sustainable, self-respecting, open to others, and self-aware. I thought that took tremendous courage. Yes, it is true that people sometimes "simply" bottom
out and have no choice but to do something else. But in these cases,
the something else was mostly a daily uphill battle, and temptation
was everywhere. In the long run, it probably would have been easier
to go back to what they had been doing and let themselves slowly and
unconsciously die an ignominious death. Instead, most of them faced
deep cravings, acknowledged their own defenses for the first time,
endured the social humiliations of the system they were part of, faced
the multiple losses attached to their substance abuse, attempted intimacy with themselves and others, often for the first time, all while
not being able to lean on their most reliable and powerful defense:
substances and their capacity to dull pain and help us forget.

They talked to me. They seemed relieved by that, for the most
part. They felt seen and understood, cleaner, lighter. And that gave
us both hope. I was inspired by what they were able to do, and I was
encouraged that the work we were engaged in was helping them. I
myself was learning that what we were both bearing together, how
we were both finding our way separately, but together, was helping
us both become stronger people, as therapist and as patient.

My paradoxical relationship to this topic is as a curious, somewhat
guilty, but admiring observer. I don't know how resilient I am. I trust

and hope that witnessing others' "hero's journeys" makes me stronger by osmosis. I look on my life gratefully for the gentleness of it thus far. It is not that there were not and are not issues or struggles. But the kinds of things that erode or tear away people's foundations have not been part of my experience. After all this study and clinical work over a number of years, I have so much respect and curiosity for the processes of resilience, which I still find somewhat mysterious.

A foundational statement in AEDP is that "nothing that feels bad is ever the last step" (Gendlin, 1981, p. 27). But sometimes this is really hard to believe in the face of unmitigated trauma or unparalleled loss. Indeed, it is not a statement of fact; it cannot be. There is *plenty* of evidence that bad wins, and often (Baumeister et al., 2001). It is, rather, an article of faith. If you believe it, you look for it. If you look for it, you often find it. And when you find it, your faith in the probability of healing, restoration, resurrection, and repair is deepened.

Ours is a wisdom field. Like good cheese or wine, we should get better with age and experience. But it does not always happen that way. I suspect that part of how it happens, when it happens, is that we remain open to continuing to learn even as we become more proficient and expert. There is sufficient balance in different kinds of experiences: of having our perspective and approach to our work confirmed or validated such that we develop a certain confidence and groundedness (assimilation), and of having our perspective challenged or stretched that we need to learn by accommodating something new (assimilation and accommodation were introduced by Piaget 1952). I want to share with you a story of a session I had with Siobhan in the course of writing this chapter that functioned for me as both types of learning about resilience. I was affirmed in my understanding, but I was also challenged toward a deeper understanding than before and to become even more open to precisely the thing I was writing about.

Missing the Forest for the Trees: The Story of Siobhan

Siobhan is a woman in her late thirties, a divorced mother of two. Her story illustrates the crucial importance of being open to true resilience, to allowing ourselves to be surprised, impressed, awed, and moved by the capacity of another, or of ourselves, to hold onto ourselves no matter what might be happening to us. The gift of this session happened one morning, just as I had been thinking about and starting to write this chapter.

Siobhan was referred to me a year before as her fifteen-year relationship was unraveling. In my first phone conversation with her, she told me she had been in a number of therapies over her lifetime, and she wanted to make sure I could deal with her strong part, but not let her get away with hiding her vulnerable part. She was now living on her own for the first time in her adult life, with her two young children, sharing custody and care with her former partner.

She is a strong person, a formidable and very likable woman, a successful artist turned successful business person who is respected and sometimes adored by colleagues and bosses alike. She works hard and has a lot of energy and a good deal of confidence. She has held for decades the tension between feeling spurned, objectified, and undesirable and knowing that people admire her, wonder at her strength, and even envy her.

Siobhan was born with a rare birth defect that caused several parts of her body to be deformed or disfigured. In later childhood and adolescence she underwent reconstructive surgeries in an attempt to restore a "normal" appearance to these parts of her body. Breaks from school were frequently spent in surgery and recovering from it. She dealt with her own anxiety, pain, insecurity, and anger around all of this but also wound up having to "take care" of her mother, who was frequently tearful, anxious, and emotionally intrusive. When she was in her late teens, a good friend cried about her going through surgery again and asked her if she really needed to keep doing this. This friend's deep empathy led her to decide that enough was enough. There were no more surgeries after that. She would never be perfect, but she would no longer pursue it.

In the meantime and through all of this, she discovered that she loved to paint. She became a serious art student and balanced a grueling schedule between time in the studio and school throughout her youth. We talked at different points about her sense of being different from others: sometimes superior, sometimes inferior. We explored the felt difference of real compassion and understanding from others versus what felt like pity and their relief that it was "not me." We talked about how all of this and more contributed to a somewhat avoidant attachment style, which assumed that she would not be understood or accepted by others, that she would have to do more than her fair share in a relationship, or that others would ultimately use her for her strength.

In this session, she talked about her experience of others' jealousy toward her, especially now as she is in a job she really likes and has fallen in love with a man who seems to understand and adore her, and as her relationship with her children had improved considerably since her separation and divorce. Siobhan slowly, somewhat timidly, spoke about her own experience of herself as "bright" (meaning happy) and loving and grateful for life. She tearfully recounted reading a story about a woman with an incredibly similar past who, despite having many positive experiences as an adult, ultimately killed herself. And with some sense of wonder, she said that she does not and never has understood suicide. She revealed more about a deep sense of the gift of life and even about her own selfhood, being a "bright," kind of easy person who had adapted to many challenges and kept pursuing more life. And as she said more, and shyly revealed this true self, there was no judgment of others or of herself. There was, rather, a sense of wonder, curiosity, and gratitude for what she called a "gift" of how she is, always has been, and how she sees life and the world. She said, "I don't feel like it is really mine to talk about," without in the least disowning it. She was telling me that she has always known and trusted that *nothing that feels bad is ever the last step.*

She felt, at a certain point, incredibly vulnerable revealing all of this to me and staying with it. Eventually, she wept for several minutes, something she had not yet done in our work together. They sounded like deep tears of grief. She emerged to tell me about one therapist who told her she needed to remember and process the difficult feelings she had had during and after the surgeries. Another spiritual guide insisted that she needed to acknowledge the anger at her mother that manifested as her disease "I wasted so many hours," she said, sorrowfully.

I think what she was saying to me was that while she suffered what she suffered, and while it had some of the negative consequences one would expect, it was not who she is or was. The bright, optimistic, grateful self that she has always known to be her true self, but that few people have known what to do with, is not a defense against unprocessed pain. It is the self that helped her metabolize that pain, that prompted her to get help when she needed it, allowed her to keep reaching for the things and people that gave her life, lifted her spirit, and related to her as a person and not simply as an admired or pitied object. And this self allows her to feel a deep compassion for other people.

It is interesting and so ironic. With many people, we are looking for that glimmer, that self that is differentiated from that which is aversive to it. It is shadow because it is largely unconscious and unaware. In Siobhan, she learned to become apologetic and self-effacing about that strength, about her own resilience. What is most vulnerable in her are not the parts that cannot deal but the mysterious part that truly can. It really brought home to me how easy it is for us as therapists (myself included) to project our own imagined feelings onto others who have suffered in ways we might not have and to go on a hunt for that suffering or that pain, rather than really marking and celebrating the ways in which people get through so many of life's blows and the mystery of how that happens. Part of doing this work is allowing ourselves to be open to and embracing of that mystery. As Masten said, "Resilience appears to be a common phenomenon arising from ordinary human adaptive processes. The great threats to human development are those that jeopardize the systems underlying these adaptive processes" (2001, p. 234). It is the ordinariness of resilience that is really extraordinary.

How Resilience-Oriented Therapy Nurtures Therapists

When initially thinking about and outlining this book, I thought a chapter on therapist resilience was warranted, although there are plenty of other books addressing the subject of how therapists can take care of themselves. There is even one titled The Resilient Clinician by Robert Wicks (2007), which I recommend. Wicks's patients are, in fact, largely therapists, many of whom have experienced burnout—or, to use a more appropriate term for our field, "compassion fatigue." So, the prescription about how to lead your life or organize your practice or take care of yourself is something I feel neither qualified nor inclined to offer here. And yet clinicians' resilience, both its potential and its capacity, is a very important piece of doing the kind of resilience-oriented work that does not avoid the abysses for fear there is no light below. Moreover, therapists' resilience facilitates their recognition of the parts of others that help them survive and thrive despite adversity.

It is in this spirit of inviting reflection on what the work is like for each of us that I shared a little piece of my own self, of my own journey with resilience-focused work. I did not want to offer the generous voices of my colleagues without adding my own. I had invited a number of my colleagues who have at least some training in AEDP to share their thoughts and reflections about what has been transformed in them by doing an expressly resilience-oriented, affective-experiential type of therapy, as well as how they have seen the unfolding of their patients' resilience. I asked colleagues on the AEDP listserv to share their thoughts about what ways they have been influenced by training in AEDP to think about or look for clients' resilience, how they have been personally challenged by the work, how they have become more resilient (if they have), and how their clients have become more resilient. I am very grateful to them for their thoughtful and thought-provoking responses and their willingness to allow me to quote them here. First, let me take a moment to place this discussion in the context of the essence of resilience as has been laid out in this book.

The Essence of Resilience for Therapists

If the essence of resilience is the self's differentiation from that which is aversive to it, then therapists' resilience has to include being able to hold onto a self that is not overcome by other people's pain or pathology—what we may commonly think of as "boundaries." One of the most powerful ways I know of attaining that kind of resilience without relying on avoidance or disconnection in relationships that need our real presence is to have or develop a deep faith in the resilience potential of the people with whom we are working.

If resilient capacity can manifest as conservation/resistance or expansion/transformance, it should be obvious that for therapists, as well as any other group of people, the more developed and complex expression of resilience is transformance oriented: open toward one's own growth and toward that of the other. It is true that some therapists are their best, most integrated, developed, and complex selves in their roles as therapists. It is easier to trust in the resilience potential or see the resilient capacity of the other than of oneself. But when it is working optimally, resilience-focused psychotherapy is mutually beneficial to therapist and patient alike. Therapists witness, help elaborate, and are inspired by the strengths and adaptations of their patients. They are encouraged to be more open and compassionate to their own places of pain or struggle, or they are inspired to try something different in their own lives in response to a challenging situation or relationship. And, as discussed throughout this book, the perspective therapists have on the resilience of their patients allows patients to see themselves differently, to have more compassion, to deepen their understanding of themselves and others, and even to be freer to have more options about what to do differently to improve their lives. We are all healed and made stronger and more resilient in witnessing and being part of the process of healing.

The Gift of Resilience-Focused Training on Therapists

Conceição, Iwakabe & Pascual-Leone gave a paper in 2014 (in preparation) at the Society of the Exploration of Psychotherapy Integration (SEPI) examining research they did with experienced AEDP clinicians on their own experiences of growth and change. Their findings reinforce many of the things I found more informally through my survey. My colleagues had a lot to say about how learning AEDP specifically enhanced their own personal and professional resilience, as well as their understanding of the resilience of their patients. Acknowledging that an inner drive toward health and access to internal resources is not a new idea proffered by AEDP, or even psychology, one psychologist who works primarily with couples and families stated, "There's something about the way we lead with that belief from our very first encounter with a patient that feels innovative, freeing, and refreshing in this era of demonization." Another colleague, referring to the search for transformance strivings, wrote that "even the infinitesimal has weight."

Most respondents said that their own capacity to be with intense affect, whether their patients' or their own, had been greatly expanded by learning AEDP. One psychoanalyst stated that it "taught me to be more courageous and to tolerate more (the) affect of others and to express myself more directly in any moment." Stretching one's comfort zones was an almost universal response. Not surprisingly, this was related not simply to the invitation to be more explicit in general but especially to being more explicitly appreciative of patients, their attempts at adaptation, and the positive feelings between the therapist and patients, including appreciation, admiration, awe, delight, respect, and love.

One of the things that several people mentioned as helpful to the restoration of resilience was the importance of deepening positive affect as much as negative or painful affect, as was discussed at length in Chapter 7. Perhaps what we are learning is that they are not mutually exclusive and it is not, in fact, constructive to ignore or bypass positive affects or experience in our determination to process negative or painful ones. Either is a way in, and once there, the perspective that highly positive affective experiences provide is uniquely broader, more encompassing, and more compassionate than that which is achieved by a more exclusive focus on "problems." Many patients, mired in symptoms or problems, need help accessing that which is positive and sustaining. One man realized, in the wake of an extremely positive experience of feeling loved and belonging, that so much of his capacity for positive affect was smothered by unprocessed negative affect: "I feel like having let some emotion out, my defenses are down and I can let the good things in . . . Because when I feel like my defenses are up, they keep a lot of good things out and the good things can't get in because there's a barrier that's preventing things from coming in. And now I feel as though I am allowing some new things to come in. Like that river is running again" (Russell & Fosha, 2008, p. 186). It seems to me highly unlikely that this man would have had this insight about the collateral effects of unprocessed negative feeling without, first, having an intensely positive and healing experience and, second, taking the time to stay with and reflect on the experience and its meaning for him.

In reading all of these generous and thoughtful responses to my questionnaire, I began to realize that what resilience-focused work requires from the therapist is hope that healing is possible and faith in our patients' capacities to self-right and to live from a place of transformance versus resistance or constriction. That hope itself makes us more resilient therapists who can weather the ups and downs of clinical practice with some flexibility and acceptance. This hope is built up either through our own real experiences with our own failures, struggles, pain, or loss or through the kind of eye-opening inspiration that comes from being truly present with another who is overcoming these difficulties.

Resilience as Interdependence

The moments in life that try us to the point where our internal resources are no longer sufficient to put us back together raise the issue of community and the need for support and connection that many of the therapists in my survey mentioned. Over and over, therapists in this community articulate the safety they feel (sometimes for the first times in their professional lives) to be themselves, to reveal their vulnerability or uncertainty, to not be on top of it or know it all. Several people contrasted their experience in this kind of community, which models itself on its explicitly empathic, emotionally engaged, resilience-oriented approach, to other professional communities in which they felt less safe because they were marked by so much competition or a sense of coolness or detachment that did not invite them in as human beings. Being met, understood, helped, and supported undoes aloneness and helps us to know experientially how to do that more for the other who is our patient. This support is a critical piece of doing emotionally engaged work in a way that does not overwhelm us as clinicians and helps us maintain some space from the pain of others without being separate or remote from them. It is therefore not only the theoretical and technical orientation of the model itself but, in a real way, the actual interactions among therapists in this community that provide support and a way of looking at ourselves and others with compassion and curiosity.

Resilience as Increased Capacity to Bear All Things

A consistent theme echoed by therapists was how this work has stretched their capacity to tolerate intensely positive and intensely negative affect both in themselves and in others. One woman said she felt a lot more courageous in the face of others' affect and in expressing herself more directly to others. Another stated it this way: "My own resiliency continues to increase as I witness and experience with my patients their own increased capacity. It also grows when I am invited into territory that is uncomfortable to me, and to do the necessary work to tolerate those places myself so that I can be with my patient in her places that evoked this discomfort in me."

This capacity to bear more has allowed a number of therapists feel more competent as therapists, which in turn increases their own resilience capacity. A few therapists mentioned that they believe they have become better, more competent therapists through learning this kind of work, and that in itself is a source of resilient capacity for them. All therapists who participated in the survey agreed that their patients have become more resilient in the course of doing this kind of work in general, and many took the time to share specific stories of cases. One clinician sensed that his own greater capacity for feeling led to a greater connectedness to himself and to his patients, which in turn helped him and his patients to trust in and be hopeful about the process together.

Hope

Hope, even if not precisely that word, was also echoed as a manifestation of therapists' resilience and as an essential piece of doing this work well. There is the explicit hopefulness of the theory, of the concepts of transformance and resilience potential and of how these inform one's stance and approach. Then there is the lived experience of daring to be more hopeful as a therapist and having that risk be rewarded many times over. Both of these pieces—the theory and the lived experience—enhance therapist resilience and stamina. A deep belief in the capacity for self-preservation and the plasticity of how that expresses itself in increasingly healthy ways with support helps the therapist notice small but important changes and trust in the self-righting of a self system that desires healing. One colleague expressed it this way: "It has helped me to believe/ know that everything about being human is potential—all psychological concepts now include for me the prospect of repair, growth, transformation, possibility. Before . . . I would have thought of resilience as a strength formed at a critical period and pretty much limited in its capacity to grow." The transformation of this woman's perspective has been repeated to me in different words many times over the years. Whether it is our own direct experience of transformation in or out of therapy or how the witnessing of our patients' healing affects our understanding of pathology and possibility, we are inspired. This participation in the experience of healing transformation engenders a deeper sense of hopefulness about our work, ourselves, others, and the world. I have tried to capture this in the Circle of Hope shown in Figure 8.1.

FIGURE 8.1. Circle of Hope.
Figure created by Diana Fosha, used with permission.

Hope is recursive and cumulative, a positive feedback loop. To be clear, by *hope* I do not mean the wishing-on-a-star, crossing-our-fingers kind of hope. I mean it more like faith and trust. Merriam-Webster's online dictionary provides two definitions that fit: "to desire with the expectation of obtainment" and "to expect with confidence." It must start with a little bit of hope that comes from somewhere, maybe if from no other place than having no choice but to hope (think of Barack Obama's book title: *The Audacity of Hope*). That little bit of necessary hope is already a manifestation of the resilience potential. It must combine with some bit of vulnerability, by which I mean a willingness to take a chance or to risk something in order to be open to something new. This gives us the freedom and enough safety to be curious in our seeking rather than certain about what we will find. This kind of curiosity invariably leads to the discovery of something new. In the case of being a therapist working from a resilience-oriented standpoint, that may involve glimpses of true self experiences, of transformance strivings, of parts that need healing, of reasons for defenses, of fragments of compassion (our own or our patients'). This brings understanding and with it comes compassion. These are necessary ingredients for healing, for beginning to see the whole picture, for our perspective to be broadened enough to include with compassion those parts of us that we have been inclined to relegate to shadow or to not acknowledge at all. And the experience of healing, whether we experience it directly or have the privilege of witnessing it, deepens our hope in approaching woundedness, defendedness, and resistance with confidence all over again.

Our own hope is very important because we communicate it implicitly, explicitly, and energetically. Our patients borrow it and lean into it until they discover that it is also coming from within. This accumulative cycle of hope is also true for patients vis-à-vis themselves and whatever they are struggling with. Instead of reacting against themselves when they are suffering or troubled, they can touch some hopefulness, perhaps borrowed, but enough to be vulnerable to their experiences. How many times have we felt grateful in hearing a patient say for the first time, "and I heard your voice in my head say . . ."? This allows them to be curious enough to spend the time to find out what is really going on with them. Sustained curiosity does not long go unanswered. Discovery of what the issue is in the moment or even a glimpse at the larger picture is the eventual response. Understanding is broadened, self-compassion deepened, and therefore, by definition, healing is taking place. They become more and more able to accept all parts of themselves and their experiences with compassion and hopefulness about their capacity to be okay and to heal in the future. People recognize this as healing. By definition, it feels good, positive, and true to them. They often smile and laugh even when the truth is painful.

Trusting the Transformational Process

In order to do deep affect work, one needs to trust the process of transformation, the thrust of healing. Clinicians who are just coming to affect-oriented, experiential work often have ambivalent feelings about what they are watching on the videotape. They are drawn in by the emotional depth of the experience the patient is having and recognize it as powerful and transformational, but they also, not infrequently, report feeling nervous or scared, or admitting that they would have backed off precisely at the point that the therapist they are watching continues to encourage an even deeper processing of emotional material or a deeper or more explicit sense of connection between therapist and patient to help metabolize the emotion. They have not yet come to trust that processing emotions to completion inevitably leads to a better place. This takes time and exposure to internalize and to trust—not only that the patient will survive and be better off for it but also that the therapist knows how to be there with him or her in this powerful place in a powerful, transformative way.

It takes exposure and practice to feel resilient ourselves as clinicians. To know that we can tolerate our own deep affective experiences and those of others, to know that we can help regulate someone when they are overwhelmed or invite them into feeling when they are overregulated, and to be able to be profoundly intimate with another person who is not spouse, child, or parent requires a lot of experiential exposure and a repeated willingness to take a risk. We never stand outside the possibility of being hurt, rejected, or humiliated, because if we did, our vulnerability would ultimately be hollow.

And so we must learn in a right-brained way that we are, in fact, resilient—but not invulnerable—in the face of our own pain and struggle and in the face of others'. We have to have experiences of remaining connected to ourselves (i.e., differentiated) and getting through difficult situations (including difficult sessions) while remaining connected to the person of the other. But in order to get there and in order to trust that such is a worthwhile endeavor, some of us need to have our left brains convinced, or at least somewhat persuaded, that this is really okay for our patients and for ourselves.

An article by Richard Harrison and Marvin Westwood (2009) speaks to that need. These clinical investigators were interested in examining what factors sustained the well-being and prevented vicarious traumatization of experienced clinicians who work with traumatized populations. One might have expected that they would have emphasized strong emotional boundaries, a strict balance between personal and professional life, and so on. After all, vicarious traumatization, as it was defined by McCann and Pearlman (1990), results from empathic engagement—our empathy makes us vulnerable. And it is easy to extrapolate from this that keeping an emotional distance is protective and necessary. It is quite the opposite of the approach that is offered in this book, which involves the therapist's vulnerability, emotional availability and engagement.

In fact, what Harrison and Westwood (2009) found was very supportive of this kind of approach from the perspective of the therapist. While boundaries and balance were found to be important, they instead found that what they call "exquisite empathy" was a protective factor among these clinicians. *Exquisite empathy* was defined as "a discerning, highly present, sensitively attuned, well-boundaried, heartfelt form of empathic engagement" (p. 213). They elaborate:

> When clinicians maintain clarity about interpersonal boundaries, when they are able to get very close without fusing or confusing the client's story [for their own], this exquisite kind of empathic attunement is nourishing for therapist and client alike, in part because the therapists recognize it is beneficial to the clients. Thus the ability to establish a deep, intimate, therapeutic alliance based upon presence, heartfelt concern, and love is an important aspect of well-being and professional satisfaction for many of these clinicians. (p. 213)

This idea of exquisite empathy is predicated, in part, on the differentiation of the self of the therapist from the traumatic (i.e., that which is aversive) story of the patient. The therapist's resilience is also tied to his or her capacity to be outside of that which is traumatic while being fully present to it and to the person who has experienced it. There is tremendous freedom in being fully present, loving, kind, helpful, witnessing, and instrumental. As Harrison and Westwood note, resilient clinicians "shared an overarching positive orientation, conveyed in terms of an ability to maintain faith and trust in: (a) self as good enough; (b) the therapeutic change process; and (c) the world as a place of beauty and potential (despite and in addition to pain and suffering)" (p. 211). One of the participants in my survey put it this way: "In those deep reciprocal experiences, it seems that giving/receiving blends as we experience it together."

A logical question that may arise for many reading this book is how one does the kind of work that is described in this book and maintain one's own resilience. The underlying assumption of that question is that working in an empathically connected, emotionally engaged way makes one vulnerable to either vicarious traumatization or some kind of fatigue or exhaustion. But what Harrison and Westwood (2009) found is also what I have found in my own personal professional experience, among the close colleagues I have the pleasure of knowing, and among the people who took time to respond to my questionnaire. In the words of one colleague, "My image of the more traditional therapeutic stance that I did in the past was that I was driving a car with the breaks on. That was exhausting and led to 'burn out'—hard on the tires—whereas the other was often re-vitalizing." Practicing in a way that is focused by hope, holds a deep faith in the self-righting capacities of the individual, and is most concerned with detecting and elaborating transformance strivings and glimmers of resilience is protective, liberating, and even transformative, of the therapist as well as of the patient.

It is my hope that whatever desire drew you to read this book, whatever curiosity you have about enhancing resilience in your patients and in yourself, has been deepened and strengthened in the reading of it. I hope that you have gleaned some tips from the transcripts and from the discussion of theory and technique. But more, I hope you have been inspired, as I have, to find and resuscitate the resilience potential of your patients, to become more sensitive to transformance strivings, and to feel more confident about and grounded in the affectively alive and embodied process of healing and change that restores and enhances resilience.

REFERENCES

Adler, A. (1964). *The individual psychology of Alfred Adler.* H. L. Ansbacher and R. R. Ansbacher (Eds.). New York, NY: Harper Torchbooks.

Ainsworth M. D. S., Blehar, M. C., Waters, E., & Wall, S. (1978). *Patterns of attachment: Assessed in the strange situation and at home.* Hillsdale, NJ: Erlbaum.

Alexander, F., & French, T. M. (1946). *Psychoanalytic psychotherapy: Principles and application.* Lincoln, NE: University of Nebraska Press.

Algoe, S. B., & Haidt, J. (2009). Witnessing excellence in action: The "other-praising" emotions of elevation, gratitude, and admiration. *Journal of Positive Psychology, 4,* 105–127.

Algoe, S. B., Haidt, J., & Gable, S. L. (2008). Beyond reciprocity: Gratitude and relationships in everyday life. *Emotion, 8,* 425–429.

Alvord, M. K., & Grados, J. J. (2005). Enhancing resilience in children: A proactive approach. *Professional Psychology: Research and Practice, 36,* 238–245.

Basch, M. F. (1976). The concept of affect: A reexamination. *Journal of the American Psychoanalytic Association, 24,* 759–777.

Baumeister, R. F., Bratslavsky, E., Finkenauer, C., & Vohs, K. D. (2001). Bad is stronger than good. *Review of General Psychology, 5,* 323–370.

Beebe, B., & Lachman, F. (1994). Representation and internalization in infancy: Three principles of salience. *Psychoanalytic Psychology, 11,* 127–165.

Benjamin, J. (1990). An outline of intersubjectivity: The development of recognition. *Psychoanalytic Psychology, 7*(Suppl.), 33–46.

Berscheid, E. (2003). The human's greatest strength: Other humans. In U. M. Staudinger (Ed.), *A psychology of human strengths: Fundamen-*

tal questions and future directions for a positive psychology (pp. 37–47). Washington, DC: American Psychological Association.

Billings, A. 1983. G., Cronkite, R. C., & Moos, R.H.. (1983). Social-environmental factors in unipolar depression: Comparisons of depressed patients and nondepressed controls. *Journal of Abnormal Psychology, 92,* 119–133.

Block, J., & Kremen, A. M. (1996). IQ and ego-resiliency: Conceptual and empirical connections and separateness. *Journal of Personality and Social Psychology, 70,* 349–361.

Block, J. H., & Block, J. (1980). The role of ego-control and ego resiliency in the origination of behavior. In W. A. Collings (Ed.), *Minnesota symposia on child psychology,* Vol. 13 (pp. 39–101). Hillsdale, NJ: Erlbaum.

Bollas, C. (1979). The transformational object. *International Journal of Psychoanalysis, 60,* 97–107.

Bollas, C. (1987). *The shadow of the object: Psychoanalysis of the unthought known.* London: Free Association Books.

Bonanno, G. A. (2004). Loss, trauma and human resilience: Have we underestimated the human capacity to thrive after extremely aversive events? *American Psychologist, 59,* 20–28.

Bowlby, J. (1980). *Attachment and loss,* Vol. 3, *Loss: Sadness and depression.* New York, NY: Basic Books.

Bowlby, J. (1982). *Attachment and loss,* Vol. 1, *Attachment* (2nd ed.). New York, NY: Basic Books.

Bowlby, J. (1989). *A secure base: Clinical applications of attachment theory.* London: Routledge.

Bradley, M. (2010). *The three stages of healing: Trauma conversion and resilience* (course workbook). Brentwood, TN: Cross Country Education.

Bridges, M. (2006). Activating the corrective emotional experience. *Journal of Clinical Psychology, 62,* 551–568.

Bryant, F. B., & Veroff, J. (2007). *Savoring: A new model of positive experience.* Mahwah, NJ: Erlbaum.

Calhoun, L. G., & Tedeschi, R. G. (2001). Posttraumatic growth: The positive lessons of loss. In R. A. Neimeyer (Ed.), *Meaning reconstruction and the experience of loss* (pp. 157–172). Washington, DC: American Psychological Association.

Calhoun, L. G., & Tedeschi, R. G. (Eds.). (2006). *Handbook of posttraumatic growth: Research and practice.* Mahwah, NJ: Erlbaum.

Cicchetti, D., & Rogosch, F. A. (1997). The role of self organization in the promotion of resilience in maltreated children. *Development and Psychopathology, 9,* 799–817.

Cohen, S., & McKay, G. (1984). Social support, stress and the buffering hypothesis: A theoretical analysis. In A. Baum, S. E. Taylor, & J. E. Singer (Eds.), *Handbook of psychology and health* (pp. 253-287). Hillsdale, NJ.

Cohn, J. F., & Tronick, E. Z. (1987). Mother-infant face-to-face interaction: The sequence of dyadic states at 3, 6, and 9 months. *Developmental Psychology, 23*, 68–77.

Cohn, M. A., Fredrickson, B. L., Brown, S. L., Mikels, J. A., & Conway, A. M. (2009). Happiness unpacked: Positive emotions increase life satisfaction by building resilience. *Emotion, 9*, 361–368.

Conceição, N., Iwakabe, S. & Pascual-Leone, A. (2014). *A qualitative study of therapists working at the edge of their experience: Their change processes and development.* Paper given at the Society for the Exploration of Psychotherapy Integration XXVII SEPI Conference, MAY 18–20, 2012, Evanston/ Chicago, USA.

Corliss, J. (2013). *Positive psychology: Harnessing the power of happiness, mindfulness, and inner strength.* Boston, MA: Harvard Medical School.

Cozolino, L. (2006). *The neuroscience of human relationships: Attachment and the developing social brain.* New York, NY: Norton.

Csikszentmihalyi, M. (1996). *Creativity: Flow and the psychology of discovery and invention.* New York, NY: Harper.

Damasio, A. R. (1999). *The feeling of what happens: Body and emotion in the making of consciousness.* New York, NY: Harcourt Brace.

Darwin, C. (1872). *The expression of the emotions in man and animals.* New York, NY: St. Martin's Press.

Davanloo, H. (1990). *Unlocking the unconscious: Selected papers of Habib Davanloo.* New York, NY: Wiley.

Doidge, N. (2007). *The brain that changes itself: Stories of personal triumph from the frontiers of brain science.* New York, NY: Penguin.

Ecker, B., & Hulley, L. (1996). *Depth-oriented brief therapy: How to be brief when you were trained to be deep—and vice versa.* Jossey-Bass social and behavioral science series. San Francisco, CA, US: Jossey-Bass.

Ecker, B., & Hulley, L. (2000). Depth-oriented brief therapy: Accelerated accessing of the coherent unconscious. In Carlson, J. (Ed); Sperry, Len (Ed). *Brief therapy with individuals & couples.* (pp. 161-190). Phoenix, AZ, US: Zeig, Tucker & Theisen.

Ecker, B. Ticic, R., & Hulley, L. (2012). *Unlocking the emotional brain: Eliminating symptoms at their roots using memory reconsolidation.* New York, NY: Routledge.

Ellison, K. (2006). *The mommy brain: How motherhood makes us smarter.* New York, NY: Basic Books.

Ezriel, H. (1952). Notes on psychoanalytic group therapy: Interpretation and research. *Psychiatry, 15*, 119–126.

Fergusson, D. M., & Horwood, L. J. (2003). Resilience to childhood adversity: Results of a 21-year study. In S. S. Luthar (Ed.), *Resilience and vulnerability: Adaptation in the context of childhood adversities* (pp. 130–155). New York, NY: Cambridge University Press.

Fosha, D. (1992). The interrelatedness of theory, technique and therapeutic stance: A comparative look at intensive short-term dynamic psychotherapy and accelerated empathic therapy. *International Journal of Short-Term Psychotherapy, 7,* 157–176.

Fosha, D. (1995). Technique and taboo in three short-term dynamic psychotherapies. *Journal of Psychotherapy Practice and Research, 4,* 297–318.

Fosha, D. (2000a). Meta-therapeutic processes and the affects of transformation: Affirmation and the healing affects. *Journal of Psychotherapy Integration, 10,* 71–97.

Fosha, D. (2000b). The transforming power of affect: A model for accelerated change. New York, NY: Basic Books.

Fosha, D. (2002). The activation of affective change processes in AEDP (accelerated experiential-dynamic psychotherapy). In J. J. Magnavita (Ed.), *Comprehensive handbook of psychotherapy,* Vol. 1, *Psychodynamic and object relations psychotherapies* (pp. 309–344). New York, NY: Wiley.

Fosha, D. (2003). Dyadic Regulation and Experiential Work with Emotion and Relatedness in Trauma and Disordered Attachment. In M. F. Solomon & D. J. Siegel (Eds.). *Healing Trauma: Attachment, Mind, Body, and Brain.* New York: Norton.

Fosha, D. (2004a). "Nothing that feels bad is ever the last step:" The role of positive emotions in experiential work with difficult emotional experiences. Special issue on *Emotion,* L. Greenberg (Ed.). *Clinical Psychology and Psychotherapy. 11,* 30-43.

Fosha, D. (2004b). Brief integrative psychotherapy comes of age: reflections. *Journal of Psychotherapy Integration. 14,* 66-92.

Fosha, D. (2005). Emotion, true self, true other, core state: Toward a clinical theory of affective change process. *Psychoanalytic Review, 92,* 513–552.

Fosha, D. (2006). Quantum transformation in trauma and treatment: Traversing the crisis of healing change. *Journal of Clinical Psychology/In Session.* 62 (5), 569-583.

Fosha, D. (2008). Transformance, recognition of self by self, and effective action. In K. J. Schneider (Ed.), *Existential-integrative psychotherapy: Guideposts to the core of practice* (pp. 290–320). New York, NY: Routledge.

Fosha, D. (2009a). Emotion and recognition at work. Energy, vitality, pleasure, truth, and desire and the emergent phenomenology of transformational experience. *The Neuropsychotherapist. Jul/Sep 2013 (2),* 28-51.

Fosha, D. (2009b). Emotion and recognition at work: Energy, vitality, pleasure, truth, desire & and the emergent phenomenology of transformational experience. In D. Fosha; D. J. Siegel; & M. F. Solomon (Eds.),. *The healing power of emotion: Affective neuroscience, development and clinical practice* (pp. 172--203). New York, NY: W.W. Norton & Co.

Fosha, D. (2012). *Immersion Course in AEDP*. New York, NY. May, 2012

Fosha, D., Siegel, D., & Solomon, M. (Eds.). (2009). *The healing power of emotion: Affective neuroscience, development and clinical practice.* New York, NY: Norton.

Fosha, D., & Yeung, D. (2006). AEDP exemplifies the seamless integration of emotional transformation and dyadic relatedness at work. In G. Stricker & J. Gold (Eds.), *A Casebook of Integrative Psychotherapy*. Washington DC: APA Press.

Fraley, R. C., & Shaver, P. R. (1997). Adult attachment and the suppression of unwanted thoughts. *Journal of Personality and Social Psychology, 73*, 1080–1091.

Frederick, R. (2009). *Living like you mean it: Using the wisdom and power of your emotions to get the life you really want.* San Francisco: Jossey-Bass.

Fredrickson, B. L. (1998). What good are positive emotions? *Review of General Psychology, 2,* 300–319.

Fredrickson, B. L., & Branigan, C. A. (2005). Positive emotions broaden the scope of attention and thought-action repertoires. *Cognition and Emotion, 19*, 313–332.

Fredrickson, B. L., & Losada, M. (2005). Positive affect and the complex dynamics of human flourishing. *American Psychologist, 60,* 687–686.

Fredrickson, B. L., Mancuso, R. A., Branigan, C., & Tugade, M. M. (2000). The undoing effect of positive emotions. *Motivation and Emotion, 24,* 237–258.

Freeman, W. J. (2000). Emotion is essential to all intentional behaviors. In M. D. Lewis and I. Granic (Eds.), *Emotion, development and self-organization* (pp. 209–235). New York, NY: Cambridge University Press.

Freud, S. (1894). The neuro-psychoses of defense. In J. Strachey (Ed.)., *Standard Edition*, Vol. 3. London: Hogarth Press.

Freud, S. (1926). Inhibitions, symptoms, and anxiety. In J. Strachey (Ed.)., *Standard Edition*, Vol. 20. London: Hogarth Press

Garmezy, N. (1987). Stress, competence, and development: Continuities in the study of schizophrenic adults, children vulnerable to psychopathology, and the search for stress-resistant children. *American Journal of Orthopsychiatry, 57*, 159–174.

Garmezy, N., Masten, A. S., & Tellegen, A. (1984). The study of stress and competence in children: A building block for developmental psychopathology. *Child Development*, 55, 97–111.

Gendlin, E. (1969). Focusing. *Psychotherapy: Theory, Research and Practice, 6*, 4–15.

Gendlin, E. T. (1981). *Focusing*. New York, NY: Bantam.

Ghent, E. (1990). Masochism, submission, surrender: Masochism as a perversion of surrender. *Contemporary Psychoanalysis, 26*, 108–136.

Gianino, A., & Tronick, E. (1988). The mutual regulation model: The infant's self and interactive regulation and coping and defensive capacities. In T. Field, P. McCabe, & N. Schneiderman (Eds.), *Stress and coping* (pp. 47–68). Hillsdale, NJ: Erlbaum.

Glantz, M. D., & Johnson, J. L. (Eds.) (1991). *Resilience and development: Positive life adaptations.* New York, NY: Kluwer Academic/Plenum.

Gleiser, K., Ford, J. D., & Fosha, D. (2008). Exposure and experiential therapies for complex posttraumatic stress disorder. *Psychotherapy: Theory, Research, Practice, Training.* 45 (3), 340-360.

Gralinski-Bakker, J. H., & and Hauser, S. T. (2004). Markers of resilience and risk: Adult lives in a population. *Research in Human Development, 21,* 291–326.

Gralinski-Bakker, J. H., Hauser, S. T., Stott, C., Billings, R. L., & Allen, J. P. (2004). Markers of resilience and risk: Adult lives in a vulnerable population. *Research in Human Development, 1,* 291–326.

Greenberg, L. S. (1991). Research on the process of change. *Psychotherapy Research, 1,* 3–16.

Greenberg, L. S., & Johnson, S. M. (1990). Emotional change processes in couples therapy. In E. A. Blechman (Ed.), *For better or worse: Emotions and the family* (pp. 137–154). Hillsdale, NJ: Erlbuam.

Greenberg, L. S., & Paivio, S. C. (1997). *Working with emotions in psychotherapy.* New York, NY: Guilford Press.

Greenberg, L., Rice, L., & Elliott, R. (1993). *Facilitating emotional change: The moment-by-moment process.* New York, NY: Guilford Press.

Greenberg, L. S., & Safran, J. D. (1987). *Emotion in psychotherapy.* New York, NY: Guilford Press.

Greenberg, L.S., Watson, J.C., Elliot, R., Bohart, A.C. (2001). Empathy.*Psychotherapy: Theory, Research, Practice, Training, 38(4),* 380-384.

Haidt, J. (2000). The positive emotion of elevation. *Prevention and Treatment, 3(1),* article 3c.

Haidt, J. (2003). Elevation and the positive psychology of morality. In C. L. M. Keyes & J. Haidt (Eds.), *Flourishing: Positive psychology and the life well-lived* (pp. 275–289). Washington, DC: APA Press.

Harrison, R. L., & Westwood, M. J. (2009). Preventing vicarious traumatization of mental health therapists: Identifying protective practices. *Psychotherapy: Theory, Research, Practice, Training, 46(2),* 203–219.

Hesse, E., & Main, M. (2000). Disorganized infant, child and adult attachment: Collapse in behavioral and attentional strategies. *Journal of the American Psychoanalytic Association, 48,* 1097–1127.

Isen, A. M., Shalker, T. E., Clark, M., & Karp, L. (1978). Affect, accessibility of material in memory, and behavior: A cognitive loop? , 1–12.

Izard, C. E., Ackerman, B. P., Schoff, K. M., & Fine, S. E. (2000). Self-organization of discrete emotions, emotion patterns, and emotion-cognition relations. In M. D. Lewis & I. Granic (Eds.), *Emotion, development and self-organization: Dynamic systems approaches to emotional development* (pp. 15–36). Cambridge: Cambridge University Press.

Janoff-Bulman, R. (1992). *Shattered assumptions: Towards a new psychology of trauma.* New York, NY: Free Press.

New York, NY, US: Free Press.

Johnson, S. M. (1996). *The practice of emotionally focused marital therapy: Creating connection.* New York, NY: Brunner/Mazel.

Kennedy-Moore, E., & Watson J. C. (2001). How and when does emotional expression help? 187–212.

Keyes, C. M. (2002). The mental health continuum: From languishing to flourishing in life. *Journal of Health and Social Research, 43,* 207–222.

Keyes, C. L. M., & Haidt, J. (Eds.). (2003). *Flourishing: Positive psychology and the life well-lived.* Washington, DC, US: American Psychological Association.

Kierkegaard, S. (1983). *Fear and Trembling.* H. V. Hong & E. H. Hong (Eds. & Trans.). Princeton, NJ: Princeton University Press.

Kirkpatrick, L. A., & Shaver, P. R. (1990). Attachment theory and religion: Childhood attachments, religious beliefs, and conversion. *Journal for the Scientific Study of Religion, 29,* 315–334.

Kirkpatrick, L. A., & Shaver, P. R. (1992). An attachment-theoretical approach to romantic love and religious belief. *Personality and Social Psychology Bulletin, 18,* 266–275.

Kottler, J. A. Blau, D. S. (1989). The imperfect therapist. San Francisco: Jossey-Bass.

Lamagna, J. (2011). Of the self, by the self, and for the self: An intra-relational perspective on intra-psychic attunement and psychological change. Journal of Psychotherapy Integration, 21(3), 280–307.

Lamagna, J., & Gleiser, K. (2007). Building a secure internal attachment: An intrarelational approach to ego strengthening and emotional processing with chronically traumatized clients. *Journal of Trauma and Dissociation, 8,* 25–52.

Lawrence, J. C. (1996). Gil Noam's fieldwork in an urban frontier.

Lench, H. C., Flores, S. A., & Bench, S. W. (2011). Discrete emotions predict changes in cognition, judgment, experience, behavior, and physiology: A meta-analysis of experimental emotion elicitations. Psychological Bulletin, 137(5), 834–855.

Levine, P. A. (1997). . Berkeley, CA: North Atlantic Books.

Lipton, B., & Fosha, D. (2011). Attachment as a transformative process in AEDP: Operationalizing the intersection of attachment theory and affective neuroscience. Journal of Psychotherapy Integration, 21(3), 253–279.]

Luthar, S. S., Cicchetti, D., & Becker, B. (2000). Research on resilience: Response to commentaries. *Child Development, 71,* 573–575.

Luthar, S. S., & Zelazo, L. B. (2003). Research on resilience: An integrative review. In S. S. Luthar (Ed.), *Resilience and vulnerability: Adaptation in the context of childhood adversities* (pp. 510–549). Cambridge: Cambridge University Press.

Lyon, B., & Rubin, S. (in press). Healing shame: A therapist's guide.

Lyons-Ruth, K. (1998). Implicit relational knowing: Its role in development and psychoanalytic treatment. *Infant Mental Health Journal, 19(3)*, 282-289.

Lyons-Ruth, K., Bruschweiler-Stern, N., Harrison, A., Morgan, A., Nahum, J., Sander, L. (2001). *Psychologist-Psychoanalyst 21(4)*, 13-17 [APA Division 39, Psychoanalysis].

Lyubomirsky, S., King, L., & Diener, E. (2005). The benefits of frequent positive affect: Does happiness lead to success? *Psychological Bulletin, 131*, 803–855.

Mahler, M. S., Pine, F., & Bergman, A. (1975). *The psychological birth of the human infant*. New York, NY: Basic Books.

Main, M. (1983). Exploration, play, and cognitive functioning related to infant–mother attachment. *Infant Behavior and Development, 6*, 167–174.

Main, M. (2000). The organized categories of infant, child, and adult attachment: Flexible vs. inflexible attention under attachment-related stress. *Journal of the American Psychoanalytic Association, 48*, 1055–1096.

Main, M., & Cassidy, J. (1988). Categories of response to reunion with the parent at age 6: Predictable from infant attachment classifications and stable over a 1-month period. *Developmental Psychology, 24*, 415–426.

Main, M., & Hesse, E. (1990). Parents' unresolved traumatic experiences are related to infant disorganized status: Is frightened and/or frightening parental behavior the linking mechanism? In M. T. Greenberg, D. Cicchetti, & E. M. Cummings (Eds.), *Attachment in the preschool years: Theory, research and intervention* (pp. 161–184). Chicago: University of Chicago Press.

Main, M., Kaplan, N., & Cassidy, J. (1985). Security in infancy, childhood, and adulthood: A move to the level of representation. *Monographs of the Society for Research in Child Development, 50*, 66–104.

Main, M., & Solomon, J. (1986). Discovery of an insecure-disorganized/disoriented attachment pattern. In T. B. Brazelton & M. W. Yogman (Eds.), *Affective development in infancy* (pp. 95–124). Norwood, NJ: Ablex.

Malan, D. (1979). *Individual psychotherapy and the science of psychodynamics*. London: Butterworth.

Marks, L. I. (2000). Perceived effectiveness of problem-focused and emotion-focused coping: The role of appraisal of event controllability and personality traits. *Dissertation Abstracts International: Section B: The Sciences and Engineering, 61*(1-B), 540.

Maslow, A. H. (1954). *Motivation and personality*. New York, NY: Harper and Row.

Maslow, A. H. (1971). *The farther reaches of human nature*. New York, NY: Viking Press.

Masten, A. S. (2001). Ordinary magic: Resilience processes in development. *American Psychologist, 56*, 227–238.

Masten, A. S., Best, K. M., & Garmezy N. (1990). Resilience and development: Contributions from the study of children who overcome adversity. *Development and Psychopathology, 2*, 425–444.

Mayes, L. C. (2005). Something is different but what or why is unclear: Commentary on the Boston Change Process Study Group. *Journal of the American Psychoanalytic Association, 53*, 745–750.

McCann, I. L., & Pearlman, L. A. (1990). Vicarious traumatization: A contextual model for understanding the effects of trauma on helpers. *Journal of Traumatic Stress, 3*, 131–149.

McCullough, L., Kuhn, N., Andrews, S., Kaplan, A., Wolf, J., & Hurley, C.L. (2003). *Treating affect phobia: A manual for short-term dynamic psychotherapy*. New York: Guilford Press.

McElroy, E. M. (1999). The effect of God image and religious coping on depression, well-being, and alcohol use in college students. *Dissertation Abstracts International: Section B: The Sciences and Engineering, 60*(4-B).

McLean, C. P., Handa, S., Dickenstein, B. D., Benson, T. A., Baker, M. T., Isler, W. C., . . . Blitz, B. T. (2011). Posttraumatic growth and posttraumatic stress among military medical personnel. *Psychological Trauma: Theory, Research, Practice, and Policy*, 1–7.

Mitchell, S.A. (2002). *Can love last? The fate of romance over time.* New York, NY: Norton.

Menninger, K. (1958). Theory of psychoanalytic technique. New York, NY: Basic Books.

Napier, N. (1993). *Getting through the day: Strategies for adults hurt as children*. New York, NY: Norton.

Nathanson, D. L. (1992). *Shame and pride: Affect, sex, and the birth of the self.* New York, NY: Norton.

Nathanson, D. L. (1996). About emotion. In D. L. Nathanson (Ed.), *Knowing feeling: Affect, script, and psychotherapy* (pp. 1–21) New York, NY: Norton.

Ogden, P., Minton, K. & Pain, C. (2006). *Trauma and the body: A sensorimotor approach to psychotherapy*. New York, NY: Norton.

Ong, A. D., Bergeman, C. S., Bisconti, T. L., & Wallace, K. A. (2006). Psychological resilience, positive emotions, and successful adaptation to stress in later life. *Journal of Personality and Social Psychology, 91*, 730–749.

Ong, A. D., Zautra, A. J., & Reid, M. C. (2010). Psychological resilience predicts decreases in pain catastrophizing through positive emotions. *Psychology and Aging, 23*, 516–523.

Orlinsky, D.E., Grawe, K. Parks, B.K., Process and outcome in psychotherapy: Noch einmal. In A.E. Bergin, (Ed); Sol Louis Garfield (Ed), (1994). *Handbook of psychotherapy and behavior change (4th ed.)*. Oxford, England: John Wiley & Sons. (pp. 270-376).

Osimo, F. (2003). *Experiential short-term dynamic psychotherapy, a manual*. Bloomington, IN: Authorhouse.

Panksepp, J. (1998). *Affective neuroscience: The foundation of human and animal emotions*. New York, NY: Oxford University Press.

Panksepp, J. (2009). Brain emotional systems and qualities of mental life: From animal models of affect to implications for psychotherapeutics. In Fosha, D. (Ed); Siegel, D.J. (Ed); Solomon, M.F. (Ed). *The healing power of emotion: Affective neuroscience, development & clinical practice*. (pp. 1-26). New York: W.W. Norton & Co.

Pao, P. N. (1979). *Schizophrenic disorders: Theory and treatment from a psychodynamic point of view*. New York, NY: International Universities Press.

Piaget, J. (1952). The fourth stage: The coordination of the secondary schemata and their application to new situations. In: M. Cook (Trans.), *The origins of intelligence in children* (pp. 210–262). New York, NY: Norton.

Porges, S. (1997). Emotion: An evolutionary by-product of the neural regulation of the autonomic nervous system. In C. S. Carter, B. Kirkpatrick, & I. Lenderhendler (Eds.), *The integrative neurobiology of affiliation* (pp. 62–77). New York, NY: New York Academy of Sciences.

Porges, S. (2001). The polyvagal theory: Phylogenetic substrates of a social nervous system. *International Journal of Psychophysiology, 42,* 123–146.

Porges, S. W. (2005). The Role of Social Engagement in Attachment and Bonding: A Phylogenetic Perspective. In Carter, C. S. (Ed); Ahnert, L. (Ed); Grossmann, K. E. (Ed); Hrdy, S. B. (Ed); Lamb, M. E. (Ed); Porges, S. W. (Ed); Sachser, N. (Ed). *Attachment and bonding: A new synthesis*. (pp. 33-54). Cambridge, MA, US: MIT Press.

Porges, S.W. (2009). Reciprocal influences between body and brain in the perception and expression of affect: A polyvagal perspective. In Fosha, D. (Ed); Siegel, D.J. (Ed); Solomon, M.F. (Ed). *The healing power of emotion: Affective neuroscience, development & clinical practice.* , (pp. 27-54). New York, NY, US: W W Norton & Co.

Porges, S. W. (2011). *The polyvagal theory: Neurophysiological foundations of emotions, attachment, communication, and self-regulation*. New York, NY: Norton.

Prenn, N. (2009). I second that emotion! On self-disclosure and its metaprocessing. In A. Bloomgarden and R. B. Mennuti (Eds.), *Psychotherapist revealed: Therapists speak about self-disclosure in psychotherapy* (pp. 85–95). New York, NY: Routledge.

Rolf, J. E., & Glantz, M. D. (1999). Resilience: An interview with Norman Garmezy. In M. D. Glantz, & J. L. Johnson (Eds.), *Resilience and development: Positive life adaptations* (pp. 5–14). New York, NY: Kluwer/Plenum.

Russell, E. (2004). On pressuring with empathy. STDP Listserv.

Russell, E. M., & Fosha, D. (2008). Transformational affects and core state in AEDP: The emergence and consolidation of joy, hope, gratitude and confidence in the (solid goodness of the) self. *Journal of Psychotherapy Integration, 18*, 167–190.

Rutter, M. (1985). Resilience in the face of adversity. Protective factors and resistance to psychiatric disorder. *British Journal of Psychiatry, 147*, 598–611.

Rutter, M., & English & Romanian Adoptees Study Team. (1998). Developmental catch-up, and deficit, following adoption after severe global early privation. *Journal of Child Psychology and Psychiatry, 39*, 465–476.

Rutter, M., O'Connor, T. G., & English and Romanian Adoptees Study Team (2004). Are there biological programming effects for psychological development? Findings from a study of Romanian adoptees. *Developmental Psychology, 40*, 81–94.

Salovey, P., Mayer, J. D., Goldman, S. L., Turvey, C., & Palfai, T. P. (1995). Emotional attention, clarity, and repair: Exploring emotional intelligence using the Trait Meta-Mood Scale. In J. W. Pennebaker (Ed.), *Emotion, disclosure, and health* (pp. 125–154). Washington, DC: American Psychological Association.

Sander, L.W. (1988). Reflections on self psychology and infancy: The event-structure of regulation in the neonate-caregiver system as a biological background for early organization of psychic structure. In Goldberg, A. (Ed.). *Frontiers in self psychology. Progress in self psychology, Vol. 3., (pp. 64-77).* Hillsdale, NJ, US: Analytic Press, Inc.

Schore, A. (1994). *Affect regulation and the origin of the self: The neurobiology of emotional development.* Hillsdale, NJ: Erlbaum.

Schore, A. (1996). The experience-dependent maturation of a regulatory system in the orbital prefrontal cortex and the origin of developmental psychopathology. *Development and Psychopathology, 8*, 59–87.

Schore, A. (2000). The self organization of the right brain and the neurobiology of emotional development. In M. D. Lewis & I. Granic (Eds.), *Emotion, development, and self-organization: Dynamic systems approaches to emotional development* (pp. 155–185). New York, NY: Cambridge University Press.

Schore, A. (2003). *Affect dysregulation and disorders of the self.* New York, NY: Norton.

Schore, A. (2012). *The science of the art of psychotherapy.* New York, NY: Norton.

Schwartz, R. C. (1995). *Internal family systems therapy*. New York, NY: Guilford Press.

Seligman, M. E. P. (2002). *Authentic happiness: Using the new positive psychology to realize your potential for lasting fulfillment*. New York, NY: Free Press.

Seligman, M. E. P., & Csikszentmihalyi, M. (2000). Positive psychology: An introduction. *American Psychologist, 55*, 5–14.

Seligman, M. E. P., Rashid, T., & Parks, A. C. (2006). Positive psychotherapy. *American Psychologist, 61*, 774–788.

Shapiro, F., & Forrest, M. S. (1997). *EMDR: The breakthrough "eye movement" therapy for overcoming anxiety, stress, and trauma*. New York, NY: Basic Books.

Shapiro, F. (2001). Eye movement desensitization and reprocessing: Basic principles, protocols, and procedures (2nd Ed.). New York, NY: Guilford Press.

Shapiro, S. (2009). It's Not About You. *Psychotherapy Networker Magazine*, Jan/Feb 2009, 23-24.

Shaver, P. R., & Clark, C. L. (1994). The psychodynamics of adult romantic attachment. In J. M. Masling & R. F. Bornstein (Eds.), *Empirical perspectives on object relations theories* (pp. 105–156). Washington, DC: American Psychological Association.

Shaver, P. R., & Mikulincer, M. (2011). An attachment-theory framework for conceptualizing interpersonal behavior. In L. M. Horowitz & S. Strack (Eds.), *Handbook of interpersonal psychology: Theory, research, assessment, and therapeutic interventions* (pp. 17–35). Hoboken, NJ: Wiley.

Shay, J. (1994). *Achilles in Vietnam: Combat trauma and the undoing of character*. New York, NY: Scribner.

Siegel, D. J. (1999). *The developing mind: Toward a neurobiology of interpersonal experience*. New York, NY: Guilford Press.

Siegel, D. J. (2003). An interpersonal neurobiology of psychotherapy: The developing mind and the resolution of trauma. In M. F. Solomon & D. J. Siegel (Eds.), *Healing trauma: Attachment, trauma, the brain and the mind* (pp. 1–54). New York, NY: Norton.

Siegel, D. J. (2007). *The mindful brain: Reflection and attunement in the cultivation of well-being*. New York, NY: Norton.

Siegel, D. J., & Hartzell, M. (2003). *Parenting from the inside out: How a deeper self-understanding can help you raise children who thrive*. New York, NY: Tarcher/Putnam.

Sroufe, L. A., & Waters, E. (1977). Heart rate as a convergent measure in clinical and developmental research. *Merrill-Palmer Quarterly, 23*, 3–27.

Stern D. N. (1985). *The interpersonal world of the infant: A view from psychoanalysis and development psychology*. New York, NY: Basic Books.

Stern. D. N. (1998). The process of therapeutic change involving implicit knowledge: Some implications of developmental observations for adult psychotherapy. *Infant Mental Health Journal, 19*, 300–308.

Stern, D. N. (2007). Applying developmental and neuroscience findings on other-centered participation to the process of change in psychotherapy. In S. Braten (Ed.), *On being moved: From mirror neurons to empathy* (pp. 35–47). Amsterdam: Benjamins.

Symington, N. (2006). *A healing conversation: How healing happens.* London: Karnac.

Tedeschi, R. G., Park, C. L., & Calhoun, L. G. (1998). *Posttraumatic growth: Conceptual issues.* In R. G. Tedeschi, C. L. Park, & L. G. Calhoun (Eds.), *Posttraumatic growth: Positive changes in the aftermath of crisis* (pp. 1–22). Mahwah, NJ: Erlbaum.

Tomkins, S. (1962). *Affect, imagery, consciousness*, Vol. 1: *The positive affects.* New York, NY: Springer.

Tomkins, S. (1963). *Affect, imagery, consciousness*, Vol. 2: *The negative affects.* New York, NY: Springer.

Trevarthen, C. (2005). Action and emotion in development of cultural intelligence: Why infants have feelings like ours. In J. Nadel & D. Muir (Eds.), *Emotional development: Recent research advances* (pp. 61–91). New York, NY: Oxford University Press.

Tronick, E. Z. (1989). Emotions and emotional communication in infants. *American Psychologist, 44*, 112–119.

Tronick, E. Z. (1998). Dyadically expanded states of consciousness and the process of therapeutic change. *Infant Mental Health Journal, 19,* 290–299.

Tronick, E. Z. (2003). "Of course all relationships are unique": How co-creative processes generate unique mother-infant and patient-therapist relationships and change other relationships. *Psychological Inquiry, 23,* 473–491.

Tronick, E. Z. (2005). "Why is connection with others so critical? The formation of dyadic states of consciousness and the expansion of individuals' states of consciousness: Coherence-governed selection and the co-creation of meaning out of messy meaning making. In J. Nadel & D. Muir (Eds.), *Emotional development: Recent research advances*, (pp. 293–315). New York, NY: Oxford University Press.

Tronick, E. Z., & Cohen, J. F. (1969). Infant–mother face-to-face interaction: Age and gender differences in coordination and the occurrence of miscoordination. *Child Development, 60,* 85–92.

Trope, Y., & Pomerantz, E. M. (1998). Resolving conflicts among self-evaluative motives: Positive experiences as a resource for overcoming defensiveness. *Motivation and Emotion, 22,* 53–72.

Tugade, M., & Fredrickson, B. L. (2004). Resilient individuals use positive emotions to bounce back from negative emotional experiences. *Journal of Personality and Social Psychology, 86*, 320–333.

Tunnell, G. (2006). An affirmation approach to treating gay male couples. *Group. 30(2)*, 133-151.

Tunnell, G. (2011). An Attachment Perspective on the First Interview. In C. Silverstein (Ed.), *The Initial Psychotherapy Interview: A Gay Man Seeks Treatment*. New York: Elsevier Insight Books.

Tunnell, G. (2012). Gay Male Couple Therapy: An Attachment-Based Model. In J. J. Bigner & J. L. Wetchler (Eds.), *Handbook of LGBT-Affirmative Couple and Family Therapy*. London: Routledge.

Vaillant, G.E. (2012). *Triumphs of experience: The men of the Harvard Grant Study*. Cambridge, MA: The Belknap Press.

VandenBos, G. R. (Ed.) (2007). *APA dictionary of psychology*. Washington, DC: American Psychological Association.

Vitaliano, P. P., DeWolfe, D. J., Maiuro, R. D., Russo, J., & Katon, W. (1990). Appraisal, changeability of a stressor as a modifier of the relationship between coping and depression: A test of the hypothesis of fit. *Journal of Personality and Social Psychology, 59*, 582–592.

Vygotsky, L. S. (1978). *Mind and society: The development of higher psychological processes*. Cambridge, MA: Harvard University Press.

Wallin, D. (2007). *Attachment in psychotherapy*. New York, NY: Guilford Press.

Watson, D., & Clark, L. A. (1992). Affects separable and inseparable: On the hierarchical arrangement of the negative affects. *Journal of Personality and Social Psychology, 62*, 489–505.

Weinberg, M. K., & Tronick, E. Z. (1994). Beyond the face: An empirical study of infant affective configuration of facial, vocal, gestural, and regulatory behaviors. *Child Development, 65*, 1503–1515.

Welling, H. (2012). Transformative emotional sequence: Towards a common principle of change. *Journal of Psychotherapy Integration, 22(2)*, 109-136.

Werner E. E., & Smith, R. S. (1982). *Vulnerable but invincible: A longitudinal study of resilient children and youth*. New York, NY: McGraw Hill.

Wicks, R. (2007). *The resilient clinician*. Oxford: Oxford University Press.

Williamson, M. (1992). *A return to love: Reflection on the principles of a course in miracles*. New York, NY: Harper Collins.

Winnicott, D. W. (1960/1965). Ego distortion in terms of true and false self. In *The maturational processes and the facilitating environment* (pp. 140–152). New York, NY: International Universities Press.

Wyman, P. A. (2003). Emerging perspectives on context specificity of children's adaptation and resilience: Evidence from a decade of research with urban children in adversity. In S. S. Luthar (Ed.), *Resilience and vulnerability: Adaptation in the context of childhood adversities* (pp. 293–317). Cambridge: Cambridge University Press.

Zautra, A. J., Johnson, L. M., & Davis M. C. (2005). Positive affect as a source of resilience for women in chronic pain. *Journal of Consulting and Clinical Psychology, 73*, 212–220.

Zautra, A. J., Potter, P. T., & Reich, J. W. (1997). The independence of affects is context dependent: An integrative model of the relationship between positive and negative affect. *Annual Review of Gerontology and Geriatrics, 17*, 75–103.

Zautra, A. J. Reich, J. W., Davis, M. C., Nicolson, N. A., & Potter, P. T. (2000). The role of stressful events in the independence of affective states: Evidence from field and experimental studies. *Journal of Personality, 68*, 927–950.

Zautra, A., Smith, B., Affleck, G., & Tennen, H. (2001). Examinations of chronic pain and affect relationships: Applications of a dynamic model of affect. *Journal of Consulting and Clinical Psychology, 69*, 786–795.

INDEX

Note: Italicized page locators indicate figures.